Adult Learning and Technology in Working-Class Life

To date little is known about the everyday activities that make up the majority of people's learning lives. This book presents a critical approach to learning using situated learning and activity theory while drawing widely on the writings of Marx, Gramsci, and various Marxist-feminists, as well as on the sociology of Pierre Bourdieu. Though many have demonstrated that schooling and adult training are deeply affected by issues of social class, this study explodes the myth that everyday learning, despite its apparent openness and freedom, can be understood as class neutral. Based on life-history interviews, selected ethnographic observations in homes and factories, and large-scale survey materials, as well as on microanalysis of human–computer interaction, this book explores learning across the various spheres of working-class life. The author draws on his own experience as a factory worker, labor educator, and academic to offer the most detailed examination of computer literacy and lifelong learning practice among working-class people currently available.

Peter H. Sawchuk is currently an Assistant Professor in the Department of Sociology and Equity Studies in Education at the University of Toronto, Canada, where he teaches in the area of adult learning and work and is a member of the University of Toronto's Centre for Studies in Education and Work.

Learning in Doing: Social, Cognitive, and Computational Perspectives

Series Editor Emeritus
JOHN SEELY BROWN, *Xerox Palo Alto Research Center*

General Editors
ROY PEA, *Professor of Education and the Learning Sciences and Director, Stanford Center for Innovations in Learning, Stanford University*
CHRISTIAN HEATH, *The Management Centre, King's College, London*
LUCY A. SUCHMAN, *Centre for Science Studies and Department of Sociology, Lancaster University, UK*

Continued on page following the Index

Adult Learning and Technology in Working-Class Life

PETER H. SAWCHUK

University of Toronto

CAMBRIDGE
UNIVERSITY PRESS

PUBLISHED BY THE PRESS SYNDICATE OF THE UNIVERSITY OF CAMBRIDGE
The Pitt Building, Trumpington Street, Cambridge, United Kingdom

CAMBRIDGE UNIVERSITY PRESS
The Edinburgh Building, Cambridge CB2 2RU, UK
40 West 20th Street, New York, NY 10011-4211, USA
477 Williamstown Road, Port Melbourne, VIC 3207, Australia
Ruiz de Alarcón 13, 28014 Madrid, Spain
Dock House, The Waterfront, Cape Town 8001, South Africa

http: // www.cambridge.org

First published 2003

Printed in the United States of America

Typeface Janson Text 10.25/13 pt.   *System* LATEX 2$_\varepsilon$ [TB]

A catalog record for this book is available from the British Library.

Library of Congress Cataloging in Publication Data
Sawchuk, Peter H. (Peter Harold), 1968–
Adult learning and technology in working-class life / Peter H. Sawchuk.
   p.   cm. – (Learning in doing)
Includes bibliographical references and index.
ISBN 0-521-81756-0 (pb.)
1. Adult learning – Canada.   2. Working class – Education – Canada.   3. Working
class – Effect of technological innovations on – Canada.   I. Title.   II. Series.
LC5225.L42 S29   2003
374′.001′9 – dc21   2002071491

ISBN 0 521 81756 0 hardback

For Jill

Contents

Series Foreword

This series for Cambridge University Press is becoming widely known as an international forum for studies of situated learning and cognition.

Innovative contributions are being made by anthropology; by cognitive, developmental, and cultural psychology; by computer science; by education; and by social theory. These contributions are providing the basis for new ways of understanding the social, historical, and contextual nature of learning, thinking, and practice that emerges from human activity. The empirical settings of these research inquiries range from the classroom to the workplace, to the high-technology office, and to learning in the streets and in other communities of practice.

The situated nature of learning and remembering through activity is a central fact. It may appear obvious that human minds develop in social situations and extend their sphere of activity and communicative competencies. But cognitive theories of knowledge representation and learning alone have not provided sufficient insight into these relationships.

This series was born of the conviction that new and exciting interdisciplinary syntheses are underway as scholars and practitioners from diverse fields seek to develop theory and empirical investigations adequate for characterizing the complex relations of social and mental life and for understanding successful learning wherever it occurs. The series invites contributions that advance our understanding of these seminal issues.

Roy Pea
Christian Heath
Lucy Suchman

Preface

This book presents a critical approach to adult learning and computer technology in the tradition of the Learning in Doing series. In it, I take up situated learning and activity theory approaches, two of the most relevant, though not the only, sociocultural approaches to adult learning currently available. However, in order to draw out the broad range of cultural, historical, and political-economic factors at play in working-class people's learning, I reflect carefully on other writings as well. These include those of Marx, Gramsci, Lukács, Marxist-feminist standpoint theory, ethnomethodology, conversation analysis, and, perhaps most important, the work of the late French sociologist Pierre Bourdieu.

I claim that learning is a reflection of the social and economic order that we produce and that, in turn, stands over us. It is differentiated and differentiating and cannot be seen as class neutral. Although there is obviously an enormous range of ways of approaching the topic of social class and learning, I have chosen to focus on the ordering of computer-based learning practice in people's everyday lives. This informs the selection of key concepts and specific technical preoccupations, and is also a direct response to a serious gap in sociological, psychological, and cultural studies and educational literatures to date. The overall argument is broken into two main lines: (a) conceptualizing learning and computer technology in terms of class standpoints and power and (b) tracing the full range of cultural and material dimensions in working-class computer learning practice.

Standing on the shoulders of a variety of writers, in terms of the first line of argument, I claim that there is a gap in our understanding of learning and computer technology. This gap is rooted in misconceptions surrounding the nature of learning and technology; inattention to learning in all its forms, including self-direct, collectively directed, and tacit;

inability to conceptualize learning across multiple spheres of activity; and, finally, the denial of the cultural, historical, and political-economic dimensions of both learning and computer technologies. Each of these missteps contributes to a model of human learning capacity that is biased against subordinate groups generally and various working-class groups specifically. I suggest that the model points to a mechanism akin to Bourdieu's concept of *distinction* in that it describes the reproduction of a sense of learning held, more or less equally by all class groups, that hierarchically orders what would otherwise be a pluralism of human practice. Sociocultural perspectives, beginning with the work of the Soviet psychologist Vygotsky and continuing to contemporary approaches such as situated learning and activity theory, are the starting point for a pluralistic view of learning.

The second line of argument is based on a variety of diverse original empirical studies that trace what is unique about learning and computer technology from a working-class standpoint. Given the onslaught of technology on the shopfloor and the dominant discourses of technological progress, computers hold a unique place in the minds of manufacturing workers in this historical period. Drawing on Gramsci, I show how working-class people are subject to a form of *technological common sense* that is used to understand and orient their computer learning practice. *Common sense* is that contradictory mix of myths, half-truths, and hard practical lessons that in fact reflect the contradictory standpoint that working people occupy in society. In terms of a critical conceptualization of learning, as I have suggested, understanding learning as a definitively social process that takes place across multiple spheres of activity (in the workplace, the home, the neighborhood, and so forth) is key. However, for working-class groups, this expansive pattern of learning is constantly under the pressure of *fragmentation*, and forms of regulation and control, that give it a nondichotomous but nevertheless identifiable class character. I argue that there is a unique set of dispositions and tendencies that emerges from and reproduces class relations, but that also provides opportunities for mundane forms of resistance and the possibility of social transformation. Drawing on the work of Bourdieu, I refer to this set of dispositions as a *working-class learning habitus*. I argue that the learning habitus is rooted in people's experiences of formal learning and a broader response to subordination through which people learn to operate in the *interstitial spaces* of institutional life. Indeed, as I show, under conditions of stable community forms, this habitus gives rise to *solidaristic* computer learning networks. I demonstrate that, although affected by other major social divisions as well, such networks depend on the production of a *proletarian public sphere* and class-specific forms of oral culture, as well as the distribution of material resources. Even under the best conditions, however, the outcome of this rich hidden (to learners and observers alike) layer of computer learning is contradictory. On the one hand, people can be seen to commodify their own everyday learning, organizing it in terms of exchange-value production and directing it toward the capitalist labor process. On the other hand, we see both organized (e.g., via trade union activity) and more spontaneous (e.g., via cooperative economic activity) deviations from this exchange-value orientation.

In the last instance, this analysis is intended to be more than a detailed look at a tightly delimited topic. Ways of making practical use of these findings are suggested throughout the book, but they are properly elaborated in the concluding chapter. Policy choices for business, policymakers, and, most important, the labor movement in terms of learning, computer technology, and positive social change are outlined.

Acknowledgments

In the introduction to this book, I write that working in an auto parts factory was the most engaging intellectual experience of my life, but of course, it wasn't the work that made it interesting. It was the engagement with people who were trying to find creative ways to resist work, to stay human within work, and perhaps to find a way to defeat work, as well as all those others who were doing their best just to get by. The positive learning I did was the result of my fellow workers. All this points to the debt I owe to my coworkers, but it also suggests the importance of the labor movement for meaningful learning. The labor movement – from its most formalized organizational and legalistic expressions down to its heart and soul in the informal solidarities that emerge in unionized and nonunionized workplaces alike – is as central for learning in working-class life as it was for the making of this book.

However, there are more specific debts that I owe as well. I'm indebted to the people who took time to talk with me and pass on their stories. These people didn't provide "data" but rather engaged with me to make sense of the relationship between class, technology, and learning. Primarily, these were members of the Communications, Energy and Paperworkers Union of Canada; the Canadian Autoworkers; and the United Steelworkers of America, as well as my nonunionized workmates in the auto parts factory. As always, some people were particularly important to the process as guides and insiders and, through the process, fellow travelers and friends. These people included Tam Gallagher, Paul Davies and Larry Williams, Lyn and Sherry James, Kevin "Sully" Sullivan, and Dan DeLeon and Cindy Spanjevic.

Though the shortcomings of this work fall on my own shoulders, I must thank the editors at Cambridge University Press, the anonymous reviewers, and Philip Laughlin, who made the process of publishing my first solo work a delight and all of whose suggestions improved the quality of the text immensely. Along related lines, I acknowledge the help of Dorothy Smith, Yrjö Engeström, and Alan Thomas for their comments on earlier drafts. Fellow students also helped me in introducing alternative ideas and literatures. Here I'm thinking of Matt Adams, Reuben Roth, Paul Raun, Patrice Milewski, Lorena Gajardo, Megan Terepocki, and Andrew Thornton. I am particularly indebted, however, to Jorge Garcia-Orgales, David Livingstone, D'Arcy Martin, and Bruce Spencer. These are the people with whom I've worked most closely over the years and who have been most intimately involved in my lifelong education. Each of them has modeled for me the mix of commitment, outrage, and intelligence that defines the best traditions of the Canadian left.

I want to also acknowledge the people who've supported me in a more general way. My mother, Betty Farrish, taught me from an early age to listen carefully, stand up, and take a side. And finally, my wife, Jill, is central to anything I've been able to do here. She has patiently supported me through my schooling and my various early work lives.

Introduction

At the end of what I thought was the last of my schooling life, I began work as a press operator at a local auto parts factory not far from where I grew up. I worked there approximately 2 years, full-time, but on a probationary basis. After those 2 years, I applied for a permanent position but was turned down. Later that year I applied to graduate school, and began doctoral studies that included the research for this book.

That period of life taught me many lessons about learning that years spent in the educational system hadn't. It was at the auto parts factory that I moved beyond the abstract ideas about social class, culture, and learning to begin to see the living dynamics and contradictions of working-class life and adult learning in the concrete. Learning was all around and crossed the boundaries of home, community, and the workplace. It took place on the shopfloor, at the pub on lunches, sometimes at courses, and often around the home and neighborhood. It involved learning for the job, but more often it involved learning that was about everything but the job. Even stranger to me at the time, though I'd arrived as a kind of "certified" learner, with a university degree no less, I was amazed to see how little my papers really prepared me for how learning in working-class life got done.

Though learning happened everywhere, the workplace held a special place as an important organizing principle in people's learning lives. From my experiences in the factory, learning came through movement as I was bumped around from job to job. Typically, I'd be shown a machine by a senior worker, having its operation demonstrated to me with instructions shouted through the noise and never more than half heard. I was stationed mostly in the cold form department, where metal was stamped into shape by giant industrial presses. Instruction included locating the buttons that made the machine cycle, the places where workers shouldn't put their hands, vague demonstrations of acceptable quality, and the number of

1

parts, that is, the worker's required production quota, for the shift. After this, I was left to my own devices. Usually a couple of dozen pieces later, something would go wrong: The parts would begin to come out with mistakes or the machine would simply stop working. I'd peer into the machine, turn it off and on, walk around it, and then (inevitably) begin to wander through the department in search of the worker who had gotten me started. If this person wasn't available, another might help me.

If the machine really had broken down, I'd become a peripheral member of a congregation of workers who'd drop what they were doing and wander over for a brief look and a kind of half-yelled discussion that consisted more of actions than of words. Sometimes after only a short time these people would scatter because word would come that a supervisor was on the way. At other times, however, people got a chance to mill around the large machine for a while. What's more, they seemed to do it in a specific pattern, with more experienced workers taking the initiative, less experienced workers trailing close behind, occasionally checking a hunch of their own, and novices like me on the outside, watching closely and staying out of the way. I was truly dependent on the group of fellow workers in my department. People who've been in the position I'm describing know that if your fellow workers do not take you under their wing, learning can turn into an experience of social exclusion and powerlessness no matter what kind of diploma or degree you have. The social and the cultural, not the certified, the individual, or the cognitive, were definitive of the learning process.

I initially imagined that if I could just get a written manual with standard procedures, I'd be fine. I could do my learning *by myself*. But there was no manual, nor could there ever be one that met the learning needs on that shopfloor. What were needed were tacit skills, practical connections, and access to the knowledge hidden in the cracks and crevices of people's lives in and beyond work. What I saw was that one's knowing – even for the most experienced worker on the floor – depended upon ongoing integration with others. Learning was *our* ability to move about the plant, it was how closely *we* could be watched, and it was the structure of *our* time and space. Learning was defined by the chances we had to participate in mundane conversation. The reality of this learning had precious little to do with classrooms that made writing a test *alone* a measure of what a person could do or know. Solidarity and social connection defined one's ability to learn. It was the barriers, and the ways people beat them and didn't beat them, and listening to the stories people would tell about trying to beat them – this was the guts of the learning process. It meant escaping boredom, solving the practical problems of stubborn machines and idiotic rules, and it meant feeling more human both within and beyond the workplace.

It might be contrary to conventional wisdom, but for me, my 2 years working in that factory and living in the community around the factory were the most intellectually stimulating of my life. These experiences brought the abstract and disinterested social sciences to life. In fact, as I looked back on these memories, I saw in them the origins of virtually every argument I present in this book. I saw the seeds of a critique of conventional adult learning theory. I saw and felt the effects of technology, and of course, I saw the pressing need for class analysis.

It has been understood for some time that social class plays an important role in people's education. An entire range of literatures that I won't review here outline this claim in myriad forms. At the same time, school and the classroom can hardly be said to be the sole or even the primary domain of learning, particularly in adult life and particularly among those who keep a distance from organized courses. From this realization there emerges a type of gap: How does social class affect learning in all its forms? This book is about seeing how social class is related to the learning that people do in a variety of social spheres including the home, the neighborhood, and the workplace. Though the book is about more than work-based learning, some of the most important discussions of learning, particularly at the policy level, require a discussion of people's lives as workers. In these terms, statements from business and government, as well as from most academic and media sources, ring with an apparent consensus: Our society and economy lack knowledge production capacity, and workers, both current and future, need to be whipped into shape. Technological adoption and computer learning in particular are thought to be central to the knowledge work process. However, to date, only a narrow band of researchers have sought to investigate the existing practices of working people in their attempts to make sense of, to cope with, and to self-educate in the face of technological change, and of these, few look beyond formal training. Fewer still have sought to investigate the everyday world of working-class informal learning and computers, and no sustained, theoretically informed research that I'm aware of has been undertaken to date that examines these broad learning processes from the standpoint of working-class people themselves.

Focusing on manufacturing workers in Canada's industrial heartland (southern Ontario), I've tried to draw on my own experience as a factory worker, trade unionist, adult and labor educator, and sociologist to offer a detailed look at computers and learning practice among working-class people. I make use of *learning life-history* interviews in which people shared their life experiences in a series of lengthy sessions that often illuminated some of their deepest desires, fears, and hopes. Supporting these data, I draw on selected ethnographic observation in homes and factories, as well as illustrative analyses of large-scale survey materials and microanalyses of human–computer interaction. Taken as a whole, this research provides evidence of the complexity, the contradiction, and above all the class-based character of adult learning and technology in people's lives.

In terms of its value to broad economic policy discussions, the evidence in this book suggests that economic shortcomings, slowed productivity gains, and the inability of organizations to meet the challenges of a globalized economy do not revolve around the lack of learning among workers. Indeed, in a historical period in which lifelong learning, knowledge work, and high-tech production options are regularly touted as magic bullets, I show the type of unused knowledge creation that currently exists among workers. What we see throughout the text are the ways in which working people learn together, often in the form of networks. And based on the analysis, I suggest that economic problems may be rooted in the social organization of work, the lack of open forms of free association at work, and, ultimately, the lack of worker control within the labor process. We see that the apparent problem of a *technological underclass* is less a reflection of the availability of equipment or people's cognitive abilities than a matter of their access to stable cultural communities that recognize and build upon the social standpoints of their members, which in turn provides a voice, opportunities, and power for these communities. I provide an account of the attempts of particular members of an important social group to cope with ongoing changes in society within and beyond work, and in so doing I challenge the myth that adult learning – even the everyday forms of learning that are, in principle, open to all – can be understood as class neutral.

The material presented in this book lies at the intersection of several different bodies of literature including adult education, labor studies, sociology of education, sociology of work, cultural studies, and technological/computer studies. It provides a discussion of adult learning in the everyday that is absent from the vast majority of studies of work culture and social class, and it provides a critical class analysis of human–computer interaction. The chapters provide a fairly detailed account of working-class perspectives, experiences, and practices surrounding how and why working people like the ones I speak with learn about computers. I argue that class processes give rise to unique patterns of learning, and I examine the meanings that emerge from class experiences in the school, the community, the union hall, and the home, as well as the workplace. I explore the material structures that shape learning practices, and I examine the role of oral communication in the reproduction of skill and knowledge, and relations of class themselves. As Michael Burawoy remarked of his own seminal study, "this is not an exercise in neo-Marxism, Marxist revisionism, or any other label social scientists may apply to the Marxism they may wish to take seriously. Rather, it is a Marxist study" (1979:xii). I too am primarily concerned with change in and continuity of class life within capitalism. By explicitly combining a Marxist framework with key theories of adult education, and with critical understandings of technology, I hope to show how working-class practices contribute to the reproduction of capitalism while at the same time producing openings for unexpected change and the potential for social transformation. This is, however, an exploration rooted in an abstraction. The specific focus on social class tends to leave out other key processes of subordination – to begin with, those based on race and gender. Concrete reality involves the interaction and simultaneity of these processes, and thus, although it is still useful to explore class as a specific social phenomenon, the study must be said to have important limitations. At points it becomes virtually impossible to separate out the effects of gender and race. In these instances, I've presented some modest discussion that, unfortunately, can only begin to scratch the surface of the real complexity of subordination in social life.

Ultimately, the implications of this discussion include the distinct possibility that the activities examined lie at a historical conjuncture in the political economy of adult learning. The emergence of the discourse of lifelong learning may be a very real and specific flashpoint for the more generalized social struggles that characterize the latest phase of capitalism. In other words, the discourse of lifelong learning, though not monolithic, may represent a previously unheard of penetration of capitalist relations into the lifeworld of human communities: a qualitatively different level of market rationalization of human activity. In the following chapters, we can begin to see the extent to which people see their lives as the production of exchange values in the form of skills, knowledge, experience, and credentials for sale in a labor market. Boundaries between home, community, and work life dissolve. We see how people are, perhaps more than ever, understanding their lives as a type of lifelong capitalist economic enterprise. Learning is increasingly understood, discursively and institutionally, through the lens of capital accumulation by which human beings are converted into what has been called *enterprising selves*.

The text is organized into two basic parts. It begins with discussions of the central concepts of learning and computer technology, followed by chapters that each focus on a different theme within the exploration of working-class computer learning. Overall, the argument is organized as an accumulation of related but distinctive discussions and claims. More specifically, in Chapter 2 I provide an explanation of what's been called *'class deficit'* theories of learning (Curtis, Livingstone, and Smaller, 1992; Livingstone, 1999; Livingstone and Sawchuk, 2000; Livingstone and Sawchuk, in press). I review several dominant theories of adult learning for their ability to make visible the social relations that shape computer learning in the everyday from a working-class standpoint. I reflect on the interlocking set of class biases in adult learning theory to organize the critique. My own analysis draws on various sociocultural theories of adult learning, and in this chapter I conclude with a critical introduction to the situated learning perspective of Lave and Wenger (e.g., 1991) and activity theory (e.g., Leont'ev, 1981; Engeström, 1987).

In Chapter 3, I situate computer technology historically in terms of relations of social class. I begin with remarks on the development of computer technologies and the social relations "cemented" in them. I draw on the work of technology historians David Noble, Lewis Mumford, and Andrew Feenberg to identify specific capital- and labor-centric approaches to understanding and developing technology. In the second half of the chapter, I focus on the meaning and experience of computer technology in the lives of the people interviewed. I outline a working-class technological "common sense" that is directly linked to class relations in the home, community, workplace, and labor market. This discussion helps us to understand the alternative perspectives on technology and provides a prologue to the more specific discussion of tool-mediated learning later on.

Chapter 4 focuses on some of the tacit elements of computer-based activity through the use of fine-grained microanalysis of interaction. By definition, the tacit is not easily expressed in interviews. Thus, these two abbreviated case studies serve as "specimens" for our development of a deeper understanding of the social processes involved in the computer learning practice that people describe during interviews. The first study deals with two unemployed men learning to use computers together in a computer lab in a Labour Education Centre in Toronto (Canada). This analysis provides a detailed look at the way people create knowledge and skill collectively through tool-mediated interaction. This case study links a major element of my critique of adult learning theory in Chapter 2, namely, the pedagogical and individualized biases of learning theory, with computing specifically. In the second case study, I present a detailed analysis of worker–computer–organization interaction. By looking at a worker's interaction with the screen texts of company software in an auto parts factory purchasing office, we see how worker activity is tacitly organized and controlled. We also see the informal ways that workers, nevertheless, learn together despite company rules.

In Chapter 5, I draw on activity theory and situated learning frameworks to present interview data that show the dynamics of how working-class people carry out their computer learning across a variety of social spheres. I demonstrate how this computer learning is tool-mediated and can involve what I refer to as *solidaristic networks* that operate at the intersection of multiple systems of activity. The analysis introduces one of the key contributions the book has to make to studies of adult learning, namely, a novel application of Pierre Bourdieu's concept of habitus. This chapter begins to outline several core features of a working-class learning habitus, the modes of participation from which it arises, and the forms of activity it tends to produce.

Chapter 6 offers a brief but focused discussion of working-class standpoints in computer activity. It draws on concepts developed in the work of Georg Lukács and various Marxist-feminist standpoint theorists. I show how issues of working-class standpoint can be used to radicalize adult learning theory generally and activity theory and situated learning approaches specifically. I provide a brief discussion of large-scale survey data showing interclass comparisons in terms of learning methods, and I compare the computer learning among workers who are unionized and nonunionized to highlight the effect of organized expressions of class standpoints on the working-class learning habitus. Finally, I review interview data from an upper-class mini-sample that further illustrates class effects on perspectives and practices involving technology and learning in the everyday.

Chapter 7 outlines the relevance of everyday conversation in working people's learning. Following the provocative work of Julian Orr (1996), I show how talk is used for working-class computer learning in two distinct ways: (1) within the course of computer-based learning practice and (2) outside of computer-based practice as a means of knowledge storage. Both forms of talk are shown to make use of specific oral artifacts or devices in such a way as to share knowledge and maintain communicative interaction despite the barriers of technical language, as well as to coordinate group membership and express class standpoints in activity.

In Chapter 8, I focus on the material barriers and contexts that face working-class computer learners. I discuss issues of social standpoint, and I include reflections on survey data that again show distinct class differences. Importantly, in this chapter I provide several brief discussions of the effects of gender and social class together, using examples that focus on experiences in workplace learning and the division of labor in the home. I point to my own previous research that provides everyday examples of how segmented labor markets and relations of language in the workplace also help to differentiate people's learning experiences in terms of race–class interactions. Finally, I evaluate recent Canadian computer access and use research to show several important gaps in its understanding and representation of working-class practices.

In Chapter 9, I discuss the process of commodification and its role in the coordination of computer learning in political economic terms specifically. As it applies to the way that people think about and carry out their learning, commodification is a process through which people integrate their lives and abilities with capitalist markets. In this process, the production of skill and knowledge becomes less and less driven by individual and community needs directly, and more and more driven by the logic and imperatives of profit making and capital. The chapter further refines the class analysis potential of activity theory and shows how class relations – and specifically what Marx called the *inner contradiction of use and exchange-value within the commodity-form* – are implicated in the motive-structure of activity. We see how exchange-value orientations in working-class computer activity represent a process of incorporation into capitalist relations, whereas use-value orientations produce activity that runs tangential or in some cases in direct opposition to the degenerative cycles of capital accumulation.

Chapter 10 summarizes the separate elements of the argument that adult learning undertaken in everyday life and across multiple spheres of activity is thoroughly saturated with relations of social class. Not only can we see that class relations play a role in the dominant ways of thinking and talking about learning, but I summarize the claims that the differential class perspectives and experiences with computer technology, the specific class-based dispositions toward the learning process, and the differential material contexts of learning practice all suggest the need for class analysis. I include a brief discussion of practical applications of the major findings and then outline two broad policy directions that the research suggests.

1 Understanding Learning, Technology, and Social Class

Concepts and Claims

To borrow an image from James Greeno, contrary to the symbol of Auguste Rodin's "The Thinker," in which thought, if not learning, is symbolized as an isolated, internalized, and perhaps even painful event, the general goal of this book is to set aside this commonsense view and look at what people really do in their everyday lives. Indeed, in researching working-class computer learning, it became obvious that the symbols associated with our commonsense view of learning were systematically misleading. An alternative perspective suggests that learning is part of the ongoing social lives of particular people, that learning is full of moments of choice and contingency, but that it is also subject to specific types of what Raymond Williams called *limits and pressures* unique to participants' social standpoint in society.

In speaking of "particular people," I mean to emphasize that social relations can never be understood, nor are they ever produced, from a universal, generic position in the world. People's activities are always accomplished from a particular point in social, historical, and material space. This recognition is crucial to the text in a number of ways. First, the idea of standpoints plays an important role in the way I conceptualize social class. Second, in terms of data collection and analysis, the starting point was a methodological commitment to hear and move out from the stories of people's everyday lives, specifically their involvement in a range of class processes. Finally, my own standpoint in the research is a bit complex. My class position, for example, mixes experiences of a working-class upbringing with adult experiences as a middle-class academic. Moreover, I can hardly claim to be a disinterested observer. My background as an adult educator, labor educator, and trade unionist, as well as a sociologist, makes this impossible. I think these basic recognitions, conceptually, methodologically, and biographically, are key to understanding the arguments I present, and of course, they set the stage for honest and productive criticism.

Computer Technology

But why computers? Simply put, computerized technology represents a critical form of tool mediation in this phase of capitalist development. Though creative technology use is often thought to be limited to the higher-income, consumer "digerati" and/or is simply thought of as a means to deskill workers, it is also the case that computer technology opens up new possibilities for both sanctioned and unsanctioned worker mediation in the world of work and beyond. In core industrialized countries, computer use is both an economic and a cultural phenomenon. Its presence sutures together people's practices across different spheres of their lives in very specific and, I argue, class-bound ways. In Canada, according to federal statistics, home computer, modem, and Internet use are all rapidly on the rise (see Table 1.1).

In the workplace we see growing computer use in virtually all occupational groups (average = 15 hours per week), with scientists, clerical workers, and managers leading the way in time use (25, 23, and 19 hours per week, respectively) and manufacturing workers averaging approximately 14 hours per week (Krahn and Lowe, 1998:104–106). Large-scale surveys by Betcherman, Leckie, and McMullen (1997) confirm that both computer use and computer training are on the rise in Canadian workplaces, but they add that access is overwhelmingly provided to those with a postsecondary education in management or professional positions. Similar trends can be seen throughout most industrialized countries; they suggest the operation of class-based processes. However, these statistical overviews tell us very little about actual, everyday, computer-based activity.

From the pages of the MIS Quarterly to PC Magazine, the computer revolution is typically fought in a black box where we never learn what people do, only that

Table 1.1. *Use of Information Technology in Canada (Percentage of Households)*

	1982	1987	1992	1995	1996	1997	1998
Home computer ownership	—	—	20	29	32	40	45
Modem	—	—	—	12	16	25	32
Internet	—	—	—	—	7	17	25

Source: Statistics Canada Catalogue 11-001-E.

they should now be able to do whatever they do faster and more easily by computing. What meaning can the "service economy," the "information economy," the "knowledge economy," and similar terms have unless they denote substantive changes either in what people do for a living or how they do it? The obvious answer is little. Yet journalists, futurists, and even sociologists routinely employ such epithets without explaining precisely what kinds of work they have in mind.... We sorely need rich descriptive data on what people do and how they do it.... (Barley in Introduction to Orr, 1996:xi–xiii)

At the same time, recent surveys in North America report that the "digital divide," revolving around occupational type and income, may not be as simple as it once was. Working-class homes and blue-collar workers specifically are increasingly being recognized as computer literate web surfers. A report from *American Demographic* magazine, for example, suggests that the class–digital division is a complicated one mediated by a range of factors beyond occupation and income.

This gap in our understanding has been recognized in isolated streams of literature; however, focused empirical studies of actual learning practice, particularly those that deal with issues of social class, continue to be rare. Studies of learning that look at informal activity, that examine the role of tacit as well as conscious forms of learning, and that integrate the cultural, political, economic, and material contexts of practice remain particularly elusive. At least part of the problem resides in the theoretical frameworks used to understand adult learning and technology use; however, an additional problem lies in the general lack of analysis of social class and class standpoints. In regard to finding effective conceptual understandings of phenomena, activity theory's notion of *tool mediation* is key. It is a concept that provides the potential to understand the way that computer artifacts actually enter into people's everyday practice.

Social Class and Class Standpoints

In this book, I begin with a conception of social class that is rooted in the observations made by E. P. Thompson in the introduction to his classic historical work *The Making of the English Working Class* (1963). For Thompson, like Marx, *working class* was, above all, a relational concept. Emphatically, despite the fact that we sometimes must resort to speaking of it as such, social class was not a category but a living relationship:

Sociologists who have stopped the time-machine and, with a good deal of huffing and puffing, have gone down to the engine-room to look, tell us that nowhere at all have they been able to locate and classify a class. They can only find a multitude of people with different occupations, incomes, status-hierarchies, and the rest. Of course they are right, since class is not this or that part of the machine, but *the way the machine works* once it is set in motion – not this and that interest, but the *friction* of interests – the movement itself, the heat, the thundering noise.... When we speak of a class we are thinking of a very loosely defined body of people who share the same congeries of interests, social experiences, traditions and value-system, who have a *disposition* to *behave* as a class, to define themselves in their actions and in their consciousness in relation to other groups of people in class ways. But class is not a thing, it is a happening. (p. 939; emphasis in the original)

Marx was equally clear on the matter. He outlined proletarian and capitalist distinctions as abstractions in which the real constitution of society by no means consisted only of the classes of worker and capitalist (Marx, 1861–1863/1987:312–332). Coming at the issue from a slightly different direction, Resnik and Wolf (1987) put it succinctly enough when they said, "class is an adjective not a noun." Indeed, although social class involves relations closely linked with the processes of paid work in which people who, in order to survive, sell their labor power to those who purchase it in order to engage in a process of capital accumulation, we should not think of class as limited to this basic set of relationships. Rather social class, as a process, is linked with production of goods and services *as well as* the full range of activities that include circulation, distribution, and consumption. Tracing these connections throughout the different spheres of life helps distinguish this approach from the classical or mechanical base/superstructure models that some Marxists use (and most Marxists are accused of using). However, although class can't be reduced to economics, we cannot afford to ignore the economic dimensions of social practice if we hope to provide anything like a broad analysis of people's learning lives. In short, the political-economic world of work, labor markets, and commodification matters. No doubt, class can be a slippery concept: Understood as a category or as an extension of the classical base/superstructure model, social class becomes mortified, a frozen description with little analytic power. However, understood as a living, historical process, the concept of social class remains as important and as illuminating as ever. In keeping with this expansive social-relational approach to class as a living process, in this book my references to "working people," "the working class," and so forth are always made with this basic explanation in mind: The working class is not some monolithic mass of people, but rather people of many types engaged in class processes from a working-class standpoint.

This relational approach to social class is not new, however. It has its origins in some of the earliest Marxist writing. It was a key component of the approach of Georg Lukács (1971) and has, in turn, partially inspired the more recent Marxist-feminist standpoint theory. It is this latter theory, developed by a diverse group of scholars, that has made perhaps the most important contributions to our understanding of the social standpoints of subordinated groups along class as well as gendered and racialized lines.

Equally fundamental to the approach to social class I take, however, is the role played by the type of materialism originally advocated by the young Marx, one that is outlined most expansively in *The German Ideology* (1845–1846/1996a). It is in this set of writings that Marx most clearly argues for the necessity of the focus on the "practical," "sensuous activity" that makes up practice in the real world. This practical activity includes ideologies and discourses, as well as the effects of tools that bear the history of the social and technical divisions of the human labor that produced them. In this way, it is my concern to understand the relationships between practical activity, class processes, and social transformation that mark the continued relevance of Marx's early work to the subject of this book.

However, it is not only the work of the young Marx that is important. His later work focuses on the political-economic forces that constitute the production and reproduction of social class under capitalism. There he specifically highlights the role of the contradiction of the commodity form: the tension between *use-values* and *exchange-values*. In brief, use-value refers to the value of goods/services/skills realized in direct human use, whereas exchange-value refers to the value of goods/services/skills mediated by exchange in a market.[1] For Marx, it was the process of commodification, that is, the production of use-value and exchange-value under capitalism, that was the key to understanding how capitalism works. It is within these processes, and how they are re-created every day, that we find the very core of the economic production of social class. In this

---

[1] Strictly speaking, in Marxist terms, the terms are not *use-value* and *exchange-value* but rather *use-value* and *value*. I retain the former terms as a means of making the concepts explicit for a broad audience. Chapter 9 focuses on the concepts of exchange and use-value specifically, but for now, as a device to bring the basic distinction between the two concepts to the fore, I suggest looking at the comparative use-value and exchange-values of diamonds and water. Water has exceptional use-value in human life but negligible exchange-value due to its relative abundance (of course, this situation is changing with environmental degradation). On the other hand, diamonds have little practical use but surprisingly large exchange-value. This comparison oversimplifies the notion of *practical use* that should be understood in an expansive way, but I hope that the comparison helps readers new to the basic ideas.

book, I argue that the process of commodification is intimately related to computer learning practice, and that this process plays a central role in producing, expressing, and perpetuating relations of social class in people's everyday lives.

Before moving beyond these opening statements on social class, however, it is perhaps necessary to address a question that some readers will have at the outset regarding my focus on manufacturing workers and the industrial, working class. After all, we are told incessantly that we live in a post-Fordist, a postindustrial, and perhaps even a postmodern age. Robots do the factory work now, not people. Social formations associated with the "old" industrial order, in particular trade unions, are said to be irrelevant. But in taking a closer look at some of these claims, we see several reasons why industrial workers may be as good a starting point as any for discussions of working-class life. First of all, to paraphrase Mark Twain, reports of the demise of the industrial working class are exaggerated. Mass media and the effects of dominant ideologies offer a partial explanation for this exaggeration, but it is just as likely that it speaks to the relative decline of the industrial sectors of core capitalist countries rather than an overall decline in industrial activity around the world as a whole. In addition, though nowhere near the levels of the second Industrial Revolution, the activities of this social group continue to make up a significant portion of the national economies in Canada and elsewhere, and as Myles (1991) so effectively argues, even in a postindustrial economy, "manufacturing matters." Indeed, new areas of the economy, the service sector for example, are rapidly being transformed by remarkably familiar Fordist and even Taylorist principles. Moreover, though robotics is being increasingly introduced, new variations of industrial work that still require people continue to reappear. In addition, on the issue of relevance, it remains important to note that organized industrial workers – warts and all – still represent one of the most coherent voices of the working class. This point takes on special relevance because working-class standpoints and perspectives, let alone intelligible class-based strategies that might emerge from them, require stable cultural communities for their development and expression. Though battered, industrial unionism can still provide a good measure of this stability and with it these forms of cultural community. So, perhaps more important than the number of industrial manufacturing jobs lost or the more or less rapid decline of the influence of the manufacturing sectors in the core capitalist countries, in this book I am interested in the industrial working class for what it can teach us about the social order and the role of adult learning and technology in it.

Finally, my focus on the industrial working class is related to the type of argument I make and the epistemological position I take in making it. My claims do not emerge from some form of positivist argument rooted in representativeness, the aggregation of findings and extrapolation. I did not tally the number of times people said they did this or felt that. I did interview a relatively large number of people in carrying out the research, and I drew on the fullness of this sample to test the relevance of my analysis. However, the heart of the analysis itself was the careful consideration of concrete descriptions of practice, with the understanding that detailed exploration of any single part of a system is a valid way of understanding the system as a whole. In other words, each part contains within it the essential principles, though differently expressed, of the totality. My assumption is that the industrial working class, like any other of the myriad subgroupings subject to class processes from a working-class standpoint, provides a microcosm through which we can gain a better understanding of the intersection of social class, technology, and learning in general.

Adult Learning Theory

The relevance of computer technology and issues of social class in today's society, the concern for practical, everyday activity and informal learning, as well as the challenges of the data are all important contributors that shape my discussion of adult learning theory. This research builds on previous work (Sawchuk, 1996, 1997, 1998a, 1998b, 1999a, 1999b, 2000a, 2000b, 2002; Livingstone and Sawchuk, 2000, in press), and in particular extends earlier investigations of informal working-class learning networks. In this early work, I discovered the need for a coherent, systematic means to make visible the learning that working-class people do that so often goes unnoticed or is obscured by dominant perspectives on learning. In this book, I challenge existing literatures on self-directed, transformative, incidental, and experiential learning. I suggest that the vast majority of theories of adult learning cannot adequately conceptualize and document learning that includes conscious as well as tacit dimensions; that is individually directed as well as collectively organized; and that is rooted in specific political-economic contexts. My emphasis is on informal, everyday forms of learning that occur outside of formalized educational settings because, simply put, this is where the computer learning of the people I spoke with was rooted. As a response, I draw on two sociocultural theories of learning that I argue allow us to better understand learning from subordinate standpoints throughout its full range of variation. Indeed, I suggest that these approaches democratize our understanding of learning, counter the obscuration that many theories of adult learning achieve, and allow us to understand the practices of dominant and subordinate groups on an equal footing.

Sociocultural theories of learning, specifically activity theory (e.g., Engeström, 1987; Cole, Engestrom, and Vasquez, 1997) and situated learning theory (e.g., Lave and Wenger, 1991), have the potential to open up informative discussions of learning in all its forms and among the entire spectrum of social participants. As I explain in Chapter 2, dominant theories express and help to reproduce a class bias by emphasizing certain features of the learning process over others. The result is the tendency to ignore, deny, denigrate, or degrade the learning of subordinate groups such as the working class (Livingstone and Sawchuk, 2000). In this way, we might say that the first step in analyzing the class relations of computer learning is to change the way that learning itself is understood.

Additional Concepts

The application of the concept of class standpoints and political economy to the issues of computer learning, I think, makes a relevant contribution to the activity theory and situated learning approaches. Both of these approaches continue to enjoy sustained growth and development, and they are certainly valuable additions to current understandings in the field of adult education. However, activity theory and situated learning scholarship has been slow to explore the effects of major social divisions. Nardi (1996) has commented that in the area of computer-based activity specifically, researchers have generally not sought to deal with "the messy, intractable world beyond the laboratory, beyond the human–machine dyad" (p. 3). Seeking to use these theories of social participation to understand class processes means examining the possibility of competing standpoints and conflicting cultural formations, and in my view requires an appreciation of issues of *multivoicedness* (Engeström, 1999). In this book, social class is understood as a process through which people actively accomplish their everyday lives. If we begin with a sociocultural perspective on learning that defines the learning process as a mediated system of participation, then we must also recognize that although people exercise freedom in their participation with each other as individual human agents, they are hardly free to participate in any way they chose. People have different experiences by virtue of their standpoint in the social world, by virtue of their relationship to tools that mediate their participation, and by virtue of the distribution of material and cultural resources. Their participation reproduces patterns that define major social divisions, though these patterns can also undergo changes that are unexpected. Thus a model of adult learning that can help us understand the class dimensions of learning practice must recognize this practice as both differentiated and differentiating, all the while associated with opportunities for individual and social transformation.

Understanding the relationship between past experience, current learning, and the reproduction of working-class life requires, in my view, concepts that were developed with these types of sensitivities and interests in mind. In order to better understand working-class life and its relationship to adult learning and computer technology, I draw on concepts that come from outside conventional activity theory and situated learning frameworks. Building on a brief but critical review of Bourdieu's concept of habitus and field (e.g., 1977, 1984), I discuss the notion of a *working-class learning habitus*. This refers to the dispositions, habits, and preferences that people develop and use as a means of selecting and being selected into various class-based learning practices or modes of participation in activity. As one writer described it, the concept of habitus is "an elegant instrument to express the nonintended reproduction of the social structure by the intended action of individuals in their everyday-life" (Koch, 1996:198). It does not describe a body of rules or codes of behavior, but rather refers to a type of preobjective, precognitive framework for practice. Ultimately, the learning habitus is related to the generation of class divisions, and at points throughout the book, I argue that the social process of generating *learning capacity* is analogous to the process that Bourdieu explored in his description of the generation of aesthetic judgment or *distinction* (1984). Thus, the application of the concept of habitus provides us access to a sophisticated body of thought that has consistently sought to understand the everyday practice of dominant and subordinate groups, the political-economic dimensions of cultural practice, and the contingency and continuity of social life in capitalist societies.

One final concept I import into my discussion of activity theory and situated learning deals with working-class orientations to computer technology specifically. This orientation affects people's computer learning in a profound way. I describe this orientation as a "working-class technological common sense" that builds on the notion of common sense developed in the work of Antonio Gramsci (1971). Like the use of habitus, the work of Gramsci helps us better understand the relations of social class and the political-economic significance of these perspectives on computer technology. Gramsci's work specifically highlights how this form of common sense emerges from a mix of ideologies: namely, dominant notions of technological progress, on the one hand, and the perspectives that emerge from the contradictory experience of working-class life, on the other. An analysis of common sense provides the basis for an understanding of people's own practical reasoning and sense of purpose in undertaking computer learning and situates them within a broader process of cultural hegemony. And it contributes to our understanding of the class dimensions of what activity theorists refer to as the broader *goal* and *motive* levels of computer-based activity.

Data Sources

This book draws on several original sources of data to support its claims, though the arguments depend disproportionately on interview data. Interviewees were recruited through a research initiative called the Working-Class Learning Strategies Project (WCLS) (see Livingstone and Sawchuk, in press). This original pool of interviewees was selected based on a stratified sample of employees in workplaces representing several key economic sectors. The data I use for the analysis in this book, however, dealt specifically with people (and their home partners, when available) working in the auto and chemical sectors. The small sample of elite and corporate executives that I discuss in Chapter 6 were selected through a random sampling of individuals listed in the 1997 *Directory of Canadian Corporate Executives*. In-depth, semistructured learning life-history interviews were conducted with 73 people overall. A range of demographic information is available in Appendix 1, but basically these people included: 42 men and 31 women averaging 39 years of age. The interviews themselves typically involved several audiotaped sessions per interviewee, each session lasting between 1 and 3 hours. Interviewees were asked to provide concrete descriptions of their learning practice, and, where appropriate, they were encouraged to actively think aloud about how they understood learning and technology and to discuss the contexts within which these understandings emerged. The sessions were organized as a type of life-history interview, a technique that has the potential to produce not only long but deeply personal levels of engagement. In keeping with this approach, the interviews took place in locations in which people felt most comfortable, such as their homes or local hangouts (coffee shops, pubs) and occasionally within special areas of the workplace where this could be arranged. Especially when interviews were conducted in the home, this opened up the possibility of making direct connections to the practices that people were describing. In other words, there were often opportunities for demonstration and engagement in actual learning processes. Often I was invited to sit down at the home computer while people showed me materials or equipment they were working with, and occasionally we took a walk to a neighbors' house, where informal discussions continued. Though transcribed audiotapes hardly do them justice, the many examples of this type of engagement provided important background to the analysis. Complementing these experiences, I also was able to visit and tour several of the plants where people worked. Of course, because I included many of my former workmates in the auto parts factory in the list of interviewees, I had a particularly intimate knowledge of the activities in and around this plant. Despite the fact that the research was not organized as an ethnographic study, these types of direct observation were crucial in developing a deeper understanding of context and practice. Of course, not all the interview data could be given the attention they deserved, and selection of specific excerpts was based on their ability to help describe and summarize the kinds of patterns seen across the data as a whole.

At the same time, exploring the social, informal, tacit, and collective dimensions of learning, even in semistructured interviews, was challenging. People don't generally know how to talk about learning as a social phenomenon, that is, individualistic accounts are hegemonic. Most felt that learning was an individual, conscious act of cognition rather than a situated social practice. In several areas of the book, I discuss how the way people can and cannot talk about their learning is itself a class process. However, in more general terms, the difficulty that people have in providing full accounts of their own learning is something that activity theorist recognized from the very start. Leont'ev, for example, was quick to point out that little of what constitutes learning is actually consciously recognized by the learner. So, to generate interview data on the learning process required what Dorothy Smith described as *active listening*, a process through which an interviewer can "read through the text" of the interview to discover the social organization of practice to which it refers.

The simple notion of the everyday world as problematic is that social relations external to it are present in its organization. How then are their traces to be found in the ways that people speak of their everyday lives in the course of interviews of this kind? We do not expect them to speak of social organization and social relations. The methodological assumptions of the approach we are using are that the social organization and relations of the ongoing concerting of our daily activities are continually expressed in the ordinary ways in which we speak of them, at least when we speak of them *concretely*. How people speak of the forms of life in which they are implicated is determined by those forms of life. Wittgenstein opposed the philosophical practice of lifting terms out of their original home and their actual uses in order to explore their essence. I am taking the further step of arguing that the way terms are used in their original context, including their syntactic arrangements, is "controlled" or "governed" by its social organization and that the same social organization is present as an ordering procedure in how people tell others about that original setting.... Given that we do not disrupt the process by the procedures we use, open-ended interviewing should therefore yield stretches of talk that "express" the social organization and relation of the [original] setting. (Smith, 1987:188–189; my emphasis)

Smith's discussion of "active listening" and "reading through" is essential to understanding the way I use the interview data in this book. For it is through a sustained focus on descriptions of events, and a detailed analysis of the social organization of practice that they announce, that we can begin to see the class character of adult learning and technology in people's lives.

Other data sources that I draw on in this book include two microinteraction case studies. The wish to carry out these case studies in fact grew out of preliminary analyses of the interview data. Interview data told me little about what tacit learning really looked like in practice or how computer practice is mediated by hardware, software, and specific cultural-material contexts at the level of micro-interaction. The first case study analyzes audio/videotape to carry out a fine-grained analysis of activity in a computer learning lab. The two men I recorded were informed of my research intentions, though there was little indication that these affected their activity. I chose a Labour Education Centre in order to find examples of working people actively engaging in computer learning, and the subjects themselves were selected based on the fact that the shape and size of the rather cramped room made their activity the easiest to record. The second microinteraction case study emerged from informal conversations with a clerical worker who worked at the same factory I did. I'd been asking her about computers in her work area informally for over a year before I decided that I could learn a great deal about the tacit dimensions of learning and computers if I studied her work more closely. I couldn't get access to the job, so I created a "mock-up" research protocol to explore the activity. The mock-up is a basic technique that has been used successfully by analysts facing similar constraints of access. For my study, it involved audiotaped explanations of particular work processes aided by the use of a series of paper printouts, of computer screens from the workplace software. Using these printouts, the interviewee was able to ground her explanation in concrete activities, providing access to tacit features of daily work activities and computer-mediated interaction.

The final set of data I use in the book is drawn, with permission, from Canada's first national survey of informal learning practices, which was administered in 1998 by the New Approaches to Lifelong Learning (NALL) Research Network (see Livingstone, 2000). The NALL survey produced a sample of 1,560 respondents overall; however, for the purposes of relatively clear comparison, I created two class groupings involving only 612 of these respondents. The formation of these two class groupings depended on the use of a statistical formula developed to be used in the statistics software package SPSS by Livingstone and Hart (see the discussion in Livingstone and Mangan, 1996). Using these two groupings, I illustrate several interclass variations in learning and technological use that, when considered in conjunction with the other analyses, help make us aware of class differences across larger groups of people.

Central Claims of the Book

To conclude this chapter, I want to make explicit the different claims within the book. The most basic claim I make in the chapters that follow is that working-class people are actively engaged in a much wider array of computer learning practices than has been previously documented. To the degree that these activities have been recognized, I claim that they have been poorly understood. I claim that these working-class computer learning practices in fact cannot be properly appreciated if viewed under the rubric of individualized cognitive events distinguished by formalized, pedagogical, or expert–novice relations. These practices are integrated with everyday life and mediated by artifacts including computer hardware and software, organizational settings, oral devices, class habitus, trade unions, and working-class culture. I demonstrate how working people encounter a variety of barriers and challenges that shape this learning and produce unique forms of working-class learning practice. I argue that these learning practices both express and contribute to the reproduction of the contradictory character of class life in advanced capitalist society generally. I show how class dimensions are inherent in interviewees' perspectives on computer technology, their reasons for entering into computer learning, and their general orientation toward education and the learning process. I claim that interviewees' relationship to the material structures of computer learning, as well as the types of dispositions, narratives, and forms of membership in specific social networks, also express and reproduce as well as transform class relationships. Finally, I argue that interviewees' relationships to the contradictions of the commodity form are a central political-economic dimension of their learning. The chapters that follow develop on each of these themes.

2   A Historical Materialist Examination of Theories of Adult Learning

> [People] made clothes for thousands of years, under the compulsion of the need for clothing, without a single [person] ever becoming a tailor.
> Karl Marx, *Capital*, Volume 1

Should we take the idea of learning itself to be unproblematic? Or is it possible that the way we think about learning is historical, a product of its time rather than a timeless, universal human process? If it is the latter, then we might notice that what stands for adult learning now is less an expression of value-free human capacities than of the specific social organization of society. As Marx put it almost a century and a half ago, the emergence of the concept of the *tailor* had little to do with the practice of making clothes. Could it be that people developed knowledge and skills for thousands of years without ever being considered learners?

The principal goals of this chapter are to establish a sensitivity to the historical, political-economic, and class dimensions of adult learning theory itself, to review theoretical approaches that obscure working-class learning, and finally, to offer a discussion of alternatives. In the review of key adult education literatures, the goal is to highlight the core dominant themes that run through it. Such a review demonstrates how a hegemonic bloc of basic class-deficit themes unites very different approaches in a way that may be unique to the current historical period. Building on this critique, we see the need for a critical sociocultural approach to adult learning based on the work of the Soviet cultural-historical school of psychology, activity theory, and concepts emerging from the theory of situated learning. This process of critique and the suggestion of possible alternatives, by questioning the identity of the concept of learning itself, represent the first steps toward a critical understanding of the relationships among adult learning and technology in working-class life.

Before going any further, however, some brief comments on the use of the concept of *cultural hegemony* are in order. I draw on this concept because it helps us understand the relationship between the separate, articulating components of a bloc of themes. What I suggest is that this model of how cultural domination is accomplished in modern societies is applicable to contemporary thinking about the concept of learning. Specifically, it helps us to understand how both the dominated and the dominant play an active role in the construction of what it means to learn in this day and age. According to Gramsci, the term *hegemony* expresses important dimensions of the power relationship in modern society: It describes a group's *domination* of other groups, and it describes a dominant group's *leadership* of the dominated. In this model, hegemonic relations involve a system of alliances within a dominant *historical bloc* dependent upon, as is often quoted, the "powerful system of fortresses and earthworks" of civil society (Gramsci, 1971:161). Of course, in the current period, education, training, and, by extension, learning practice can be understood as key areas of civil society. Raymond Williams, building on Gramsci's work, described hegemony as a concept that allows analysts to understand the totality of domination relations that corresponds to the reality of social experience (1997:37). Hegemonic relations, according to Williams, represents a whole body of practices, expectations, assignment of energies, and ordinary understandings of the world in terms of meanings and values.

Working from Gramsci and Williams in this way provides an important means of understanding the different ways of thinking and speaking about learning. Gramsci highlights the fact that specific forms of language often ratify deep historical continuities and become an important terrain of social struggle in particular periods. The concept of hegemony helps us understand the political economy of adult learning theory because it suggests an alliance of articulating interests that together constitute a powerful system of relevance that defines what is and what is not legitimate learning practice in our daily lives.[1] In principle, the historical bloc that dominant articulating themes produce privileges certain practices while obscuring, denigrating, or denying others. The use of the concept of hegemony offers a valuable heuristic that makes viewable an order to

---

[1] The activation of these tendencies is similar to the process that Latour (1987) described in his notion of *inscription*, in which a set of articulating assumptions represent a specific mode of understanding and representation of social reality by which control, domination, and the compliance of others are ultimately achieved.

what, in the context of academic debate, can appear to be a set of dispersed and competing theoretical programs.

The recognition of several of the themes I will discuss is not, however, particularly new. For many, these themes represent the defining features of modernism. I borrow them from Marx's own methodical critiques of bourgeois philosophy. Nevertheless, their identification in the context of adult learning literature, with specific linkages to the learning of working-class groups, offers a chance to open up new insights and fresh debate. The themes I will trace include (a) individualist/cognitivist-rationalist tendencies, (b) universal/ahistorical tendencies, and (c) formalized learning/expert–novice tendencies. Together these themes bind the potential of conventional adult learning theory to meaningfully recognize the learning of working-class groups, thus forming a significant class bias that shapes our ways of viewing, acting upon, strategizing about, policymaking for, and understanding adult learning (see also Livingstone, 1994; Livingstone and Sawchuk, 2000, in press). In general terms, theories that individualize the learner and reify learning into a cognitive-physical act make invisible the relations of collectivity and cooperation upon which subordinate groups like the working class have historically depended. Any approach to learning with the hope of articulating the experience of working-class life must engage directly with everyday activity constituted by (rather than simply taking place within) the historical political-economic relations of the period. The argument is, then, that theories of adult learning that universalize the standpoint of the learner hide the contradictory historical and political-economic relations that constitute working-class life. Finally, it is important to note that for subordinate groups, the learning that takes place beyond the classroom is of vital importance. Theories of learning premised on conventional notions of pedagogy or facilitation, or even those based strictly on the relations between expert and novice, do not provide a meaningful understanding of working-class learning more broadly.

Cultural Deficit Theories of Social Class

Theories of social action are the ultimate conceptual expression of the adult learning process. Though many have not done so explicitly, all theories of adult learning must in some way grapple with the relationship between structure and human agency, the relationship between macro and micro processes, the reproduction of social life, and the dynamics of social change. Indeed, the most relevant models of adult learning, including those of Mezirow, Giroux, Friere, Lave, Wenger, and Engeström, are the ones that most explicitly reference a broader theory of the social. Thus, before entering into a review of adult learning theory, it is important to consider briefly examples of theories of working-class capacities, working-class cultural forms, and the reproduction of class society.

Dominant accounts of working-class culture have an important reciprocal relationship to the types of hegemonic themes that run through adult education literature. As we noted in Livingstone and Sawchuk (2000), for most academic researchers today, working-class culture, if registered at all, is devoid of positive significance. Though it is obvious that people remain dependent on the wage system of capitalism, issues of social class are increasingly thought to be irrelevant. The cultural forms, expressions, perspectives, and dispositions of working-class groups are portrayed in the media as merely oppositional (reactive and uncreative) and episodic (centered on specific events, strikes, protests, etc.). The result is that in both popular media and intellectual spheres, working-class agency in active and creative cultural forms is sorely misrepresented.

Important examples of this approach in the intellectual sphere can be found in certain elements of the work of Pierre Bourdieu[2] (e.g., 1984; Bourdieu and Passeron, 1977) and Basil Bernstein (1971, 1990, 2000). Both can be seen to express versions of a *cultural capital* theory, and both have drawn on basic Marxist language in developing their approaches to class relations. Nevertheless, the work of each is so rich that a critical appreciation of their contributions is important for moving beyond the limits of a cultural capital theory of working-class practice. In the context of learning activities specifically, both authors place an emphasis on forms of class-specific cultural knowledge using grounded empirical investigations of how class reproduction, schooling, and learning are intertwined, though Bourdieu's focus tends to be on the social conditions of utterances, whereas Bernstein's relies on a discourse analysis of the utterances themselves. The writings of both are applicable to broader sets of social practice, but at their core it is claimed that children of the affluent classes, who have acquired familiarity with bourgeois cultural forms at home (through exposure to their parents' knowledge, manners, and linguistic practices), possess the means of appropriating school knowledge

---

[2] The recent work of Charlesworth (2000) seems to build on this same tradition. Like Bourdieu, Charlesworth offers an extremely sensitive account of the most dominating elements of working-class life, but offers few hints of the ways that subordinate groups can and do produce openings, forms of resistance, and so on.

relatively easily. Both authors insist that the cultural and linguistic tools imparted to the upper and middle classes account for their higher rates of success in schooling. Working-class children, in contrast, find their lack of familiarity with these cultural forms to be a major obstacle to successful school performance.

As the final volume of his influential series *Class, Codes and Control* (Volumes 1–4, 1971–1990), Bernstein produced *Pedagogy, Symbolic Control and Identity* (2000). As in earlier work, he begins and ends with a focus on the principles of communication as the nexus of the reproduction of modes of control in the context of pedagogical relations.[3] His notions of the *pedagogical device* and the *pedagogizing of knowledge* constitute his most fully developed attempt to generalize his theory of education to a theory of learning more broadly. However, schooling, as a cultural/material system, exerts powerful discursive control over notions of *learning*, and in this sense, we might say that in order to identify most easily the positive expressions of subordinate forms of *pedagogical discourse*, we would do well to look in the places where subordinate groups collectively exercise the most discretionary control (e.g., in neighborhoods, trade unions, social movements, and so on). As Apple (1992) has observed, Bernstein's point of entry to understanding codes and control has perhaps always emphasized a middle-class rather than a working-class standpoint, and in the end, the result is the charge of *class deficit* theorizing that has followed Bernstein's work from the beginning (e.g., Dittmar, 1976; Bennett and LeCompte, 1990; Livingstone, 1997b; Livingstone and Sawchuk, 2000).

Bourdieu's work, discussed fully in Chapter 5, seems to offer another form of the same problem, particularly as he develops his notion of different forms of (cultural and educational) capital. To their credit, both Bourdieu and Bernstein have carried out extensive empirically grounded

---

[3] Bernstein's arguments specifically highlight class-based differences in *elaborated* and *restricted* linguistic codes that cause differential levels of routinization and predictability of speech, i.e., the extent to which each facilitates (elaborated code) or inhibits (restricted code) an orientation to symbolize intent in a verbally explicit form. For Bernstein, these are windows into social capacities for expression and self-control that are dominated (and rewarded in schooling) by middle-class students. However, in these formulations, we see a range of narrow assumptions about legitimate forms of social organization and cultural practice: Elaborated codes align with the assumption of individualist, even competitive, contexts; restricted codes align with social cohesion and consensual/negotiated contexts. Fuller critiques of Bernstein's work can be found in Curtis, Livingstone, and Smaller (1992) and Sadovnik (1995). The underlying dynamic is that the former emphasizes the "I," whereas the latter emphasizes the "we" orientation toward social action. Again, see the discussion of Bourdieu in Chapter 5 for further details on this element of his work.

verification and refinement of their work. Both have made important contributions to the explication of relations of class reproduction, but as many have found, their accounts tend to remain one-dimensional descriptions of the status quo rather than real explanations of it.

Adult Learning in Working-Class Life

R1:   People learn whether they want to or not; sometimes they just balk at it!

R2:   [nodding] They don't recognize it as learning. I guess it's because at school it's fed to you. You have to learn. You gotta do it. "Do your math!" This is the time you do this and this and this. When you're at home it's just an endless process really. (Autoworker and partner, W17a/b)

In examining interviewees' descriptions of learning embedded in excerpts such as this one, in thinking about the types of activities that I recorded ethnographically, and in reviewing the learning that I analyzed in terms of micro-interaction, it became clear to me that the way interviewees spoke of learning did not fit easily into the dominant theoretical frameworks of adult education. In general, the people I interviewed seldom departed explicitly from hegemonic understandings of the learning process, just as they seldom spoke explicitly about issues of social class. Indeed, the preceding excerpt provides a suitable starting point for discussions of working-class experiences because of its relative uniqueness in its identification of a gap between what people do and what they can name as learning. The excerpt weaves together issues of formal education and the invisibility, yet importance, of learning in the flow of everyday life, and openly announces a type of resistance to the dominant discourse of learning. These themes are key to my critique of existing theory, but before beginning, in this section I want to situate the types of class tensions that informed the learning experiences of the people described in this research.

In addition to Bourdieu and Bernstein, a vast array of writers have drawn clear connections between schooling and the reproduction of class relations. Strips of transcribed talk I analyzed often included references to formalized learning experiences in both workplace training and school. In most accounts of working-class learning, experiences are either implicitly or explicitly framed by notions of formal learning that serves the role of the "other" in the meaning that is expressed. People define, explain, and understand their ongoing practices against a backdrop of formalized learning, and in so doing root their practice in opposition to the antagonistic cultural contexts that schooling represents for working-class children. In fact, one of the most apparent difficulties I encountered in developing an understanding of learning in working-class life involved drawing distinctions between the formal institutional roles and relations of education (e.g., teacher, student) and more general processes of learning. For speakers, there is a level of convenience here, as institutional roles and relations provide important markers or signs that learning is occurring. These markers might include, for example, the opening and closing of "lessons," evaluation, or reference to an identifiable "expert" or canonical form of knowledge, and so forth. However, the learning that expresses and develops upon a working-class standpoint in a positive frame tends to operate either in opposition to or beyond these markers and institutions.

However, class-deficit theories of adult learning do not simply underestimate, ignore, or misconstrue the cultural experiences of working-class groups in formalized learning; they also tend to neglect the role of collective and interactive social processes that define learning more broadly. It is this missing component that disputes, on the one hand, the suggestion of unfettered agency of the individual (e.g., self-directed learning) and, on the other, the strictly reproductive character of social practice in class society. In discussions with workers, though the gain in individual skill and knowledge in the final instance is easily recognizable, the individual planning functions within this development are harder to identify. Rational choice–based models of social action and adult learning, premised on conventional notions of the autonomous individual, miss the boat entirely. Rather, the vast majority of planning, if it can be called this, is the product of one's participation in social systems. It is these collective systems, with their shifts in individual and group patterns of participation, that account for changes in individual skill and personal knowledgeability. In other words, shifting patterns of participation and the planning dimensions of learning are far more often interactive accomplishments rather than products of individual agency.

Although the role of formal learning cannot be ignored, the task of understanding learning in the flow of everyday life is the core challenge for understanding learning from the standpoint of subordinate groups such as the working class. Analysts must concede that broadening the boundaries of learning beyond the classroom and beyond self-directed and intentional learning forces us to come to grips with the fact that learning can be found anywhere and everywhere. And as I want to highlight in this chapter, the conceptual means of delimiting the phenomenon, necessarily a politicized choice in systems of value and relevance, becomes an important and contestable issue essential to understanding working-class learning.

The tensions between working-class practice and various theories of adult learning that guide the following section were ones that arose first in listening carefully to what workers said when they talked about their learning. Experiences that interviewees did not name as learning (they were "balked at") were nevertheless examples of participation that led to changes in personal and collective forms of practice, skill, and knowledge-ability. As I remarked at the beginning of this section, the "fit" between working-class practice and the dominant ways of thinking and talking about learning is not a good one. It was in the course of some of my first research interviews that I began to see that an understanding of the discourses of learning, both professionalized and popular, was central to understanding the class dimensions of learning practice. As I argue later in the book, this lack of fit actually signals something significant. It suggests the idea of *learning capacity* as an analogue to the process that Pierre Bourdieu describes as *cultural distinction*: a mechanism that allows the class-specific forms of experience, skill, and knowledge of the dominant minority to be both valorized and universalized.

To conclude these opening sections of the chapter, we can reflect on the following statement from a chemical worker. In it are the roots of several of the lines of tension and critique I've introduced. In a few short lines, it suggests a class-based critique of schooling, inverts the discourses of legitimate learning, asserts the relevance of situated social participation as the heart of working-class learning, and highlights the types of mediated agency that can be achieved in organized representations of class interest.

Education? I don't have any, I don't believe in it. I left school when I was fifteen. Never stayed on further than I had to. . . . My real learning came when I joined the miners' strike. You learned what the state apparatus is, keeping people in order, protecting the issues. That was my education. (W51)

A Historical Materialist Approach to Adult Learning Theory

Each time that in one way or another, the question of language comes to the fore, that signifies that a series of other problems is about to emerge, the formation and enlarging of the ruling class, the necessity to establish more "intimate" and sure relations between the ruling groups and the national popular masses, that is, the reorganization of cultural hegemony. (Antonio Gramsci quoted in Giroux, 1987:1)

Although others have drawn together more general reviews of adult learning theory (e.g., Selman and Dampier, 1991; Mezirow, 1991a, 1996; Hart, 1992; Merriam, 1993; Welton, 1995; Usher, Bryant, and Johnston, 1997; Foley, 1999; Illeris, 1999; Poonwasie and Poonwasie, 2001), the goal of this section is to select from the range of theories of adult learning and to review those that may in one way or another have something to contribute to an analysis of working-class learning specifically. The theories I will evaluate are Knowles's andragogy (1970, 1975, 1977), Tough's self-directed learning (1967, 1979), Mezirow's transformative learning (1991a, 1991b, 1994), critical/radical pedagogy as represented in the work of Giroux (1983) and the collected authors in Livingstone (1987), and finally, the notion of conscientization in the work of Freire (1970, 1996). In each case, I compare the approach to the set of hegemonic themes outlined earlier. Tracing these themes through each theory provides both a rationale and a starting point for my preference for sociocultural approaches to adult learning.

In beginning this mapping exercise, it's important to mention the work of Malcolm Knowles, and specifically his notion of *andragogy*, "the science and art of helping adults to learn" (1980:43). For mainstream North American adult educators, this text remains, implicitly, one of the seminal pieces of theoretical work in the field, and in this sense it cannot be ignored. The important contribution of Knowles's work for this discussion lies in his claim that adults are more or less autonomous beings whose learning takes place within a developmental and social context fundamentally different from that of children. It was Knowles's work that helped lead the way to North American discussions of the *facilitation* rather than the *pedagogy* of adult learning. In its own place and time, this conceptualization of the adult learning process was an important, even radical, departure. At the same time, Knowles's work provides a starting point for a historical materialist critique of adult learning theory as well. As others have pointed out (e.g., Pratt, 1988; Collins, 1995; Garrick, 1996), the notion of the autonomous adult and Knowles's uncritical *humanist psychological foundation* (Selman and Dampier, 1991:33) creates a fundamental problem that is more than likely beyond resolution for the purposes of a topic such as working-class learning. In the concept of andragogy, there is simply no means to differentiate between social standpoints beyond those of expert facilitator and participant. This fact dulls any real possibility of recognizing that major social divisions in society are closely interwoven with the adult learning process. Nor are there explicit means of moving beyond institutionalized and/or facilitated processes of adult learning that leave out so many subordinate groups. Learning without such facilitators, as well as tacit and collectively led learning, is unaddressed and unaddressible given the conceptual framework. Draper (1998) has gone so far as to suggest that, in fact, andragogy was not a theory of learning at all but rather simply delineated categories of basic phenomena from which theory might emerge. Nevertheless, understood in its historical context, Knowles's work is important to our understanding of adult learning, as he is one of the first North American theorists to seriously problematize conventional notions of pedagogy from the perspective of the adult learner.

One of the scholars most closely identified with theorizing about autonomous, informal, and self-directed adult learning is Allen Tough (1967, 1979; see Percy, Burton, and Withnall, 1994). In developing his seminal work on self-directed adult learning, Tough sought to understand and identify adult learning as the ways in which adults seek to produce some "lasting change" in themselves through intentional self-directed learning projects. Not only can the far-reaching effects of Tough's work be read as testimony to the relevance of a sustained, theoretically informed research program that until recently was so often missing among academic writers in the scholarly field of adult education,[4] but the shift in the object of inquiry beyond the reach of Knowles's facilitator and into everyday life offered rich and important new terrain at the time. Tough documented the massive extent to which adults learn outside formalized settings, and he determined that people regularly undertook a median of eight distinct learning projects yearly, which accounted for anywhere from just under 100 to as many as 2,000 hours per year (average = 500 hours per year). His legacy remains the initiation of one of the first sustained, systematic, research-based engagements by adult education research with the everyday lives of learners. Like the work of Knowles, however, Tough's self-directed learning concept requires some interrogation. In the first instance, despite his sampling of a range of occupational groupings, Tough's research remains largely class, gender, and race blind. Power relationships and the systematic distribution of time, resources, and human energy play an important role in shaping adult learning, are each subject to the major

---

[4] In his review of the state of adult learning literature, Rossing (1991) notes that as of the early 1990s, there were very few theoretically informed and evidence-based research programs within the field of adult education. At least up to that point, according to Rossing, the field tended to be dominated by an energetic, if generally atheoretical, group of scholars, Knowles and Tough among them, for whom traditional humanist, psychologically based approaches were taken as a given.

social divisions of society, and are not addressed in the work. We are presented with the conclusion that subordinate groups learn less rather than learn different things in different ways. In addition, learning defined as lasting change in the individual is blind to the fact that there are specific discourses of learning that define relevant learning as well as relevant learners. Moreover, the work misses the point that a great deal of learning cannot be talked about because it is tacit, protensional and/or must be performed, often with others, rather than reported individually. Forms of educational research that cannot move beyond either the autonomous individual or the assertion that only self-conscious descriptions of intentional personal change signify the learning process cannot begin to grasp the relationship of social class and learning.

One of the more heavily discussed contemporary formulations of adult learning theory on the North American scene for the last decade has been Mezirow's theory of perspective transformation or transformative learning (1991a, 1991b, 1994, 1996). Mezirow styles his theory as a defense of universal rationality in opposition to what he describes as a "diverse group of social cognitivists" on the one hand and the "postmodernist threat that society's power and influence inevitably corrupts" on the other (1996:171). Unfortunately, beyond the polemics, Mezirow's actual engagement with the work of either is not very impressive. Moreover, as others have pointed out, Mezirow's application of Habermas to the context of adult learning is selective and incomplete. The theory of transformative learning centers on relations of communicative action that Mezirow claims are key to understanding learning that synthesizes the disparate and competing forms of rationality. As in the discussion of Knowles and Tough, in this approach we are left with what Newman (1994) has correctly described as a vision of free-floating communicators, unfettered by material constraints that play such an important role in shaping learning among subordinate groups. Hart's (1990) critique is perhaps one of the most relevant, centering on Mezirow's suggestions of universalism in the communication process. Mezirow's preference for the lofty heights of high abstraction over the real, concrete circumstances of learning life invariably leads to serious difficulties.

In contrast to transformative learning, a more fully developed engagement with critical theory and Western Marxism more broadly can be found in the tradition of critical/radical pedagogy (Freire, 1970; Corrigan, 1979; Giroux, 1983; Simon, 1985; Livingstone, 1987). Here we find a superior explication of the complexity of education and learning relations in advanced capitalist society. The work of Paulo Freire is implicated in the tradition, but in transporting it to the context of advanced capitalist countries, writers such as Giroux and Corrigan, for example, have offered superior analyses of educational life in a variety of forms expressing the complex relationship between the reproduction of culture, subjectivity, and human agency. The relevance of this approach for the purposes of this book lies in its commitment to a careful consideration of praxis from the standpoint of the oppressed themselves (Giroux, 1979, 1981; Livingstone, 1987) as opposed to an abstract critique of rationality, as in Mezirow. The critical pedagogy approach is well summarized by Simon's (1985) definition of critical pedagogy, in which he outlines three interrelated processes: transformative critique that conceives of knowledge as socially produced, legitimated, and distributed; a recognition that knowledge expresses and contributes to particular material interests; and the active negation of objective characterizations of knowledge so as to reveal their relationships with power and control. However, almost two decades since its emergence, as Wardekker (1997) points out, critical pedagogy still appears to be in search of "a concretization of the elusive ideal of emancipation" (p. 3). In addition, rooted as it is in pedagogical relations, critical pedagogy's interests remain largely fixed on the domain of formalized education, analyzing the struggle of subordinate groups in these systems, and unfortunately, it can tell us little about the informal contexts of struggle in which so much adult learning takes place. Though Freire himself was deeply committed to the notion of learning outside formal schooling, critical pedagogy in the North American context appears to have been only minimally concerned with actively researching and theorizing a broader conception of learning per se. This has not gone unnoticed by critical pedagogy theorists themselves. Wexler, Martusewicz, and Kern, for example, make an important clarification by insisting that critical pedagogy should necessarily include building from "existing practically-inspired educational movement as well as more informal critical education discourses within far broader social movements" (1987:227). Despite the constructive critiques and massive theoretical syntheses over the years, it would appear that a line of systematic, empirically based research focused on learning in the everyday has yet to emerge fully in the critical pedagogy tradition in any but isolated forms.

As a touchstone of critical pedagogy but with implications that move beyond it, the work of Paulo Freire, and particularly his notion of *conscientization*, deserves special attention. As early as the 1960s, Freire had begun developing his notion of conscientization and a "pedagogy of the oppressed" in the midst of his own activism that would eventually span Latin America and Africa, as well as parts of Europe, North America, and Australia. Perhaps the most illuminating feature of the conscientization concept was its explicit commitment to understanding relations of learning as grounded in specific racialized, gendered, classed, and regionalized standpoints of the second and third worlds. As Freire notes, the standpoint of the oppressed provides the basis (vis-à-vis *generative themes*) upon which a critique of schooling, curriculum, and social life ultimately rests. Indeed, conscientization is firmly rooted in the Marxist tradition of revolutionary praxis. Learning is understood as rooted in social practice in the concrete world and in what Freire and Macedo called an *act of knowledge* (1987:52). Freire was well aware of the power of hegemonic discourses of learning and education. He identified the way conceptions of schooling, studying, and literacy, in fact, contributed to the reproduction of forms of consciousness and learning practice:

The preoccupation of this text with the act of studying seems obvious; for example, combating the ideological, though not always explicit, belief that one only studies in school. School may be considered, from this view, *the* matrix of knowledge. Outside of academia there is no knowledge, or the knowledge that exists is believed to be inferior, to have nothing to do with the rigorous knowledge of the intellectual. In truth however, this disdained knowledge, "knowledge made from experience," has to be the point of departure in any popular educational effort oriented toward the creation of a more rigorous knowledge on the part of the people. While an expression of the dominant ideology, this myth about academia deeply influences the people, sometimes provoking disdain for themselves due to their feeling that they have little or no "reading." It becomes necessary, then, to emphasize practical activity in concrete reality (activity that never lacks a technical intellectual dimension, however simple it may be) as a generator of knowledge. (Freire and Macedo, 1987:77–78)

Not coincidentally, Freire notes the writing of Vygotsky as one of his prime influences. A practical-critical, activity-based approach to learning, not the least important element of which is its grounding in and effect on *historical memory*, as developed by Adorno through to Freire and Giroux, offers an important opening for my focus on learning in the everyday among groups of industrial workers in Canada.

At the same time, the concept of conscientization as a theory of learning has its limits. These can be traced in two interrelated areas: the theorization of collective action and the dependence on pedagogical relations of knowledge production. In the first case, although grounded by Freire in collective political action implicitly, the concept of conscientization itself does not offer a means of making visible the actual social nature of the learning processes of subordinate groups. In other words, how is it that people actually produce their own transformation socially? This suggests a bias toward conscious goal-directed and cognitive dimensions of learning and social action. In general, however, we are left with engaged description rather than a conceptual means of carrying out systematic analysis. Second, like critical pedagogy more broadly, conscientization seems to assume an "enlightened" other. Like Knowles, Freire assumes a facilitator in cultural circle activities. In this way, Freire has not sought to understand spontaneous and self-led, collective forms of learning beyond cultural circles altogether. Under the basic Freirian approach, the type of learning that takes place in the flow of everyday working-class life, although being the basis of facilitated sessions, would not be registered analytically in its own right. In sum, Freirian critical pedagogy remains too rooted in (1) the moment of critique and (2) the work of the pedagogue. Although the work of Freire and critical pedagogy help us to unmask ideologies, they do little to help us to understand the masking and unmasking practices that go on in the daily lives of the oppressed outside pedagogical relations.

Vygotsky and the Cultural Historical School

The preceding critique of adult learning theory prefigures a call for an alternative. In order to begin to better understand the alternative intellectual traditions that have looked at learning as a form of historical human activity, we would do well to take a moment to consider the exercise that activity theorist Yrjö Engeström (1987) undertook in charting three distinct historical lines of development. At the heart of each lineage is a discussion of its ability to recognize and analyze the active process of tool mediation that provides an account of the dialectical nature of structure and human agency in practice. Each offers an alternative to the Cartesian separation of mind and body, and the bias of individual, subjective and conscious direction of human action. For Engeström, the first lineage is rooted in the semiotics of C. S. Peirce. Engeström argues that although Peirce produces a detailed treatment of the process of mediation between subject (or interpretant) and object vis-à-vis the sign, the mediational process is still restricted to its intentional, abstract-logical, and purely linguistic dimensions. In turn, the lack of connection between symbolic mediation and the realm of concrete action inspires Engeström to conclude that the formulation loses much of its "anti-Cartesian" potential. As such, the Peirce lineage is subject to some of the same type of criticism offered in the previous section, which focused on dominant themes of individualism and rationalism. The second lineage Engeström outlines originates in the social psychology of George Herbert Mead. In this work, again we see a tool-mediated process of meaning production vis-à-vis the basic formulation gesture/adjustive response/result. However, Engeström's critique of Mead suggests that, once again, we are faced with a limited conceptualization of human practice as a process of communication separated from the production of sensuous material practice mediated by tools that may be material as well as symbolic. Accordingly, Mead's "sidetrack" into material dimensions of practice in *Mind, Self and Society* does not do enough to demonstrate the relationship between communication and the overall cultural and material structure of social life and social change.

It is Engeström's third lineage that has the greatest affinity to the purposes of this book. This line of development has its origins in the cultural-historical school of Soviet psychology and the work of the Russian psychologist Lev Vygotsky (1978, 1986, 1994). This tradition emerged from an attempt to understand learning as a historical form of human activity with an explicit concern for the problematics of peasant and working-class groups. It was the work of Vygotsky, meeting with colleagues such as Luria and Leont'ev in his small one-bedroom apartment, that gave rise to the development of what is known today as an *activity theory of personality and learning*, a theory based on social relations in labor, tool mediation, and language (Leont'ev, 1978). An important feature of the development of this tradition was, in fact, the period in which it took place. During the earliest phases of the attempted development of the Soviet Union into a state socialist society, there were open declarations and ideological support for the social scientific valorization of the lives of previously oppressed classes. Having attended the famous Shaniavsky People's University (home of the leading anticzarist scholars of prerevolutionary Moscow), Vygotsky was to become heavily influenced by the works of Spinoza, Hegel, and especially Engels and Marx (Blanck, 1993). Indeed, Vygotsky's program was aimed at nothing less than a reorganization of psychology based on Marxist principles:

It is my belief, based upon a dialectical materialist approach to the analysis of human history, that human behaviour differs qualitatively from animal behaviour to the extent that the adaptability had historical [elements]. . . . Naturalism in [bourgeois] historical analysis, according to Engels, manifests itself in the assumption that only nature affects human beings and only natural conditions determine historical development. The dialectical approach, while admitting the influence of nature on man, asserts that man, in turn, affects nature and creates through his changes in nature new natural conditions for his social existence. This position is the keystone of our approach to the study and interpretation of man's higher psychological functions and serves as the basis for the new methods of experimentation and analysis that we advocate. (Vygotsky, 1978:60–61)

In collaboration with Vygotsky but under the guidance of Luria (1976), related ethnographic and linguistic research conducted with workers also began to provide important insights into the interrelations between modes of production and modes of thinking and learning. Following Vygotsky's premature death in 1934 and an extended period of suppression, Vygotsky's work began slowly to reemerge in the post–World War II period, and in the past two decades it has seen a particularly vigorous growth in the West.

The core contribution of Vygotsky's work lay in the argument that learning is a sociocultural rather than simply a cognitive phenomenon (1985:46). It is mediated by symbolic as well as material tools and by particular modes of social participation that allow first intersubjective and eventually higher-order functions of cognition and individual action. That is, the concept of learning presupposes both a social and a historical nature (1978:88). In these terms, Vygotsky's notion of *turning* is vitally important. Turning, or interiorization, defines the process in which external social relations and sociohistorical systems are transformed into the internal mental actions, outcomes, and embodied states we associate with notions of knowledge and skill. In *Thought and Language* (1986) his line of analysis focused specifically on cognitive and linguistic development. He concluded that later forms of the intellect and speech, specifically the development of (in an illuminating inversion) *inner speech* and *verbal thought*, are constituted in and constitutive of cultural-historical relations (Vygotsky, 1986:51). Vygotsky's empirical work, however, was centered primarily on issues of child development rather than adult learning, though he did not exclude issues of the labor process and the cooperative/collective features of social activity more broadly. Both in his own time and in ours, researchers working from his ideas have been able to examine the specific character of adult thinking and learning as cultural-historical and participatory rather than individualized, internal, natural, or innate.

Building on the paradigmatic break that Vygotsky made possible, the development of a recognizable cultural-historical theory of activity is generally ascribed to Vygotsky's colleague A. N. Leont'ev (1974, 1978,

1981). It is the work of Leont'ev that is typically considered the bridge between Vygotsky's original work and the development of modern theories of adult learning in this genre. In "The Problem of Activity in Psychology" (1974), *Activity, Consciousness, and Personality* (1978), and, in particular, *Problems of the Development of the Mind* (1981), Leont'ev outlines the central critiques of psychology put forth by the cultural-historical school and pays special attention to the foundational role of Marx's critique of bourgeois philosophy. For Leont'ev, Vygotsky provided a truly revolutionary extension of Marxist analysis: "Only after the work of L. S. Vygotskii ... did the meaning of Marxism become fully understood" (1978:11). Vygotsky initiated the development of a structured approach to understanding learning as participation in social practice defined by dynamic transformations, change, and interrelations with other social systems.[5]

Sociocultural Theories of Adult Learning: From Vygotsky to the Present

The critique of individualized, cognitivist, and behavioralist models of human learning initiated by the work of Vygotsky serves as the historical point of departure for a more focused discussion of sociocultural approaches to adult learning. By understanding these origins, we can better turn our attention to theories that share, more or less directly, a concern with the elaboration of the situated, historical, and social character of adult learning. These approaches offer progressive alternatives to the limits of adult learning theory discussed earlier.

To situate the relationship between Vygotsky and contemporary developments in the tradition, however, we need to take a closer look at Leont'ev's theory of human activity. Rooted in the work of Vygotsky, activity theory has been said to have undergone a number of "generational" developments (Engeström, 1996). The first generation, centered on the notion of human action and human learning as mediated by cultural tools, can be associated with the original work of Vygotsky himself. In turn, Leont'ev's development of the concept of *activity* is associated with the

---

[5] Interestingly enough, in regard to my wish to trace the dominant theme of formal pedagogical relations in theories of learning, Vygotsky's own writings assert a faith in the *essentially* progressive nature of formal schooling, a commitment that Van Der Veer and Valsiner critique as a type of imagined "educational utopia" (Vygotsky, 1994:6). Likewise, Moll (1993) has suggested pedagogy as key to the development of Vygotsky's psychological approach.

second generation of theory. Here the realization of the importance of the role of mediating cultural tools is elaborated to include broader social dimensions of practice. The analysis of social participation with others differentiates the first generation from the second. In terms of class struggle, what this development helps to bring to the fore is how collective forms of action, in the sense of historical agency, are made possible. The current generation of activity theory now has the goal of understanding more clearly how articulating systems of activity function and change. According to Engeström, in this latest iteration issues of diversity, different perspectives and the role of contradiction in developmental change are also key challenges.

Returning to the work of Leont'ev and his original formulation of the concept of activity specifically, we can see that it offers a valuable starting point for detailed discussions of technology and working-class learning practice throughout its full range of variation.

Activity is the minimal meaningful context for understanding individual actions.... In all its varied forms, the activity of the human individual is a system set within a system of social relations.... The activity of individual people thus depends on their social position, the conditions that fall to their lot, and an accumulation of idiosyncratic, individual factors. Human activity is not a relation between a person and a society that confronts him.... [I]n a society a person does not simply find external conditions to which he must adapt his activity, but, rather, these very social conditions bear within themselves the motives and goals of his activity, its means and modes. (Leont'ev, 1978:10)

It is within this early framework that we see a perspective on adult learning that necessarily required practice to be historicized and contextualized broadly. Expanding on the basic concept, activity is associated with a series of subconcepts that provide an analysis of activity with multiple layers. Leont'ev offered an explanation of the need for these different levels of activity in this way.

An analysis leading to an actual disclosure of sense cannot be limited to superficial observation.... After all, from the process itself it is not evident what kind of process it is – action or activity. Often in order to explain this, active investigation is required: substantiating observation, hypothesis, effective verification. That to which the given process is directed may seem to be inducing it, embodying its motives; if this is so, then it is activity. But this same process may be induced by a completely different motive not at all coinciding with that to which it is directed as its results; then it is an action.... In spite of what it seems to be from the superficial point of view, this is a way that confirms the objectivity of its bases to a high degree inasmuch as this way leads to an understanding of the consciousness of man derived from life, from concrete beginnings, and not from the laws of consciousness of surrounding people, not from knowledge. (Leont'ev, 1978:173–174)[6]

Leont'ev's conceptualization of activity moves Vygotsky's observations into a workable model of adult learning. Specifically, it provides the means to begin to analyze everyday learning systematically, with or without reference to conscious reflection, as something more than simply a shapeless flow of experience. It roots this flow of experience in specific forms of social organization that include historical as well as political-economic dimensions.

---

[6] Although this is obviously not fully elaborated, the following can be considered key terms of the basic activity theory approach according to Leont'ev (1974, 1978):

Activity: subject, object, actions and operations; "activity is the minimal meaningful context for understanding individual actions" (1978). The famous example of Leont'ev (1981:210–213) is the primeval collective hunt, in which participants, in order to catch game, separate into two groups: catchers and bush beaters. Bush beaters frighten the game toward the catchers. When compared with the goal of hunting – to catch game for food and clothing – the actions of the bush beaters are irrational; they can be understood only as part of the larger system of the hunting activity.

Subject: a person or group engaged in an activity.

Object: held by the subject and motivates activity, giving it a specific direction; behind objects there "always stands a need or a desire, to which the activity always answers."

Actions: goal-directed processes; different actions can be undertaken to meet the same goals; "just as the concept of motive correlates with that of activity, so the concept of goal correlates with that of action" (1974:23).

Objects and actions relations: typically undergo transformation, though with some stability over time.

Operations: "methods by which an action is realized. Their uniqueness is that they respond not to motive and not to a goal of action but to those conditions under which the goal is assigned" (1978:164); "Actions are related to goals, operations to conditions. Let us assume that the goal remains the same; conditions in which it is assigned, however, change. Then it is specifically and only the operational content of the action that changes" (1978:65)

Central technical focus: mediation of activity by sociocultural and historical artifacts.

Goal: "like a law determines the mode and character of action.... Let us take the case of a person's activity energized by food. Food is his motive; however, to satisfy this desire for food he must carry out actions not immediately directed at obtaining food. For example, his goal may be to make a hunting weapon. Does he subsequently use the weapon he made, or does he pass it on to someone else and receive a portion of the total catch? In both cases, that which energized his activity and that to which his action is directed do not coincide.... [A]ctions are not special, separate entities that comprise activity. Human activity exists only in the form of actions or chains of actions" (1974:23–24).

Tools: "[a] tool is a material object in which are crystallized not actions or goals, but modes and operations" (1974:26); "A tool, for example, viewed apart from its connection with a goal, becomes as much an abstraction as an operation viewed apart from its connection that the action it realizes" (1974:28).

In terms of the most recent development of activity theory, in my view the work of Engeström can be recognized as a particularly important program of research. His core theoretical contribution to date is the subject of his book *Learning by Expanding* (1987). The theory of expansive learning is based on the idea of *ascending from the abstract to the concrete*, a notion that draws on the work of the Russian philosopher Evald Ilyenkov (e.g., 1982), a key writer in the field of Marxist dialectics. Following Il'enkov's elaboration of the role of contradictions as the motor of change and development in activity systems, Engeström's theory describes how practice undergoes the type of change that defines the learning process. Accordingly, rooted in the internal contradictions of the activity system, an *expansive cycle* involving individuals questioning and eventually moving beyond legitimated forms of practice is produced. New patterns of individual participation and even new patterns of overall activity ensue. In related work, Engeström focuses on analyses of activity outside of schools specifically (e.g., court systems, the doctor's office, hospitals, etc.), and this work is particularly instructive here. His research on expertise (1992), for example, provides an important empirical analysis of how "expertise" is a coproduction within an entire activity system. Making use of detailed interactional analysis, the activity system Engeström describes is composed of the individual participant, coparticipants, the material and conceptual tools of the activity system, and the negotiated objects, goals, and motives of ongoing learning practice, as displayed graphically in Figure 2.1. Exemplifying a third-generation approach, Engeström shows how activity systems are enmeshed within a "multi-dimensional network of [other] activity systems" that interact, support, destabilize, and interpenetrate (1992:13).

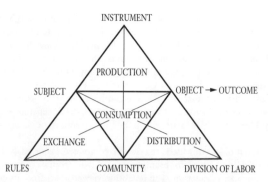

Figure 2.1   Activity theory triangle.

Perhaps most important to an analysis of the processes of social differentiation within the learning process, however, is the issue of social standpoints, and the third generation of activity theory offers openings for a critical examination of class standpoints in activity systems. It helps us pose new questions that build on and extend previous research such as that of Engeström (1992) and Wertsch (1991), whose discussions of standpoint revolve around issues of *heterogeneity of expertise* and *multivoicedness*. For example, we could begin to explore the notion of *core and peripheral relations* in activity systems, which, in turn, suggests the need to think about multiple centers of activity systems based loosely on particular standpoints. Through articulation with other forms of activity, an activity system might be understood as composed of competing and overlapping sets of cultural rules and conventions. Narrow conceptualizations of activity might presume a system of relevance favoring orientation to particular "legitimate" objects and goals despite the fact that these may be contested. Indeed, thinking in terms of relations of legitimation and conflict may help us to provide accounts of how social relations of power are played out in the course of learning practice. In general, the potential to theorize these types of relationships depends on a recognition of different standpoints in activity, as well as articulating systems of activity, and highlights the relevance of the most recent iteration of activity theory development.

Activity theory, however, is not the only contemporary example of a sociocultural approach to adult learning. A theory with similar preoccupations can be seen in the work of Jean Lave and Etienne Wenger. These authors, both together and separately, have contributed a good deal to discussions of the social character of learning in their development of an influential model called *legitimate peripheral participation* or *situated learning* (1991; see also Lave, 1988, 1993; Wenger, 1998). In their seminal book, these authors draw on ethnographic materials to provide a program of inquiry into learning as a dimension of social practice generally.

Social practice is the primary, generative phenomenon, and learning is one of its characteristics.... In our view learning is not merely situated practice... learning is an integral part of a generative social practice in the lived-in world. The problem... is to translate this into a specific analytic approach to learning. (1991:34–35)

The analyses of the practices of grocery shopping (Lave, Murtaugh, and de la Rocha, 1984), recovering alcoholics, navy quartermasters, butchers, and tailors (Lave, 1988; Lave and Wenger, 1991) convincingly open new ways of thinking about the concept of learning. For Lave and Wenger

(1991), learning is defined as a collective practice in which novices shift their patterns of participation in relation to experts and participants shift their collective patterns of participation and knowledgeability toward new forms of expertise within a *community of practice*. This concept of community has rough similarities to the concept of activity system, but unlike activity theorists, Lave and Wenger spend comparatively little time discussing the role of tool mediation. Nevertheless, the authors define the notion of *situated* practice as follows:

[I]n the concept of situated learning we were developing, however, the situatedness of activity appeared to be anything but a simple empirical attribute of everyday activity or a corrective to conventional pessimism about informal, experience-based learning. Instead, it took on the proportions of a general theoretical perspective, the basis of claims about the relational character of knowledge and learning, about the negotiated character of meaning, and about the concerned (engaged, dilemma-drive) nature of learning activity for people involved. That perspective meant that there is not activity that is not situated. (1991:32–33)

This approach makes an important contribution to a deeper understanding of learning in people's everyday lives beyond organized classroom settings, and beyond individualized and narrowly circumscribed events. At the same time, however, key conceptual elements can be refined to contribute more effectively to an analysis of relations of learning and class life specifically.

One feature of the situated learning approach that deserves attention concerns the issues of micro-context and cultural material power. Although Lave and Wenger comment on the essential need to theorize about issues of conflict and cooperation, to date few grounded analyses drawing on the situated learning approach have focused on these issues explicitly (see Holland and Lave, 2001, for an exception). The problem may lie in the ideas surrounding the structures of opportunity and participation that Lave and Wenger develop through discussions of *legitimacy* and *peripherality*.

Legitimate peripherality is a complex notion, implicated in social structures involving relations of power. As a place in which one moves toward more-intensive participation, peripherality is an empowering position. As a place in which one is kept from participating more fully – often legitimately, from the broader perspective of society at large – it is a disempowering position. Beyond that, legitimate peripherality can be a position at the articulation of related communities. In this sense, it can itself be a source of power or powerlessness, in affording or preventing articulation and interchange among communities of practice. The ambiguous potentialities of legitimate peripherality reflect the concept's pivotal role in providing access to a nexus of relations otherwise not perceived as connected. . . . There is not a place in a community of practice designated "the periphery" and, most emphatically, it has no single core or centre. . . . We have chosen to call that to which peripheral participation leads, full participation. Full participation is intended to do justice to the diversity of relations involved in varying forms of community membership. (1991:36)

Peripherality (like marginality) is a relational concept. It is impossible to understand it without assuming a type of center. In order to refine the concept, we might wish to ask, peripherality and legitimacy according to whom? In my view, appeals to experts and expertise cannot fully explain the dynamics of peripherality or the conflictual dynamics of legitimacy in the lives of working-class learners. Such refinements are clearly not beyond the scope of situated learning theory. Just as clearly, however, these refinements would benefit from careful explorations of different social standpoints in practice, as well as of the means by which legitimacy is established beyond basic skill and knowledge differences. This book, I hope, will contribute to refinements like these by extending the tradition to an investigation of adult learning in working-class life specifically.

Summary

I began this chapter with a quotation from Marx's *Capital* that, to my mind, suggested the importance of historicizing our understanding of the concept of learning. The preceding discussion attempted to build on the basic notion of class-deficit theorizing to show its relevance to a critical understanding of the adult learning process. Elaborating on this concept, I then briefly explored the need to challenge the specter of formal learning from a working-class standpoint and then offered an opening critique of the dominant themes of autonomy, individualism, and conventional understandings of rational planning in theoretical discourses on the adult learning process. Just beneath the surface of these first two sections of the chapter were suggestions of the types of dispositions that shape working-class learning practice, as well as the first approximation of a working-class learning habitus.

I used these dominant themes to animate a critique of selected adult learning theories. I suggested that these themes formed a hegemonic bloc displaying deep continuities with advanced capitalism. Together these themes help to construct particular ways of understanding the production of skill and knowledge. Marx would surely have identified these ways of thinking and talking about learning as a process of *fetishization*: the transformation of a complex set of relationships into an object, a "thing," yet each of the theories I examined offered a contribution to an emergent class analysis of adult learning.

In the second half of the chapter, I shifted from a critique of dominant approaches to alternative models of adult learning. I began by introducing the cultural-historical school of Soviet psychology and the work of its central founding member Lev Vygotsky. I outlined the break in the study of human learning that Vygotsky's work made possible before moving on to a discussion of more contemporary approaches. Building from Leont'ev's definition of activity, with its various dimensions and levels (i.e., activity, action, and operation), I examined the latest, third generation of activity theory with special attention to the work of Engeström. I concluded this final section with a critical discussion of an additional sociocultural approach to adult learning called situated learning (Lave and Wenger, 1991). In both cases, I suggested areas of refinement important for an analysis of working-class learning. Together these reflections offer a starting point for a program of inquiry that seeks to avoid the traps of class-deficit theory and that directly critiques individualism, bourgeois psychology, universalism, and the formal schooling bias. Through the application of these concepts, an analysis of learning becomes an analysis of the forms of historically, politically, and economically situated social participation.

In general, I suggest that the dominant themes within learning theory are dominant for a reason. They express, ratify, and show important continuities with the basic principles of private property, market exchange, and capital accumulation that, although not monolithic, play a definitive role in defining social life in advanced capitalist countries such as Canada. A critical examination of the concept of learning itself is the necessary first step in a class analysis of learning practices. Sociocultural approaches to adult learning, including the original cultural-historical school and the work of Vygotsky, are well equipped to historicize the dominant thematics and open up new understandings of adult learning in working-class life.

3 "That's Technology"

Understanding Working-Class Perspectives on Computer Technology

> For half a century, along with television, space flight, nuclear weapons, and automobiles, computers have formed the technological backdrop for the [North] American mental landscape. Revered as the consummate representatives of an ever more technological civilization, they are tools for work and toys for play, assistants to science, fixtures of daily life. They are icons of efficiency, social status, and a high-tech future.
>
> Paul Edwards, *The Cultures of Computing*

> See that's a funny word, technology.
>
> Autoworker (Ontario, Canada)

According to Theodore Roszak (1994), the word *computer* entered the North American public vocabulary in the 1950s. As Roszak says, this was a time when the most advanced models were still room-sized beasts that burned enough electricity to present a serious cooling problem. Today, the sophistication and power of both the devices and the rhetoric have expanded considerably. Everywhere we are inundated with images of the high-tech "info-bahn" world. However, as a host of critical writers and researchers on computer technology have consistently noted, it is doubtful that the rhetoric has come anywhere near living up to its claims. In fact, we are presented with a contradiction: expanded power, efficiency, and influence of computers on the one hand, and questionable evidence of meaningful, shared positive benefits for the vast majority of people on the other.

Digging a little deeper into the different effects that computer technologies have on the population, we see that the United States Bureau of Labor Statistics reports that there will be a massive growth in the rate of employment in the computer sector by 2005 (certainly a positive finding for people who depend on a wage to live). On the other hand, in a (U.S.)

population predicted to grow to between 280 and 300 million, we see that the total number of people actually employed in this sector will not make it to the half million mark. Looking at computers in the workplace in Canada, Krahn and Lowe's (1998) examination indicates, in terms of computer use on the job, management, science, and professional occupational groups more than triple those who work in the primary, service, and manufacturing sectors (66.8% and 21%, respectively). Moreover,

[i]f Canada is becoming a knowledge society, it is mainly as a result of workers' own education intitiatives.... Yet large numbers of employees perform work that is low-skilled and requires less education than they have. More than 20 percent of employees feel overqualified for their jobs, a problem that is somewhat more common among non-union workers than union members.... There is a common fear that the information technology revolution, coupled with economic globablization, means Canada will lose out to foreign competitors unless workers become better skilled. This idea does not stand up to scrutiny. For instance, there is a surplus in computer literacy in this country. In 1994, over two-thirds (68 per cent) of the employed were computer literate, but only half of all employees (and even fewer self-employed people) actually used a computer in their work. More generally, job structures often deprive workers of opportunities to use their education and talents. (Lowe, 2000:170)

These types of statistics draw our attention directly to the class-based character of technological change under advanced capitalism. Indeed, several contributors to the work of Schön, Sanyal, and Mitchell (1999) suggest that computer technology is driving the working poor out of the mainstream economy in the United States. In general, we see both an overestimation of the knowledge-based work of technologists and programmers, on the one hand, and a bifurcation of the technological opportunities in the workplace based on occupational status, on the other. Likewise, the basic computer access and use statistics presented in Chapter 1 (Table 1.1) indicate important changes in the home and the workplace. Clearly, there has been some sort of technological revolution. However, I suggest that the character and dynamics of this revolution tell us more about the relations of class, occupation, and capital accumulation than about the developmental trajectory of computer technology itself. From a working-class standpoint, computers represent a revolution in which positive features (e.g., some growth in higher-quality "knowledge work"; the potential for greater discretionary time due to automation; the potential for lower consumer costs) are wildly overblown and negative features (e.g., technologically based unemployment; work intensification;

deskilling; heightened surveillance and dislocation from mainstream society) are just as wildly understated.

Despite this growing awareness of the computer revolution, for the vast majority of Canadian manufacturing workers, the infusion of computers directly into their work lives is, in many ways, only a little over a decade old. Indeed, the majority of people who actively used computers, specifically forms of networked personalized computers, in the workplace whom I interviewed indicated that computers had appeared on their shopfloor only in the first half of the 1990s. Greenbaum (1998) explains this seemingly belated appearance as related to corporate strategies concerning computer integration (including the design principles these strategies command in the technological development sector). She indicates that the design principles changed from a concern for automation in the 1970s and 1980s to a concern for communicative integration of workers into the labor process. Communication in this case is limited to managerial objectives and is largely one-way (i.e., workers move information up the command chain). Thus, it entails a heightened ability, as Greenbaum argues, to "coordinate re-divided labour" across a wider range of distant sites of production. According to Menzies (1996), for blue-collar workers in particular the structure of capitalism is shifting toward "quick-response" and "just-in-time" manufacturing. Workplaces are being reengineered into global cybernetic systems permitting centralized financial and managerial control, intensification, commodification of activity, unprecedented fragmentation, and increased surveillance of the labor process. Such "advances," however, do not represent a real break from current practices under capitalism, but rather an intensification of its basic logic in a new form.

It is business as usual with a vengeance. . . . With the information highway signalling the network-integration phase of a computerized restructuring which dates from the 1970's, the industrial paradigm is shifting [to] exploit the highway network as a "unified system" of production, marketing distribution, and consumption. This isn't a strictly technological development, nor a deterministic one. A host of ideological and historical choices are at work, including deficit cutting and government downsizing; privatization, free trade, and deregulation, plus downward ratcheting of social and labor standards. (Menzies, 1998:87–89)

Much of this picture of computer technological development and the perspectives that are produced in relation to it were, in many ways, prefigured in Marx's original discussion of the forces of technological development, work intensification, and changes in the relation of constant to variable capital now almost a century and half old (Marx, 1867–1868/1990: Vol. 3).[1]

Whereas in the previous chapter I dealt with approaches to adult learning that open up our understanding of class differentiation, in this chapter I focus on computer technology in order to situate it historically and in relation to capitalism and class experience. Computer technologies, however, must be understood broadly in relation to more general theories of technology, though we must be careful to tease apart academic approaches from contemporary popular discourses of technology. In other words, strictly speaking, the term *technology* should include any mediating tool of human activity, ranging from a pencil, to a computer, to a language, to any rational organization of material resources. However, in the industrialized world, ask someone to talk about technology and his or her response largely begins and ends with a discussion of computers. This chapter attempts to address both of these ways of thinking and talking about technology, but with a clear emphasis on computers specifically. The following sections inform two main lines of discussion: first, historical and theoretical perspectives on technology and their role in understanding working-class standpoints in practice; and second, a discussion of working people's experiences, perspectives, and patterns of activity in relation to computer technology specifically. Both set the stage for a critical understanding of adult learning and technology in working-class life. From the perspective of the activity theory framework, this chapter provides a better sense of the relationship between the goal and motive levels of activity from the perspective of working-class people. I suggest that working-class perspectives on technology provide important clues and background knowledge for making explicit the goal and broad motive of people's activity. Implicated in this discussion of the goal and motive levels are the dispositional "tools" that people bring with them and use to mediate their participation (i.e., the class habitus).

As I remarked at the start of the book, the addition of other concepts to existing sociocultural approaches to learning is meant to draw attention

---

[1] For those who are less familiar with Marxist language concerning different types of capital, *variable capital* refers to investment in "labor power," i.e., the work that people contribute to the labor process. *Constant capital* refers to investment in machines. In general, the significance of the distinction between the two terms relates to the claim Marx made that only variable capital contributes to the generation of surplus value that is necessary for capital accumulation. An "immanent contradiction" of capitalism, then, is that as the ratio of constant to variable capital rises, the rate of surplus value generation tends to fall.

to what I see as key class dimensions of practice. Bourdieu's concept of habitus is an example of this. Likewise, as it highlights a range of ideological or dispositional tools that mediate activity, the work of Antonio Gramsci helps to situate perspectives on computer technology within a broad socioeconomic framework. For this generation of workers, as the quotation from Edwards at the beginning of this chapter indicated, computer technology holds an almost mythical place in the popular imagination. This popular imagination plays an important role in what people do in their daily lives, what they are willing to accept, and how they organize their responses despite the fact that it rarely enters into people's conscious, goal-directed action. For working-class people, this popular imagination translates into action and understanding in a distinct way by virtue of their standpoint in the range of class processes in the workplace, education systems, community, and home. For all class groups, practices surrounding technology from childhood to adulthood are filled with contradictory meanings and fragmented experience. Together these half-synthesized notions are expressed by the concept Gramsci (1971) called *common sense*. From a working-class standpoint, abstract, positively framed descriptions of computer technologies in terms of efficiency and control are mixed with descriptions of competing negative effects (e.g., job loss, loss of operator control, safety concerns in the workplace). However, the contradictory character of common sense consists of more than just half-truths, folk myths, and fairy tales; it expresses a kind of truth in the sense that it is actively produced out of the contradictory character of class life itself. In other words, these contradictions are not as much dependent on individual abilities to make what Gramsci called *good sense* as they are a reflection of the contradictory experience of life under advanced capitalism.

Situating Computer Technology Historically

Computer technology hasn't simply descended from the heavens to the earth. It has been brought into being by specific historical and political economic relations. In his groundbreaking work *The Forces of Production* (1984), David Noble provides an impressive documentary analysis of just how such forces have conspired to provide us with the kinds of technologies, specifically microcomputer technologies, that working people are faced with today. Noble demonstrates how elites – in the context of the postwar industrial-military complex in the United States – actively produced the types of information technologies that have led to contemporary production applications and the modern microcomputer.

Briefly, according to Noble (1984), the concerted activities of specific corporations, principally General Electric, Westinghouse, RCA, AT&T and IBM, were essential for the appearance of the computer technologies we know today. Noble is quick to point out that this is an accomplishment achieved not by the use of private research and development, but rather through the conscious, forceful, and direct appropriation of material resources and use of political power resulting in unprecedented access to public funding. This conscious use of power helped to amass huge profits for elites during World War II through military contracts and was then extended to create and then reap the benefits of the American military-industrial complex during the cold war era. Noble shows how this private control over public monies and the extension of the reach of these programs into public research institutions such as the Massachusetts Institute of Technology led directly to specific early forms of computer technology such as Computerized Numerical Control (CNC). These same concerted efforts continued well past the immediate post–World War II period in North America in increasingly complex forms as manufacturing technologies expanded into spheres of distribution, marketing, communications, and consumption vis-à-vis microcomputers (e.g., see Menzies, 1996; McChesney, 1998).

Despite the fact that computers now play important roles beyond the workplace, returning to these historical roots, we see that CNC technologies emerged from, were designed for, and were further modified in the practical world of work based on the specific requirements of business. It is through this process of mediation that computer technologies have come to take on their underlying capital-centric qualities. However, what makes this even more clear in Noble's work are the alternative technologies that could have just as efficiently achieved the purposes of technological research and development at the time, but that differed only in their ability to concentrate control in the hands of employers. The key example in this regard was Record/Playback (R/P) technology. The distinction between CNC and R/P lies in the fact that with R/P technology the practical skill and knowledge of workers remained central to the programming of the machinery. In this way, R/P forms of computer technology could be considered more labor-centric. Control was left in the hands of the worker. However, as Noble puts it, "to the software engineer, this places far too many cards in the hands of the lowly machinist" (1984:190).

A similar dynamic in which power and control directly influence available technologies in their general form is described in pan-historical terms in the work of Lewis Mumford.

[F]rom late neolithic times in the Near East, right down to our own day, two technologies have recurrently existed side by side: one authoritarian, the other democratic, the first system-centred, immensely powerful, but inherently unstable, the other man-centred [*sic*], relatively weak, but resourceful and durable. (Mumford, 1991:14)

In our times, this trajectory of technological development is a clear example of how political-economic relations actively affect the production and development of tools that somehow still seem to retain their guise as value neutral. The concrete political and financial mobilization in the industrial, governmental, military, and higher education spheres by elite groups has actively cut short the possibility of labor-centric computer technologies such as the R/P system. Decades of formal as well as practical experimentation, research, and development (and enormous public resources) were directed instead to CNC technologies and its line of development, narrowing the possibilities of R/P and similar democratizing, labor-centric technologies.

New alternatives do and will continue to appear, as Mumford's comments suggest. McChesney uses the Internet as a (potentially) progressive example of this kind.

The Internet has opened up very important space for progressive and democratic communication, especially for activists hamstrung by traditional commercial media. Some have argued that the Internet will eventually break up the vice-like grip of the global media monopoly and provide the basis for a golden age of free, uncensored, democratic communication. Yet whether one can extrapolate from activist use of the Internet to seeing the Internet become the democratic medium for society writ large is another matter. The notion that the Internet will permit humanity to leapfrog over capitalism and corporate communication is in sharp contrast to the present rapid commercialization of the Internet. (McChesney, 1998:21)

As the detailed practical analyses of Cockshott and Cottrell (1993), Bansler (1989), Ehn (1988), Belanger (2001), Sawchuk (2001a, 2001b, in press), and others demonstrate, alternative uses and development of computer technologies remain possible. To draw on some political and labor-based examples, we can look at my own union's (Canadian Union of Public Employees) internationally groundbreaking Solinet, the International

Labor Organization's Course Reader software (Belanger, 2001), or examples such as Russia's original GlasNet, various forms of distance education (e.g., Open Universities in the United Kingdom and Canada), and the plans for an online international labor university (Lee, 1997). Indeed, the myriad small-scale, local initiatives including activist list-serves, the relatively old-fashioned Bulletin Board Systems (BBS's), and the like continue to function in various social spheres, all of which suggest a persistent democratizing pressure emanating from below. The labor-centric model of technologies will continue in whatever form it can, not only because alternative forms and visions of genuinely democratic social life continue, but also, as Wilkinson (1983) and others noted some time ago, because the actual positive social effects of capital-centric technologies remain elusive.

Critical Approaches to Computer Technologies

Discussions of computer technology implicate an entire range of psychological, social, and political issues. However, we can also link these discussions of computers with more general theories of technology by discerning at least four basic approaches. This four-type model draws on a general reading of a range of key theoretical texts including Ellul (1964), Mumford (1991), Dreyfus (1992), Sejersted and Moser (1992), Ihde (1993), Feenberg (1991), and Negroponte (1995), as well as the more exhaustive (and exhausting) review of North American – based business and state-based policy/reports (e.g., Printing Industries of America, 1994; Industry Canada, 1997). Briefly, these can be divided into technocratic, critical/essentialist, constructivist, and the "democratic rationalism" of a critical theory of technology (Feenberg, 1991).

The first approach most often seen in business and state-based policy writing, in a sense, cannot really be understood as theoretical in the sense that its claims are not evidentiary, nor are they based on a openly articulated set of concepts. Nevertheless, this approach has enormous effects on how we think about and experience technology. It is a largely ahistorical approach to technology, is fixated on computer technology specifically, fails to consider different standpoints, and generally seeks to reproduce the general dynamics of capitalism and neo-liberalism more broadly. The result is a massive reification of technologies, figuring them as autonomous and sometimes even active social agents. Computer technology within this casting is given a positive or neutral role. More elaborate political economic formulations of this technocratic approach are rooted in the work of intellectuals beginning with Dahrendorf (1959) through Kerr (1969) and Bell (1973). More often than not under this approach, technology takes on a kind of autonomous, creative, deterministic role. This, in turn, gives rise to exaggerated notions such as that of the "knowledge worker" (Bell, 1973) in the postindustrial age (further popularized in Naisbitt, 1982). Toffler's (1980) suggestion that technology leads societal change takes the final step by reversing subject–object relations.[2] It is this position that Noble and others directly refute in their mapping of the historical power relations of the computer age.

A more critical but largely essentialist treatise against technology forms something of a mirror opposite to that of the technocrats, though it is only the former that provides detailed historical scholarship. The critical essentialist approach, then, focuses on general social structures of society and the functions that technologies serve in a given society. Technologies take on values in relation to the structures that produce them and cement in them a history of power relations, environmental degradation, and alienation. Writers such as Ellul (e.g., 1964) and Heidegger (e.g., 1977) exemplify this style of the critical approach.

However, we should remember that the roots of technocratic and critical/essentialist approaches to technology depend on the activation of specific technologies in everyday life at work and elsewhere, as well as an intricate and expansive semiotic network of, as Edwards (1995) puts it, "a dense and energetic fabric of signifying forms."

Computers were the enigmatic objects of profound hopes and hatreds even before their invention during the Second World War. They have always been as much symbols as practical devices: 'giant brains', standards of precision, signs of scientific values, evidence of omnipotence. Ideas about artificial intelligence, a networked society where computers instantaneously handle calculation, communication and control, and the view of the human brain as a biological computer are now commonplaces. We can make sense of the material roles of computers as tools only when we simultaneously grasp their roles as cultural metaphor. (Edwards, 1995:69)

This constructivist approach to computer technology is the third of the four general theoretical approaches. It depends specifically on these forms of signification (Ihde, 1993). The meaning and effects of technology are determined by their use and not before. Hubert Dreyfus (1992), for example, provides one of the most enduring accounts of how computers cannot mimic human interaction with these types of constructivist ideas in mind.

---

[2] It follows from this that the computer can be chosen as *Time* magazine's "person of the year."

One of the most relevant critical discussions of technology in terms of social relations and the activation of technologies in social life, however, is provided by Hacker (1990). In conversation with sociologist Dorothy Smith, Hacker explains this perspective toward technology in this way:

Hacker: You know that one definition by Marx that makes so much sense, that work could be an act of human freedom and expression of human creativity. Because work then sounds like play and it sounds like having block parties and it sounds like people getting together and enjoying – doesn't matter if they're building a house or damming a river, maybe. And technology is the way we organize energy and materials to get work done. I don't have a feeling that people [are advocating] "hands off" nature. But it's the "gentle touch" that would be more pleasurable, I think, for both.

Smith: I hadn't really thought of technology in that way before. I suppose technology has come to have a thoroughly bad name.

Hacker: Yeah, yeah.

Smith: So to see technology as it could be, as embedded in really human relations is kind of surprising. And as enhancing people's capacities to . . .

Hacker: To be playful!

Smith: To be playful.

Hacker: Yeah, like firecrackers as opposed to gunpowder. (p. 202)

Although Hacker perhaps underemphasizes the way historical social relations do play a role in the potential uses of specific forms of technology through their history of design, we nonetheless see that specific technologies take on their meanings and subsequent effects in specific cultural and material contexts and uses. Approaches such as Hacker's begin to approximate the fourth and final theoretical approach to technology. However, it is the work of Andrew Feenberg that perhaps best exemplifies a critical middle ground between essentialism and technological determinism, on the one hand, and a dehistoricized social constructivism, on the other. Like Hacker, Feenberg pays close attention to the role of dominant and subordinate standpoints in society and the role these standpoints play in potentially liberating social practice.

[Ordinary people] encounter technology as a dimension of their lifeworld. For the most part they merely carry out the plans of others or inhabit technologically constructed spaces and environments. As subordinate actors, they strive to appropriate the technologies with which they are involved and adapt them to the meanings that illuminate their lives. Their relation to technology is thus far more complex than that of dominant actors (which they too may be on occasion). (1999:iv)

It is this balance that best reflects the situated, tool-mediated approach to working-class learning that I take in this book. The concept of tool mediation in activity, an idea developed in the work of Vygotsky, suggests that tools transmit culture and shape practice. As Latour (1994) has argued, tools shape people's goals and interests and, in a sense, have built into them the relations of design from which they emerge. At the same time, tools must be activated by human agents, and in the context of activity there is always room for unexpected results. A critical tool-mediation approach inherent in activity theory is aligned with the type of critical theory of technology that writers like Feenberg put forth. Indeed, it can express the learning dimensions of social practice in such a way as to provide the basis for understanding how technologies (tools/artifacts of any kind) mediate ongoing contingencies of activity and express historical relations of their production and use.

Common Sense and Working-Class Perspectives on Computer Technology

In his *Selections from the Prison Notebooks* (1971), Gramsci defines common sense as "[that] incoherent set of generally held assumptions and beliefs common to any given society" (p. 323). He goes on to indicate that

[this] does not mean that there are not truths in common sense. It means rather that common sense is an ambiguous, contradictory and multiform concept.... (423)

The argument I put forth in this book is concerned with the horizons of general theories of technology insofar as they can help shed light on working-class computer learning practices and the more general issue of class perspectives on computer technology, all of which play a role in shaping the overall structure and meaning of learning. The work of David Hakken (1993) provides a useful starting point for discussions of class-based technological common sense in his study of working-class computer learning in northern England. Using open-ended interviewing and community ethnographies, Hakken outlines a form of technological common sense. For example, workers in a local adult education technology program, whose comments follow, explain that their perspectives and concerns involving technology spring from a concern for jobs, for not getting left behind, but at the same time show a sense of attraction to the modern. These understandings compose a contradictory complex of beliefs and experiences.

I can't take it all in [it's doing things] ... and you can't see it doing any of those things. If only I could see t'bus going to there, and picking it up, and moving it. If you're younger, you accept things.

I've just got one question. Will computers make people redundant?

Progress in one way is very good, but in another, not very nice when people don't have a job.

I thought the computer had a brain ... I saw it on television falling in love with the operator.

We've got to do computers. You read it, that these are the jobs of the future.... You either keep abreast or you get left behind. (All from Hakken, 1993:14–20)

These quotes demonstrate a powerful range of feelings and observations that, taken as a whole, express the character of people's desires and fears related to technology in their lives. Particularly pronounced in Hakken's interviews is the fear of how technology will affect people's working lives, fueled equally by mystification and lack of information. Hakken summarizes as follows:

Indeed, computerization had become an important symbol, both of political doubt and of the kinds of change processes that must be dealt with for the doubt to be overcome. Politically as well as linguistically, the working class in Sheffield is of two minds about computerization. One mind-set sees it primarily as a threat, to be avoided where possible, if only by structuring personal consciousness. The other mind-set approaches computerization positively, as a new means to accomplish accepted goals. Often both mind-sets were held by the same person. (1993:23)

In my own interviews with industrial workers, we can see striking similarities in the weave of competing class and perspectives on technology. Consider this range of quotes:

Your whole life is going to revolve around computers.... Computers, wow! Personally, I'd just as soon do without them but I know that they're coming. (W50)

That's progress. You can't stand in the way of progress, anyhow. (W6)

Technology you know to me it's a funny word. The future, they say the future is on technology, new technology for the future. They're trying to design new things, come up with new things I guess that's what technology is, inventing things. (W7)

It's going to be it in the future. (W12)

They run everything now, you have to have it, you know there is no way you can be in any type of technical business without one. You know it's into everything, every home, somehow you're connected with it. (W19)

We see that many of the same themes that Hakken identifies encompass the social life of working people generally but are rooted more or less directly in the class experience of the workplace and the labor market. Within both sets of comments we see a persistent contradiction concerning a future that, although not necessarily preferred, is described as inevitable. Contradictory elements of a class-based common sense emerge in their clearest form, however, when people begin to talk of concrete practices surrounding computer technologies. This example provides a glimpse of the duality that exists in working-class perspectives on computer technology.

R: God, you can't live today and be computer illiterate, you're out in left field if you don't have any knowledge. I don't really want to have to learn it but. . . .

I: Do you use a computer at work then?

R: No I don't use one there. We don't really need one.

I: So will you buy a home computer then?

R: Probably not. (W38)

A contradictory common sense, as Gramsci describes it, should not be dismissed as some form of false consciousness. It is, as I suggested at the start of the chapter, a reflection of contradictory positions in the cultural life and information flows in real communities and real workplaces under advanced capitalism.

Working-Class Technological Common Sense Rooted in the Workplace, the Labor Market, and the Home

We've seen that a working-class perspective on computer technology seems to be deeply influenced by one's position in the labor market as a wage earner. However, the degree to which these comments reflect a necessary linkage between a position in the labor market and forms of computer learning is expressed more clearly by this person. Working for an employer who is actively engaging in contracting out services, this woman talks of another "world" of secure employment, better-paying work, and the connection of this world to computer technology.

There are some layoffs coming and that, you know. So I'm on the list, what happens to me when there is a layoff coming up and so where do I go? And when you're on your own and you have three kids to support, so, two now but, you know, where do you go if you don't have your education or you don't pick up something? And by just staying there... you're not learning anything else unless you go out and learn computer, or learn how the other world is running. You know, unless you get yourself involved in something outside the workplace. (W3)

Or, consider the comments of this autoworker, who, having worked for a company for 17 years and having successfully completed high school and part of college, makes a fairly straightforward connection between his employment situation and his knowledge of computers.

I feel if I don't get some kind of knowledge of it I'm going to be handicapped like not being able to write. That's like the thing, if I don't figure out how to work this I'm going to be sitting there and not know what to do and everyone else is just going by. Can't move on, you know you're stuck in one spot. (W19)

What's perhaps most interesting is the degree to which this man and most other interviewees eventually outline the narrow simplicity of computer technologies in the workplace and the relative ease of mastery under suitable conditions. These are not merely casual comments; they are charged with strong emotions. As I was to find out in the course of this research, computer technology, almost across the board, provides the means for many workers to discuss some of their deepest fears, hopes, and desires for themselves and their family. These are rooted in political-economic relations and, in particular, extend to households with young children. Here another autoworker uses humor to draw a direct connection between computer literacy, a declining manufacturing base in the context of free-trade agreements in North America, and the future needs of one's children.

I: Do you think kids should be learning more about computers in school?

R: Yes! Definitely, because that's where the future's going to be.

I: How so?

R: Well, as far as manual labor, *Manuel's* labor's gonna be in Mexico. Manuel labor is gonna be in Mexico. [laughter] ... Anyways. No, the technology of today are gonna be doin' away with manual labor. Instead, they're gonna go all high tech. You're gonna be able to do everything from the computer. That's where the future's going to.... I know one of the guys in our department actually, he's dead, dead, dead broke but he's got a good computer system because it's good for the kids. (W5)

In Canada, more than 50% of households with children have computers (Statistics Canada, 2000), and this link between family life and computer learning comes up repeatedly in discussion of technology and learning in working-class life. However, computer learning is also central to working people's feelings about employment and life trajectories. Indeed, one source for large-scale survey research in Canada that can provide additional insight into the set of beliefs and perspectives just highlighted is a massive study conducted in the early 1990s by a national trade union. The Communications, Energy, and Paperworkers Union of Canada's *Technology Adjustment Research Programme* project (Garcia-Orgales, 1992) carried out an extensive survey of its members. Issues of computerization and technological change were seen to be central to the feeling of insecurity in terms of personal employment and the viability of the workplace. Over 75% of respondents claimed to "feel insecure about the future of the firm or plant."[3] In this context, computer-based learning was selected as far and away the most important current and future interest among workers, helping to make visible the weave of work with home life and views of life chances.

In the ways just illustrated, experience with computer technology, the ideas and discourses that surround it, and the struggle for stability in the face of it form a central signifier for working-class life under capitalism. It reaches into people's work as well as their home and community lives in a variety of ways. A theory of technology that does not somehow grasp these concerns, the social organization of everyday life they express, and the motive of activity they represent cannot help us understand the differentiated and differentiating modes of participation that define working-class learning and technology.

The Active Production of a Working-Class Technological Common Sense in Everyday Practice

As we saw in the previous section, the notions of inevitability and progress associated with computers are fundamental elements of the popular discourse of technology. I've argued that these elements

---

[3] Indeed, the vast majority of these rank-and-file workers cited international trade policies such as the North American Free Trade Agreement as central to this insecurity. This further accentuates the degree to which political-economic factors play an important role in everyday consciousness and the framing of activities. This general finding, as we'll see, is closely linked with, among other activities, an interest in computer learning.

are interwoven with concrete and contradictory everyday life experiences of people engaged in various processes from a working-class standpoint to produce a particular type of technological common sense. The most apparent contradictions within this common sense include the fact that although computers created wealth and were good for society, this form of technological change often involved job loss, created new hazards, and increased boredom and alienation in the workplace. Furthermore, interviewees told story after story of how the computer-based knowledge and skills that are necessary for manufacturing work were relatively simple to acquire. However, one of the most important ways that this common sense was expressed in practical action was seen in the learning practices of working-class households. Most interviewees, as the quotation from Feenberg indicates, were neither cheerleaders for computer technology nor negative about technology in their lives. Instead, as Feenberg says, they were simply striving to "appropriate the technologies with which they are involved and adapt them to the meanings that illuminate their lives." In this way, they displayed pragmatic acceptance as well as quiet resilience in the face of social forces seemingly beyond their influence. Though a minority of people viewed the computer revolution as an opportunity for class mobility, most saw it as a necessary part of the social landscape, providing the means of achieving some level of basic economic stability. Both perspectives led to the extension of computer-based learning beyond the workplace and into the home and community, involving adults as well as children.

The following interview provides an important clue as to how the dominant perspectives on technology are infused into working-class technological common sense. There is, of course, a consistent message broadcasted to the population vis-à-vis the school curriculum, state initiatives, and the privately owned mass media that computer literacy is both lacking and required by the citizenry. However, the following excerpt belies the claim that this common sense emerges passively from experience, and highlights the active role of the workplace and those who own and control it. In the basement recreation room of this autoworker and his partner (R1 and R2, respectively), the conversation focuses on how people get the information they have about computers, as well as how and why computer technology becomes an interest of the average working people. It describes an incident that is not uncommon for those who work for large industrial employers. The excerpt begins when the partner mentions a guest speaker whom the auto company had brought into the plant to speak to the workers about computer technology.

R2:   [to R1] Who's that Mr. Smith at work, that you saw at the Company and he had these cards and he said/

R1:   Oh, Dr. Jones? Oh, God! Alright. He's from Toronto, okay? This guy is – calls himself a cyborg, alright? He was a guest speaker at the Company's quarterly report [to employees]. And he's got artificial lenses in his eyes; he's got a valve in his heart; he's got a knee replacement; he's got a hip replacement. Oh, he had three or four other things.

I: Little, like [a robot]/

R1:   Yeah. That's why he called himself a cyborg. And his thinking was, if you have a computer and you don't have a modem, okay, it's only a piece of junk sittin' in the corner because of the vastness of knowledge that's capable out there now. Every computer should be on the modem. Every kid should be hooked up. He says, "You adults, if you want to learn more, you will learn, but children need it now." That's when to start 'em on it.

I: Okay. So how long ago was this that you heard this guy [Dr. Jones] talk?

R1:   Oh, we had a quarterly meeting where he was there in person, and he was a guest speaker.

I: Oh, so all employees?

R1:   Yeah.

I: And, did that have an effect on you gettin' even deeper into it [computers], or more/

R1:   Yeah. About different things and stuff like that, about the technology of it, eh? . . .

R2:   Well, even that TV advertisement, Candice Bergen, she's on the phone and she says, "Call accountant!" And it's an automatic thing and it goes right through to an accountant and it just dials without her having to punch in the number or remember the number. . . . That's technology! (W4a/b)

Together, these interviewees outline the resources, experiences, and contexts informing the dominant perspectives on technology woven into the complex that can be described as a technological common sense. Nor were these descriptions unique. Specific resources and contexts are actively created, emerge directly from a market logic, and attempt to exert greater control over workers by dominant interests expressing a specific worldview. These flows of information run through the nightly event of television watching as well as the celebrated rituals of managerial and guest presentations at the factory. Both events are examples of the active campaigns of corporate education that flow through the everyday lives of workers. Digging a little deeper, we can see other ways in which messages like these are, in fact, examples of class processes. For example, these messages take on their class character as the recipients are positioned in particular roles that are beyond narrow limits, quite passive in character. Emphatically, for the creators of these messages, the experiences are actively produced. So, although the messages are the same, they take on their class character through the active/dominant versus passive/subordinate standpoints through which people participate in the communication process.

The effects of these mechanisms of cultural hegemony, despite the vast resources that support them, are not a foregone conclusion, however. People I interviewed engaged in concrete activities that eroded some of the dominant assumptions. As one woman put it, "a computer will not fix your sink" (W41). It is these attitudes, emerging from mundane life, that account for the contradictory mix of information and beliefs that Gramsci suggests in his original definition of common sense. These disconnects from the dominant discourse are rooted in the taken-for-granted experiences of everyday class life, once again highlighting the importance of a theory of everyday life for an understanding of learning among subordinate groups.[4] A discussion that includes this alternative viewpoint can be found in the next interview. Taken from an afternoon spent in discussion with an autoworker and his partner, it begins with an explanation of the difficulties of industrial wage labor and ends, to my mind triumphantly, with a claim that brings issues of technology firmly and irreverently down to earth in the lifeworld of local community relationships. Again, we see a process in which people actively engage with a dominant discourse and, in the course of this engagement, reveal its contradictory nature by drawing on concrete examples from their own class standpoints. The excerpt

---

[4] Dominant discourses are not, it must be emphasized, separate from everyday activity but are accomplished practically. The difference between the two types of practices lies in the extent to which activities are integrated with more general sets of social relations. Dominant discourses are integrated and thus help to integrate the practices (which correspond with their logic) into a network of extralocal social (e.g., market) relations. Breaks from dominant discourses and the social practices with which they correspond are less integrated with more general sets of social relations beyond localities such as the home, the neighborhood, or the industrial workplace, for example. Though they may be essential for the achievement of these "dominant networks," they do not find a point of articulation within a shared "public sphere" (Negt and Kluge, 1993), they tend to become taken for granted and invisible, even to the participant.

begins with a comment the autoworker makes concerning the technological changes occurring in his plant. His partner, an unemployed driving school instructor, expands and links these comments with a broad class and gender analysis. This couple quite reasonably resent the insecurity and degradation of community life that they associate with current technological change. Their perspective is rooted in their class standpoint in the broader processes of computer development and application.

R1:   I gotta sort of be a little realistic too; how long is my bullshit job going to stay there? It's hard to say how long before they push that work out into a different company someplace.

R2:   People have been saying for years that they're going to have robots doing the, making cars and that, and everybody else is going to be standing on the street, nobody going to buy the cars because the robots aren't getting paid okay, well that's technology. It's hard on people, you can talk about it anyway you want, but that's been said for thirty years now, you know, and it's just getting worse and worse, and worse. I don't understand a lot of things, like even this whole country. Imagine, like these people from the prime minister right on down, every politician was brought up, well I would say almost everyone of them was brought up in a well-to-do family, and they've never known what it's like to scrounge. They haven't a clue how the rest of us are living. What the hell do I want to be on the, the cyber-net for, or whatever the hell you want to call it. I want to get out of my house get into my little truck and go to the grocery store, and the hardware store and the drugstore and all this garbage and I want to say hello to people. I do! (W17a/b)

Here we see an outline of the cultural and material relations that undergird virtually every working-class account of technology I came across in the course of my interview research. Discussions of computer technology, as I have suggested from the outset, served as a platform from which to investigate a whole social world of life trajectories, social origins, and fears of unemployment in working-class life under advanced capitalism.

Even against these difficulties, the desire for and pleasures to be found in stable working-class community life persist. Indeed, after the interview just presented, the three of us walked out into the hot summer day, stopping by their pickup truck to finish a cold beer each. We ended up lifting the hood of the truck, and as we did, a neighbor walked across the street. All four of us now looked under the hood of the truck, as the dashboard display hadn't been working correctly for the past few weeks. Because the truck was bought used, the owner's manual had not been included; however, the neighbor had seen this problem before. Together they disconnected and then reconnected the battery. The computer system on the truck reset itself, and the dashboard worked properly again.

Summary

I began this chapter with a discussion of the current technological revolution and the economic restructuring in Canada and the United States. Though technology does not refer to computers alone, computer-based technology dominates academic, policy-based, and popular discourse on technology. I situated the emergence of computer technology with a brief historical look at its origins in the military-industrial complex. This discussion culminated in an outline of several basic approaches to technology generally. This process was meant to integrate broad critical historical perspectives on technology with social relational analyses of ongoing learning practices. The presentation of data in the second half of this chapter sketched the basic character of the background knowledge, experiences, and concerns that working people find interwoven with notions of technology, learning, and computer-based activity. As activity theorists such as Leont'ev have argued, the broader structure of activity is essential to an understanding of the conscious goal direction of practice. This chapter did not focus on computer devices as tools but instead described the character of a set of ideological and "dispositional" tools that mediate specific forms of social practice among working people. These tools, collectively understood as a form of common sense, will help us understand the practices we explore in the remaining chapters.

The analysis of interviewees' perspectives on technology and their reasons for entering into computer learning built on the work of Gramsci to illustrate the dimensions of a working-class technological common sense. This common sense was a weave of dominant discourses that were actively produced in a variety of settings. The experiences that gave rise to this common sense were not idiosyncratic, but were continuous with the creation of active/dominant and passive/subordinate relationships as well as the logic of capitalism and, as such, class life.

This chapter suggests a way of understanding what activity theorists call the motive level of activity systems, as well as a way to see how and why technologies such as computers shape specific forms of practice. Although I'll continue to add detail to the conception of computer learning as I proceed, from this chapter we learn about people's general disposition toward computer learning (as contradictory and compelling) and how it is rooted in their participation in a number of key spheres of activity. It was in reflections on actual practice that a distinct working-class standpoint was most clearly elaborated. Computer technology served as a key signifier for working-class experience that opened up space for discussion of some of people's deepest class-based desires and fears.

4   Microanalysis of Workers' Computer Learning

Two Case Studies

From a sociological perspective, activity theory and situated learning theory are most effective when operating as middle-range theories of learning and social action. Clearly, discussions within both approaches become vague to the degree that they grapple with macroconcepts concerning the major social divisions, the structure of society, and the dynamics of social change. Though each approach is somewhat stronger in terms of microanalysis, likewise, discussions with a clear understanding of the *interaction order* (Goffman, 1983) or the *active accomplishment* of encounters (Garfinkel, 1967) have also not been prominent. Throughout this book, I attempt to integrate macroconcepts of political economy into the analysis of activity and communities of practice; however, in this chapter I focus on microanalysis. I deal with the microinteractional, tacit, tool-mediated processes that are largely assumed in discussions of learning while making suggestions about how these processes may be related to activity theory and situated learning approaches as well as to issues of political economy. The assumption I make here is that learning practice must not only be macrocontextualized, but microcontextualized as well, in order to be fully understood.

This chapter involves an examination of two case studies. The first one focuses on how people interact with each other and with computer artifacts in the course of computer learning. I have not missed the irony of the fact that although I've made much of the formal-learning and pedagogical biases of dominant theories of learning, in this first case study I analyze an audio-video recording of two unemployed men learning in a Labour Education Centre's computer lab, a social context designed explicitly for learning. Despite taking place in this institutional setting, however, the study focuses on periods of independent, collectively directed informal practice and provides several important insights into precisely how people learn to use computers together. Importantly, we see learning in real-time, moment-by-moment interaction rather than retrospectively described. In other words, I move away from analyzing people's account of their learning to observe what they do. This case study shows the operation of the microinteractive machinery of learning, and through this we get a sense of how learning is a situated social act that people perform together rather than passive transmission and cognitive absorption of information. We see that conventional notions of expert–novice or pedagogical relations need not be definitive of the learning process. Instead, learning can be seen to consist of such simple features as the distribution of access to keyboard/mouse tools in interaction, the viewability of the screen, the arrangement and movement of chairs, the positioning of people's bodies in sequentially organized practice, and so forth.

The second case study deals with a work-based learning process that highlights the mediating effects of hardware, software, and the organizational contexts of computing. It provides a view of the structure of ongoing practice in which the worker is an active agent yet is situated in an institutional context that does not actually encourage learning. I point to a range of political-economic dimensions involved, including how the imperatives of capital accumulation and the capitalist labor process directly shape opportunities and modes of participation with coworkers and specific hardware/software. Workers struggle to achieve local goals (both those of the workplace and their own personal goals) in the face of forces beyond the workplace. Although it does not have an industrial manufacturing setting, this case study provides a detailed example of how software and organizational contexts affect the way computer learning is accomplished. It demonstrates the importance of computer as well as broader organizational mediation of learning practice from the worker's standpoint.

Both analyses find inspiration in the insights and concepts of ethnomethodology (EM) and conversation analysis (CA), though including issues of political economy that go beyond the traditional scope of EM/CA analysis. In brief, EM/CA, founded by Harold Garfinkel on the one hand and by the work of Harvey Sacks and Emmanuel Schegloff on the other (see Heritage, 1984), has as its domain the tacit "seen but unnoticed" social accomplishment of everyday life. At the most minute levels of interaction, with powerful empirical commitment, both EM and CA provide valuable insights into the nature of social order. However, more specifically in the area of human–computer interaction, each case study owes a general debt to Lucy Suchman's *Plans and Situated Actions:*

The Problem of Human–Machine Communication (1987). Suchman demonstrates, through a detailed analysis of computerized expert help systems, how the human–technology interface relies on tacit, moment-by-moment accomplishment rather than a rational choice–based model of conscious human planning. Suchman's work is important because, among other things, it helped clear fresh space for an understanding of computer mediation. Furthermore, as benign as the existence of (photocopier) expert help systems may seem, the analysis created an opening for better understanding of the troublesome character of computer-mediated interaction that includes serious issues of control over technological design. Suchman herself puts it this way:

[A]s long as machine actions are determined by stipulated conditions, machine interaction with the world, and with people in particular, will be limited to the intentions of designers and their ability to anticipate and constrain the user's actions. (1987:189)

As such, I suggest that we can begin to imagine the process through which locally produced activity is subject to extralocal systems of activity that involve workplace control, intensification of work, and, expanding further, the reproduction of class processes. These considerations can enhance our understanding of how computer-mediated activity systems and communities of practice relate to the intentions of technological designers, as well as how these systems function in terms of microinteraction and the contingency of local practice.

Part 1: A Microanalytic Approach to Computer Learning at a Labour Education Centre

In this case study,[1] I draw on basic concepts from CA to explore computer learning interaction.[2] I want to show how learning must be understood as a collective, moment-by-moment accomplishment limited or enabled predominantly by social procedures on the one hand and by

---

[1] The full analysis of this transcript is available in Sawchuk (see *Discourse Studies*, in press), but for further detail on the line-by-line analysis upon which the following summaries are based, see Appendix 2.

[2] For the purposes of analysis, I've followed the basic guidelines that Psathas and Anderson (1990) have established regarding CA transcript preparation, though for accessibility for a non-CA audience, I've simplified the transcript considerably. I've left out the timing of silences, not indicated the production of inflections in speech, not signaled overlapping speech, and omitted a variety of other items important for the coordination of activity often included in traditional CA transcripts. In place of these, I've substituted my own commentary.

the specific social, historical, and material contexts on the other. Indeed, if we were to think of learning in the conventional sense, EM/CA would have little to offer us. Learning as such would be considered a "gloss" for a range of invisible and inaudible processes. The basic EM/CA approach would appeal only to those warranted facts recoverable directly from the interaction data, as it is these that are are available, moment by moment, to the participants themselves. From this orientation, as Heritage (1984) explains, the task is to directly analyze the construction of the action as it is played out, frame by frame, where it will seem methodical because of the intelligibility and orderliness that the actors themselves have produced. In other words, the social structure of activity is the participants' own accomplishment together. CA specifically requires careful attention to the minutiae of communicative interaction. As such, the substantive content of conversation is not the object of analysis. Rather, under this approach, semantic and syntactic analyses become relevant only in the context of social negotiation and sequencing. As Moerman and Sacks say, "[f]or studying conversation per se, dull materials are best" (1988:68), and in these terms the transcript in Figure 4.1 is extremely useful. Drawing on the strength of EM, this poses in a sense a very useful limit to an analysis of practice that in fact helps us to bracket our assumptions about what learning really is, that is, what it means to do "learning." This in turn, deepens how we think of learning so that issues of tacit processes and social differentiation in the everyday can be made visible.

Specifically, I comment on the semantic and syntactic organization of interaction and focus primarily on sequential analysis of the interaction between two unemployed men, Larry and Roger, learning to use computers together (Figure 4.1). I outline tacit interaction procedures that are also in some respects specific to computer-mediated dimensions of practice. The analysis in this case study focuses on a transcript of interaction in a computer lab run by a Labour Education Centre in Toronto, Canada. The lab was not a typical classroom setting that one might find in formal schooling. As the facilitator in the session explained, at the Education Centre the belief was that workers are willing and able to organize and carry out much of their own learning. Practically speaking, this meant that after orientation to a topic by the facilitator, the participants worked on their own to explore a list of the particular computer software functions. Thus, after the initial presentation, students were left to divide into informal groups and discuss issues of mutual interest as they learned.

1 R: [looking at L's screen then turning body to L's computer]

2   Uhhh, excuse me, Larry.

3 L: What's that?

4 R: Could you tell me how can I go to the, uhhh, merging. To

5   merge one? [pointing to his screen; L looking away from

6   his screen to R's]

7 L: You finished the typing, right?

8 R: Yeah [pause] Should I go to the "tools" [moving mouse

9   pointer to pull-down menu]

10 L: That's a good one.

11 R: Then go to merge? [moving through menu and highlighting

12   selection]

13 L: [pointing to R's screen] Why don't you go straight to

14   merge [R highlighting a "nonmerge" option] nnnnn,

15 L: Why don't you try that merge there? I'd try that

16   [pointing to R's screen; R highlighting "merge" option]

17   yeah merge/

18 R: Merge. yeah [R clicking on merge selection; R's computer

19   jumps to new screen]

20 L: Let's see what happens.

21 R: There?

22 L: Yep

23 R: And click on the thing?

24 L: Yeah, click on that, yeah, then it's going to get merge

25   one, yeah, you highlight it

26 R: The one [R's screen changes]

27 L: The second one, okay, then select [pause] and nowwww

28   [pause], now what?

29 R: Did it merge it?

30 L: No, uhhhh

31 R: Try this and trying to merge it? [pointing to R's screen]

32 L: Is it done? I don't think so. Didn't do the stuff

33   putting one and two together? Oh I'm not sure/ [turning

34   to face/shoulders to his own screen] Shhhh(it), Wow

35   R: But is not the correct way?

36   L: What's that? [turning to R]

37   R: It's not correct?

38   L: This is not the right way? [L turns to look for

39   facilitator]

40   R: Yeah [pause] Third, third [L turns to face R's screen]

41   L: [turns to look for the facilitator] Joe, we're kind of

42   stuck here eh?

43   [Joe is busy with others, looks at them and waves "in a

44   moment"; long pause; each looks back (at his own screen. Both

45   R and L start to work on their own computers, R checking

46   through menus, L typing at keyboard; later, R begins to

47   type as well]

48   L: You got somewhere yet? [no initiation by R; L still

49   looking at his own screen, however]

50   R: No, not yet. [long pause, each begins working at his own

51   screen, L seeming to have problems and searching menu

52   items] [pause]

53   [L turns head/body toward R's screen and slides his

54   chair toward R while beginning to speak]

55   L: So you get it.

56   R: Yeah.

57   L: So okay, you, uh, after you uh finish typing, did you find

58   out what to do?

59   R: Not yet.

60   L: [L looks frustrated, rubbing his face; both R

61   and L turn to look at L's screen; L folds his arms] You

62   know. It's the same process we did yesterday when we

63   were [inaudible].

64   R: I think you should go toooooo

65   L: Tools?

66   R: Uh

67   L: You think so? I don't remember. What did you do

68   yesterday? [full pause] Tools, so what?

69 R: [moving mouse pointer to menu, highlighting the "merge"
70   command] Merge?
71 L: /Merge. You think so? What about this? Insert
72   [inaudible].
73 R: Find [inaudible].
74 L: Think so? [long pause, each working at his own screen]
75 R: No [inaudible], repeat.
76 L: Yeah. [long pause, each working at his own screen; L gets up,
77   walks across room to look at another student's screen, and
78   initiates a conversation]

Figure 4.1   Computer learning transcript.

Learning without the Pedagogue: Analyzing the Control of Turn Taking

The transcript itself accounts for approximately 40 speaker changes. Sizable as that is for a CA analysis, even more unusual is that it accounts for a duration of approximately 30 minutes. My use of such an extended period suggests that this stretch is a single segment of inter-action/conversation. The data warrant this characterization (as a single strip of activity) for a number of reasons. First, there is a continuity of topic that is both typical of a single segment of interaction and often seen in ed-ucational settings.[3] The participants, true to the purpose and given struc-ture of the setting, are focused on a particular *business at hand* (Boden and Zimmerman, 1993): figuring out the merge function of word-processing software. Even more important to the claim that the 30-minute stretch is a single segment of talk is the fact that only one opening sequence (a summons-answer or "prequestion" adjacency pair, lines 1–3) occurs.

An *opening*, as understood by CA researchers, is a sequence that sets in motion a particular frame of activity. The openings in this computer learning frame have features that center on an easily recognizable, for-malized, initial opening and less standard subsequent ones that I argue are, in fact, not openings at all, but rather reengagement after periods

---

[3] I say *education* is only a very good possibility here because although other contextual, sequen-tial, syntactic features suggest the interaction as understandable as "educational," I could imagine other institutional settings such as work that would also work to fix or maintain continuity of topic. Indeed, Zimmerman and Boden (1993) discuss briefly this notion of *monotopical* interactions (p. 15) in a similar way.

of "suspension."[4] Specifically, the analysis of the transcript in Figure 4.1 tells us that after the opening and a series of exchanges (lines 1–27), a failed initial attempt to help (lines 28–33), and a concentrated attempt to suspend interaction (lines 34–47), the strip of interaction is put on hold by the participants. At this point, both learners focus their attention on typing up full texts on which to apply the merge function they are trying to master (lines 44–47). The learners suspend interaction (lines 50–52) for approximately 7 $^1/_2$ minutes. Further evidence that we are looking at a single strip of action with a suspension of action in the middle rather than two separate strips of action can be seen in the following: (1) suspensions of action are more ambiguous than complete stops (made even more so by the computer artifact that mediates the subjects' communication[5]); thus, suspensions are more difficult to accomplish, and this is the root of most of the action we see on lines 34–47; and (2) Larry's lack of an additional opening summons/response sequence or even a head or shoulder turn toward Roger on lines 48–49 contributes to the claim that there was no reason to reopen a conversation (as it was never closed, only suspended).

In Chapter 2, I spent considerable time outlining the implications of moving our understanding of learning beyond pedagogical relations per se; here we see learning that is much more like an everyday conversation than teacher–student interaction. The claim that the strip of talk can be considered as a more or less continuous whole is extremely relevant

---

[4] Concise explanations of the differences between various types of silence are important for the analysis. Building on the survey of CA concepts carried out in Nofsinger (1991), briefly, the general term used in traditional CA is *silences* but not all silences are the same.

> *Lapse:* at a transition-relevant place (TRP), i.e., where there would normally be a speaker change, no one talks.
> *Gaps:* at a TRP, a usually brief (1 second or less) space before a speaker self-selects.
> *Pause:* a silence during which no one speaks at a TRP and the speaker elects to continue, or when someone is distracted though not at a TRP, or when a selected speaker takes a moment to respond.

[5] During the course of interaction, the computer can play a problematic role as a quasi-participant (see Latour, 1987, 1994; Suchman, 1987). The computer complicates conversation considerably adding ambiguities related to the educational or learning context of the interaction. This artifact-as-participant dynamic is detectable in lines 11–19, for example. Here Larry and Roger not only maintain the interaction and successful question-answer sequences, but Roger's responses to Larry's directives are signaled both verbally and physically through Roger's actions, which are mediated by the computer screen text and the mouse. Another example can be found in lines 67–76, where Larry attempts to elicit a meaningful second pair part (which may have come in the form of Roger's on-screen actions rather than in the form of a conventional direct verbal response). My suggestion here is that this is another reason why extended silences of all kinds are tolerated in this form of interaction.

because, when it is seen in this way, we find that control over turn taking is shared. This contrasts to the findings of studies of educational settings, where one of the defining features of the interaction is that turn taking is controlled by the teacher (e.g., Sinclair and Coulthard, 1975; McHoul, 1978; Heap, 1991). McHoul (1978), for example, states that it is the instructor who generally chooses who speaks next (i.e., self-selects), selects the next speaker, initiates a bidding for the next turn sequence, and so on. As Heap (1991) explains, this is an accepted and even a desirable element of interaction in educational settings. In educational terms, control over turn taking is associated with an unequal distribution of knowledge and hence power, and in many ways can be said to define expert–novice relations. Early on, it is only Larry who seems to use self-selection in turn allocation (in lines 27–28 and 32–33). Roger (apparently in the novice role) must make the initial summons request (lines 1–2) followed by a question first pair part (FPP). Larry remains in control over speaker selection during this time, providing the only informatives, that is, formulating what will happen next (line 24), and issuing the only directives, that is, direct instructions (lines 13–20). However, we see that this expert–novice relationship, understood in terms of control over turn taking, use of directives, and so on, becomes blurred in the second half of the transcript, and thus control, expertise, and conventional notions of learning become problematized. Roger is much less sure of himself than Larry in the opening segment, but he nonetheless becomes positioned as the expert (in terms of the organization of turn taking), even providing (albeit weak) directives (line 64 and perhaps line 73).[6]

Considering the preceding explanation, it is arguable that learning in the everyday can be distinguishable from both formal, conventional pedagogy, on the one hand, and informal conversation, as outlined by Sacks, Schegloff, and Jefferson (1974; Sacks and Schegloff, 1974), on the other.[7] Individual modes of participation shift (i.e., there is movement

[6] It is very difficult to recover the sense of what Roger is getting at in lines 64, 73, and 75. Although line 64 seems to represent something of a directive, as it has little connection to the immediately preceding utterance by Larry, it could be a continuation of Roger's answer on line 59. The use of the pronoun in "I think *you* should go tooooo" (line 64) adds to the ambiguity. Lines 73 and 75 are even more ambiguous. It is very possible that some or all of these three examples are responses to the computer (i.e., the response to Roger's own screen actions), which would be another example of the complexity and contingency of human–computer–human collective interaction.

[7] This topic continuity is one indicator that the interaction is different from everyday conversation, which, according to Sacks et al. (1974), typically includes topic changes (as well as a range of topic introduction sequences, the need for topic-"fitting" efforts [Schegloff and Jefferson, 1974:243], and so on).

from a peripheral to an expanded form of tool-mediated participation), but this changing participation is a collective achievement that does not depend on expert–novice or pedagogical relations per se. At the same time, Larry and Roger create a continuity of topic that is quite different from the topic fitting and topic changes associated with conversational interaction. Therefore, one of the contributions that this discussion makes to our understanding of learning is its depiction of tacit dimensions of interaction that exist outside of pedagogical direction.

Distal Influences within Interaction and the Connection to Learning

The detailed analysis of interaction offers a glimpse of the tacit machinery that is the true "bricks and mortar" of both self-conscious (i.e., goal-directed) and unintentional (i.e., operational) dimensions of activity. Indeed, we can reflect on the data presented in ways that provide important examples of core activity theory concepts. Looking closely, for example, we can recognize the different levels of activity described in Leont'ev's original formulations of activity theory: operation, goal, and motive. At the operational level (techniques and skills, typically unconsciously used, related to conditions rather than to the object or conscious purpose of an activity), we see Larry and Roger carrying out skilled interaction in relatively complex forms of two-way (person–machine), three-way (person-to-person mediated by machine), and four-way (person-to-person mediated by machine with facilitator) communication. These are practices at the level of operation that produce learning according to specific conditions through the maintenance of interaction, the maintenance of topic coherence, and so forth. In terms of the goal level of activity, we might say that the merge function and its specific meaning (e.g., the software designer's use of language) are most relevant. Ask Larry or Roger what he is doing and he will tell you that he is learning the merge function. Based on analysis of the trascript alone, however, the motive of the activity remains less obvious.

The activity theory concept of motive is, arguably, paralleled in the CA tradition in Mehan's (1993) notion of *distal influences*. For Mehan the notion is meant to help smooth the rough edges of what he calls *radical situationalism* (p. 87). The motive level of activity, although not apparent in the data, nonetheless makes operations and actions possible and provides meaning and direction to specific practices. Following this, I argue that elements of the broader context are a legitimate sequential element of the interaction as well. These influences are features that mark the interaction as a specific variation of the speech exchange system.[8] For example, we can see that the participants' actions are oriented to the identity of the setting by virtue of their prompt mutual arrival at the computer lab. Referencing only the sequential accomplishment, we see that the first action in the sequence is not the opening described in lines 1–3 at all, but Larry and Roger's copresence as participants in the situation. If we were to extend the sequential analysis of computer learning beyond the 30-minute length to, say, a month, earlier we would learn a good deal in trying to make warrantable claims that the actions occurring during this month are in fact part of a single sequence of action. In this case, we would be tracing the distal influences, contextualizing action–object relations even those as (seemingly) trivial as the merge function in the context of, for example, the search for employment. Indeed, we could investigate whether the need to sell one's labor power in order to survive (a feature of social class) provides the motive structure of the activity system, and in doing this, we would be performing sequential class analysis of activity.

We can see that producing, repairing, and proceeding with social interaction, self-consciously and tacitly, is the means through which activity is accomplished. Understanding this process is part of the microcontextualization of computer learning. This process is full of ambiguity, contingent rhythms of interaction, and active decision making by skilled participants (no matter how much of a novice they happen to be). Changing control over turn taking and topic continuity are central to understanding how learning is accomplished. It should be clear that these sequences demonstrate the mutual construction of a *zone of proximal development* (Vygotsky, 1978). Although the conclusions we can draw from this short strip of talk are modest, Larry and Roger nevertheless help us problematize several of the major themes of conventional class-deficit learning theory empirically. They demonstrate that the tool-mediated interactions of two novices can produce knowledge and skill. And, they help to emphasize the fact that it

---

[8] One feature typical of classroom interaction, according to the literature, that is only weakly present in these data is the evaluative function that paid instructors must carry out. Even in the most pedagogically structured portion (lines 1–35) of the transcript, although there are some basic evaluative utterances by Larry, particularly line 10 ("That's a good one"), it is clear that there is no overall structure of "lecturing, asking questions, accepting feelings, praising, encouraging, using student ideas, giving directions, criticizing and justifying authority" (Heap, 1991:23) typical of instructional formats. In other words, there is a general absence of the institutional demand for one person to evaluate another.

is the culturally and materially regulated entry into and accomplishment of interaction that disproportionately defines one's learning capacity.

Part II: Accomplishing Organizational Sequences of Action: A Case Study of Computer-Mediated Activity in an Auto Parts Purchasing Office

We have developed computers into precise machines for control. Their capacity to produce detailed knowledge about the physical or social worlds and thereby to extend our power over them is not my main concern here. I am concerned more with their power to know their users. Sharon Dannon has provided us with a revealing example of this power being applied to the individual whom it knows and therefore produces. The point of control is a print-out of the day's work of one of the 350 employees, almost all of them women, in Trans World Airline's reservation centre. The computer works "externally" to allocate customers to seats and "internally" to monitor its operators. In this tiny fragment of working life we can trace the macro power systems of individuation and knowledge which Foucault diagnoses as the prerequisites of a modern society. (Fiske, 1993:71)

This second part of the chapter deals with the *underlife* (Goffman, 1961) of clerical work in the purchasing department of an auto parts factory by focusing on the interaction between worker, computer, and organization. Beyond Goffman, studies of workplace learning, organization, and labor process have strong relevance to this analysis, particularly the work of Kusterer (1978) on the skill of the apparently unskilled worker. His analysis parallels the argument I make here in terms of a basic problematization of skills and how those skills are acquired. In the analysis of work generally, organizational studies theorists have been less interested in either learning or the standpoint of workers. These authors have generally discussed workers' practices in terms of employee recalcitrance to be overcome in favor of management's prerogatives (see Collinson, 1994, for an overview). Labour process theorists, on the other hand (e.g., Burawoy, 1979; Thompson, 1989; Jerimer, Knights, and Nord, 1994; Lucio and Stewart, 1997), have contributed to an understanding of the cultural life of work that recognizes worker resistance, but in some cases are still saddled with either an underlying affirmation of the capital accumulation process or a mechanical conceptualization of workers' resistance to the organizational imperatives of capital. And although Braverman's (1974) seminal work on the labor process as well as Burawoy's (1979) clarifications are both instructive, neither deals with issues of learning or class relations at the micro level.

The analysis I present in this brief case study links issues of work and learning at the micro level. Although I do not conduct a situated EM analysis in the traditional sense, I do make use of a type of organizational EM that highlights how workers actively deal with the Oracle computer system software. The analysis makes use of a series of in-depth interviews with a female clerical worker whom I'll call Gwen. Over the course of several months, I met with Gwen to discuss the role of the computer system software in her working life, and as I indicated in Chapter 1, we did this using a set of computer screen texts, involved in Gwen's daily work activity, printed on sheets of paper. These printouts helped her (and me) in the task of describing what could not be described in so many words, namely, the situated, tacit knowledge production of clerical work. All in all, excluding numerous follow-up contacts for clarification, our interviews spanned approximately 6 hours of recorded conversation as we peered over the paper printouts at her kitchen table.

The analysis of the transcripts from these interviews shed light on how computer screen texts can be understood as an important constituent of the workplace structure that workers negotiate through a form of computer-mediated activity. This claim involves understanding computer systems not simply as tools of production (in this case, the production of accounting/purchasing records) but also as tools meant for the production of organizations themselves. At the same time, we can see that despite the apparently heightened level of managerial control that computerized technology provides, highlighted in the preceding quote from Fiske (1993), workers still exercise forms of agency, creativity, and control. And finally, we see how computers work in coordinated fashion with the more general organizational norms and sanctions surrounding the needs of capital in the daily work and the learning lives of workers.

In speaking of the role of agency, worker control, and the informal dimensions of organizations, it is important to recognize that forms of workplace research, beginning with the emergence of industrial sociology in the first half of the 20th century (e.g., Mayo, 1945; Roy, 1952; Goulder, 1954), have recognized the role of informal and cultural dimensions of worker control and resistance. However, it is equally true that the informal dimensions of learning at work have not been widely discussed. The analysis of *organizational sequences of action* here shows that both the formal and informal dimensions of these sequences are important for understanding the modes of participation in activity, and hence learning, in the workplace. Indeed, I argue that it is the contradiction between the control that capital asserts, vis-à-vis Oracle, and the needs of clerical labor that creates the specific types of computer learning practices we will see.

Making Use of a "Texts-in-Action" Approach to Computer Learning

There are a variety of ways to approach the topic of computer mediation at the micro level, but a relatively novel one can be found in the work of Smith (1990), Mellinger (1992), Smith and Whalen (1994), and a small group of other theorists. The defining feature of these studies is that each tries to understand *texts* as playing a key role in the (re)production of specific organizational relations. In discussing their analysis of the work of call center attendants, for example, Smith and Whalen draw on the connection between talk, computerized texts, and organizations in this way:

Analysis of the talk-text-talk sequence shows the text in action and as integral to the co-ordination of the sequence and the ordering of the component sequences of talk. However this is not sufficient to establish our claim to describe the sequence as 'organizational'. This is established as we demonstrate the standardization of recipient design in the officially required (and in part technically constrained by the software) descriptive syntax in which call-takers are trained and into which they translate the caller's vernacular. (Smith and Whalen, 1994:29)

A key element of these types of studies is their expanded view of the concepts of text, textuality, and intertextuality. A basic description of these concepts is found in Smith and Whalen (1994), where the authors insist on two key dimensions. On the one hand, the text refers to a physically sensed "materiality" (e.g., pages in a book, an application form, a specific screen text of a computerized system). On the other hand, texts also involve social and interactional elements associated with the process of *signification* (Barthes, 1979). The notion of human–computer–organization interaction represented in an analysis of organizational sequences of action has some rough similarities to the concept of activity as used by activity theorists in the sense that it attempts to integrate participants, tools, and social context as a process of mediation within a single unit of analysis. However, although the text-in-action approach offers a workable empirical program of inquiry into situated interaction, it says nothing about how this analysis relates to issues of learning per se.

Texts, like other tools, are created within a specific set of historical and socioeconomic relations, and must be "activated" throughout the course of an active social relationship (i.e., they must be read). Explicating the active and social relational dimensions of texts is the basis of what Smith and Whalen (1994) call the *texts-in-action* approach. They offer two observations that are relevant to the analysis of the following case study. First, "[t]he iterative capacity of the text, particularly the printed and now the electronic text, is foundational to contemporary forms of large-scale organization" (1994:6). Second, as constituents of an organizational sequence of action, "the technically formalized and iterable text enables coordination of activities across time and space, many times over, and with varying personnel" (1994:9). These observations point to the essential work that texts do for the modern workplace, and the authors go on to outline how texts perform a regulatory function representing a specific organizational agenda. In the case of the multinational auto parts company involved in this case study, this agenda is oriented to capital accumulation and control within the capitalist labor processes in which purchasing and accounting information from dispersed international worksites are centrally and automatically integrated through the use of a computer network.

The organizational sequence of action of interest here is the purchase order (PO) sequence. This sequence defines a segment of the labor process through which the plant orders and receives the materials it needs to maintain production. Much of Gwen's work day consists of helping to produce versions of this sequence using the Oracle computer software, in effect responding successfully to the software's series of screens throughout the work day. As Smith and Whalen say, "[t]he empty fields of the computer text are questions insistently seeking response" (1994:11). Gwen's role is to translate the needs of production into a series of contracts that ensure that the specific materials get to the plant. As Suchman (1987) and Latour (1987), would also indicate, the technology is a participant in the interaction. In basic terms, it is the computer software that, once the necessary information is entered, produces and stores centrally all the pertinent transaction information. However, it is important to note that although the addition of the Oracle accounting/purchasing system to Gwen's office is new, the PO organizational sequence of action is not. Over the 15 years Gwen has worked at the factory, the PO sequence has undergone steady development. This began with the use of standardized, manual, typewritten paper forms (duplicated and stored in physical form),[9] followed by "display writer" word-processed and printed-out paper forms (duplicated

---

[9] By stating that the various types of information are "stored in physical form," I am indicating that storage in this form is the primary method of maintaining/retrieving/using these financial records.

and stored in physical form), then WordPerfect processed and printed-out paper forms (duplicated and stored in physical form), and now using the Oracle computer system (in which data are entered and stored electronically). This historical dimension, as we'll see, allows important comparisons to be made that help us better understand the new dynamics of the technology.

The basic elements of the current PO organizational sequence of action can be described as follows. The sequence begins with a production or maintenance need (say, the need for more steel or a machine part) to which a purchasing agent responds by filling out a Requisition to Purchase form. This form initiates the production of a PO electronic record within the Oracle computer system that includes a hard-copy PO Agreement contract (a 8.5 × 11 inch purchase contract). This PO Agreement is sent via courier to the vendor company that will supply the requested item to the auto parts plant. The vendor company acknowledges the PO Agreement by sending back a copy of the agreement and then ships the requested item. Upon receipt of the item at the auto parts plant, a Packing Slip that accompanies the item and displays a number is forwarded through internal company mail to Gwen to be entered into the electronic record. This completes the basic PO organizational sequence of action, at the same time adding to the centralized purchasing and accounting infrastructure of the company.[10] It is impossible for a contract and payment to be issued to a supplier without a PO number. In fact, an important aspect of the

---

[10] It might be helpful to clarify the differences among these closely related terms for ongoing reference:

Purchase Order Organizational Sequence of Action: the entire set of organizational, work, conversational, and intertextual relations that are part of this sequence of action.

Purchase Order Electronic Record: the complete electronically stored record of information on a transaction, which may include a history of transactions with that supplier on that item if the order is an ongoing or "blanket" order. In any case, it contains a great deal of information on such things as currency rates, taxation codes, shipping instructions, authorization(s), and all supporting text reference numbers, as well as quantity, delivery dates, item descriptions, etc.

Purchase Order Agreement: an 8.5 × 11 inch piece of paper that is produced from the PO electronic record by the Oracle system. This is sent to the supplier as a call to purchase an item(s).

Requisition to Purchase: a traditional noncomputerized form that is filled out by hand by a buyer and passed on to Gwen, in many ways initiating a PO organizational sequence of action.

Other organizational texts, records, and so on all referred to occasionally in this work that are also essential subtexts or subdocuments within the PO organizational sequence of action, including drawings of items, various standardized letters (e.g., a "drawing letter" introducing drawings to the supplier), etc.

initiation of the production of a PO electronic record is that the Oracle system issues it a unique PO Number that tracks (intertextually, through time and space) the purchase, allowing for greater centralized surveillance and control over the process.

I: When you come in for the day, do you basically know what to do or does your supervisor have to tell you what to do or/

G: No, barely ever.

I: So basically you design your day based on requisition forms that are in the basket, or any that are handed to you that day/

G: Yep, packing slips that come in, yeah, so it all just kind of flows. (W13a)

Requisition forms, packing slips, drawings, drawing letters, confirmation forms – all texts within the PO organizational sequence of action governed by the software system provide the basic structure of Gwen's day, creating the rhythm of work in the department. Her daily paid work is ordered by these texts through their relationship with the structure (i.e., control and surveillance) of the workplace. It is an authoritarian computer/organizationally mediated activity.

Before we go further, however, a few additional contextual facts should be explained. The auto parts factory in this case is part of a group of auto parts plants located in southern Ontario (Canada) and the northeastern United States. They are owned by a large, diversified multinational corporation. In the purchasing department of this auto parts factory, the company has inserted accounting technology that is networked with the company's other auto parts plants in this group. Indeed, one of the important factors that Gwen returns to again and again in describing the daily problems of her work is the conflict that arises as a central authority attempts to maintain and extend rational control over the increasingly distant realities of a larger and larger number of local sites of auto parts production.

Screen Texts and Organizational Sequences of Action: Contradictory Local–Extralocal Relations

One of the central achievements of texts, as Smith and Whalen point out, is their ability to "suture the extra-local . . . to the local actualities of our necessarily embodied lives" (1994:6–7). However, what needs to be made explicit for an analysis of the class dimensions of the learning process here is the role that the capitalist labor process plays as a source of contradiction in text-mediated activity. The local–extralocal relations of production, a feature of globalized capitalism, is a daily source of mundane struggle in the workplace. This struggle, mediated by a range of associated mechanisms, such as labor market segmentation, displays racial and gendered dimensions as well, but in the purchasing office, it is the process through which the extralocal financial base of the corporation attempts to gain more immediate access and control over localized (plant) information that the class dimensions of the process seem to emerge most clearly. Computers are essential for this process.

To begin to understand the broader contradiction between the local and extralocal as played out through the screen texts of the Oracle system (and the process of computer learning), we can compare the previous paper-text methods and the Oracle method of accomplishing the PO organizational sequence of action. Of course, the main change is the centralized electronic storage of data. This entails a process that makes Gwen's work less flexible to local needs in her plant. In other words, the system makes any changes based on the contingencies of local practice particularly onerous.

G: Well it takes a lot longer. As far as my job or the person who enters the purchase orders [into Oracle], it takes a lot more time, but if you look at the pluses it is definitely worth it. . . . It takes nothing. You just zip them through quick, but it's when there's a change. It can take you hours to do a simple thing, where in the past it just took you no time at all. You could just type another order and have the same number on it, whereas with this there is so many things you can't change [in Oracle]. So it definitely is a lot more cumbersome to the purchasing department.

I: It's made your job more, but it's made somebody else's less though?

G: Oh yeah.

I: Whose?

G: I think for finance it's easier, like more automatic. Like again, I think it all boils down to the data; having that database is the big benefit. (W13a)

Gwen describes Oracle's ability to "demand" (as one of its design features) the extralocalization of all information pertinent to the financial structure of the corporation before proceeding with the organizational sequence of action at the local site.

Among the other differences between the Oracle-generated screen texts and paper texts is the additional removal of "traces" of the worker, local production, and control by the localized constituents. In the old paper-text methods, not only were specific knowledge and skills needed for the production of the report, but the physical location of the hard-copy forms, that is, localized filing, also played an important role in the process. This was referred to by Gwen as a particularly significant aspect of the earlier PO organizational sequence of action.

I: How big a deal is it to have to go searching through things for packing slips or whatever/ like is that a pretty big deal?

G: Oh, it is.

I: Do people get a little panicky?

G: They used to come down and they'd be looking for things, whereas now they can look at it on the screen.

I: So now there's a little bit more control? [for management]

G: I think so, yes. It's all there [on-line]. It's so easy. And how easy is it for someone to take out a purchase order and misfile it, and then you can't find it. Or someone's got it on their desk and two, it was always, fine, if it was last year it was right there in your office, but for the year before it was upstairs and after that it was across the road [another office of the plant] after the last seven years/over in the archives.
        (W13a)

The existence of information in paper-text form as the primary method of record keeping tends to contribute to localized control. This localization (understood by the extralocal base of the multinational corporation as "lack of control") meant that information had to be mediated by local workers to a far greater degree. This local mediation took the form of more face-to-face contact and cooperation among workers in different clerical departments.

I: So was there more face-to-face stuff with finance then [than with the paper-text method]?

G: I think so. We'd be up there digging through their files a lot, whereas now we can look at it here [on the Oracle screens]. The same thing with them. They used to be down at month end, and I used to call it "Oh, they're fluddering." They used to have to come down and just dig through our files. Looking for packing slips.

I: So it would be the equivalent of them trying to solve all the "bombed-out" ones?

G: Yeah. They'd have invoices without packing slips. Now they can look to see if there was a packing slip [on the Oracle screens], whereas before they used to have to come down and find the PO and the slip. (W13a)

While Gwen reiterates the notion that work and information were once organized locally, she also introduces a key part of Oracle's control/surveillance procedures – the *bomb-out*. The bomb-out is part of an important new vernacular in the office since the introduction of Oracle, and has been a necessary component of the development of new patterns of participation in activity and hence learning. The importance and meaning of the bomb-out in the lives of Gwen and her coworkers is due to their standpoint as clerical workers. Whereas the bomb-out is a means of control for management, it is a source of problems for workers, something to work and learn around. It refers to an instance in which Oracle has detected that the PO organizational sequence of action has been broken in some way. Gwen now describes a typical bomb-out, with special reference to the Oracle system as an active part of the process. In this case, the price of a supplier's goods does not match the number of units actually purchased. For ongoing or *blanket* orders, the Oracle system tracks the history of an item's purchase from a particular company.

> Like say if you would have a price for a minimum quantity of say five thousand pieces and another price for ten thousand pieces. When the shipment comes in and it's received, it [Oracle] tries to interface but it doesn't know which one to go to, so it [the Oracle screen text] will say "Ambiguous price or location" on the Interface Report. As far as the "SRI" [the computerized shipping, receiving and inventory system], the shipment will be received into inventory and it'll show in inventory but it won't come through to Oracle, the accounting side, because it [Oracle] won't know. It'll keep going "Oh, where can I [interface]?" It doesn't know which one to go to. And the receiver doesn't know – they just receive it. So it would just go boing-boing-boing ["bouncing" among choices, unable to make a decision], and then the bomb-out comes out on the Interface Report. (W13a)

We again see the syntactic positioning of Oracle (versus the paper-text forms) in Gwen's description. Here and in most places throughout the interview, Gwen grants Oracle an active subject status in the description of work sequences. Gwen goes on to outline how Oracle interfaces with the shipping department's computer system, and notes that when the system finds ambiguous information, it records the problem PO number in an Interface Report (an electronic record) that is printed out daily for management. In this way, the Oracle system can monitor workers automatically through its command of an enormous database of information that the clerical workers create but do not control.

Formal Organizational Sequences of Action and Informal Variations: Alternative Standpoints and Discretionary Learning

Thus far, I have described the top-down dynamics of the multi-national company and its computerized control system as they appear in a local purchasing department office from the standpoint of a clerical worker. Indeed, as they are throughout this research, issues of standpoint are paramount for understanding what's going on. For example, although I didn't interview managers in the purchasing department in this case study, it's reasonable to speculate that their accounts of interaction, the goals of activity, and even the motive of activity are quite different. From Gwen's standpoint, the computer system uses Interface Reports and the bomb-out to control and consistently reproduce particular dimensions of her work. However, technical control of this kind is rarely, if ever, complete (at least in the forms that are intended). In the world of everyday practice, workers regularly respond to attempts at control, sometimes, as in the case of Gwen, if only to do her job in ways that meet local needs of production. Local needs of production are contrasted to the extralocal needs of rational accounting and the requirements of capital accumulation. These forms of variations, in fact, highlight an important tension or contradiction within the activity system. Whatever the reason, whatever the outcome (hyperexploitation, nervous exhaustion, promotion, etc.), these practices do not, in any simple way, merely ratify or reproduce the dominant logic of the organization. Rather, they reflect participants' interpretations, their own reasons, and their own methods of accomplishing this work from their own standpoint. The *manufacturing of consent*, as Burawoy (1979) identified it, is a process that is accomplished with the active involvement of workers. Workers such as Gwen create spaces in which to exercise their own creativity and develop skills according to an alternative, practical (what Bourdieu referred to as a *pro-tensional*) logic. Importantly, it is at this point (and outside the scope of the formalized plan of the organizational sequences of action) that we see that learning, as a response to internal contradictions of the activity system, produces individual and collective knowledgeability and skill.

I use the term *informal variations* to describe these worker-led organizational sequences in order to show that they parallel the formal process (which is always a skeleton of actual processes anyway) but lie buried just below its surface. Goffman's (1961) concepts of *instrumental formal organization* versus organizational *underlife* show many parallels here. Gwen states:

> Like I'm saying this, but *you're not suppose to do it this way*, the "req" [requisition form] should be in your hand, but hey, they need it right now, but to get it they'd have to get approvals and phone whoever. But instead they say, "We need this. Could I have a purchase order?" So you don't have the req in your hand and *we're not suppose to give you a purchase order number without a requisition number* [and the accompanying information, ex. prices, item codes, etc.]. They'll have that req form [incomplete] in their hand and it'll have a req number on it and I'm giving them the purchase order number and they will write it down on that req form and I type the req number on my purchase order [on-screen]. So you can begin to track it that way [the bomb-out due to incomplete information, i.e., only a requisition number and an issued PO number are contained in the PO electronic record]. But usually by the time that would come up [on the Interface Report] you'd have the req on your desk and it could be entered and that would be done. (W13a)

In addition, Gwen describes another typical situation in which the purchasing, finance/accounting, and shipping department workers collude to override the system altogether, thereby developing another informal variation in the organizational sequence of action.

> So the packing slip will come in the back door and *not in agreement with Oracle*, but it's the only way we can do it. . . . Shipping will code the packing slip and send it up to accounting and they do their charging that way because there's no way to do it with Oracle. Well you could do it, but then again it would be a PO for a box of Band-Aids, so it's good for some things but for others it's not. (W13a)

It is becoming quite clear that there is an inherent contradiction in the activity system, ultimately driven by the logic of capital realized in the context of operations, goals, and motives of activity. As activity theorists such as Engeström (1987, 1992, 1996, 1999) suggest, these political-economic dimensions are inextricably related to the most unintentional of operations, and I argue that these elements also infuse computer-based learning with class relations. Workers like Gwen constantly must (re)produce systematic variations to the organizational sequences demanded by the company through Oracle. Here Gwen describes the regularity with which localized workers produce these variations.

I: How often does this whole *back way* happen?

G: *This backwards way happens all the time. Always. I would say about eighty percent of PO's are done that way.*

I: Why don't they [management] want it to go that way?

G: I don't know – I guess they do [laughing]! It's just that everyone is/ Like they [production workers] are working on a machine and something breaks down. They don't have time to say, "Oh I've got to write out this piece of paper and take it to purchasing and purchasing will have to place the order, and first I have to run around and get all the signatures on it." (M13a)

Competing logics of production rooted in opposing class standpoints coexist. One logic emanates from the bureaucratic, extralocal demands of a large multinational corporation in pursuit of profit and control. Another logic emanates from localized choices of workers attempting to do the best, most satisfying, and least taxing job they can by exercising creativity and initiating new patterns of relationships (cf. Burawoy, 1979).

Key Input Fields and Organizational Sequences of Action

Another way of understanding the role of computerized text systems in the context of computer/organizational mediation in human activity is to focus on the role of key input fields that appear in the PO electronic record. Whereas we can imagine the computer system as a participant in ongoing interaction, for Gwen this "conversation" is actually carried out through interaction with specific on-screen input fields (see Figure 4.2). We can again see that issues of social standpoint are important. By this I mean that the Oracle system has its own *key fields*. These are data fields through which management manages workers' practices and the activity system as a whole, either by automatic reports from Oracle or through old-fashioned manual surveillance (i.e., manually checking the contents of the electronic files). These are the fields in which breakdowns in the formal sequence of action are meant to be signaled. For example, an "Incomplete Record" message appearing in the system's status field indicates that one of Oracle's key fields has been improperly dealt with. Oracle will display an "Ambiguous Statement" message at the lower portion of the

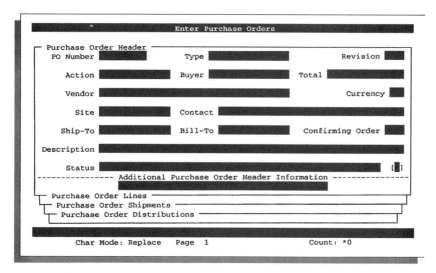

Figure 4.2   Oracle system computer screen. (From *Oracle Purchasing Release 10, Volume 1 Reference Manual*, 1997, page 1.2.)

screen if it determines that the input information does not match a series of authorized answers. If a PO electronic record remains incomplete and/or ambiguous throughout a work day, a line is entered in the daily Interface Report that Gwen's supervisor obtains each day. The report gives the PO numbers, leading management directly to the source of the problem – who, from management's perspective, is a clerical worker like Gwen.

Alternatively, the two fields that were central to Gwen's work were the PO Number and Description fields. It is the PO Number field that functions as the central means of tracing the sequence in order to keep the company's formal version of the PO organizational sequence of action on track. Gwen explains that the issuing of a PO number and the initiation of a specific organizational sequence of action, though easily done with only a computer key stroke or two, is not to be taken lightly.

> *[T]here's no way on earth that you can change that record* [the PO electronic record]. You have to cancel that order and give it a new number, which is a royal pain because it's that number that tracks the whole thing. It's gone to the supplier. It's quoted on their paperwork. It's come through to the plant. So you have to make sure that when you issue a new PO number you have to change it everywhere.....
> *There's just not the room for error where before [with the paper-text method] it was so easy to correct.* You don't do your purchase orders over because the big thing is that you do not want to have to issue a new PO number

> because that just creates problems, like until everyone gets it
> straight . . . so you go to all this trouble to avoid canceling and
> reorganizing a purchase order. (W13a)

Here, at the level of the informal variations in the formal organizational
sequences of action, is where Gwen exercises her discretionary engagement with Oracle in collusion with a network of coworkers, engineers,
and secretarial staff at the supplier company. It is in fact here that Gwen
(et al.) responds to the internal contradiction of the activity systems to
provide the opportunity for changing participation in a community of
practice. The computer software and organizational procedures, however,
are not the only important structural features that affect how participants
respond to contradictions in this organizational sequence of action. In
the following dialogue, we see Gwen's reflection on learning, followed by
concrete descriptions of other factors that influence it.

G: And it's on the job that you learn all the little things that are behind the
      scenes. It's not just copy typing; you gotta recognize that that's not the
      right account number, or you recognize that name.

I: You recognize names and faces when you see the PO number?

G: That's right.

I: And I guess you need to know who to phone and know the person at
      the supplier too, so it's a whole network.

G: Yeah it is. . . .

I: So how would you go about handling problems or if you didn't know
      something?

G: Probably coworkers who've been through the same training and are
      basically doing the same things as you. Then maybe ask the consultant
      who's been there, then maybe this Marie, who's suppose to know a lot.
      Not the buyers and the purchasing agents and the supervisor, phfft
      [snorts]. You won't get anything from them.

I: This may seem like a silly question, but how's your desk area laid out?
      Like, is it easy to contact your coworkers?

G: Well, if I was asking my supervisor, it would be easy, I have easy
      contact with him. I can just turn my chair and call in to him. But I'd
      have to get up and go around to talk to somebody else.

I: So there's, like, cubicles.

G: Yeah, I'd have to get up and go around the cubicle.

I: So that's not the best thing. It would almost be good to take down the
      cubicles.

G: No. [pausing] Because there's all that stuff going on. Or [I'll sometimes just use] the phone.

I: [Talking to] coworkers?

G: Well the consultant upstairs, but I guess if you're right in the middle of something, you don't want to have to stop and send an e-mail or something. You want an answer right then. And there will be, I'm sure you need to keep a set of notes, which I had been doing, and we still haven't had our meeting, but they said anything we perceive to be a problem, write it down. What's happening with this, what's happening with this. We're supposed to just get together and talk about it.

I: When do you get a chance to talk with these people [coworkers]? Do you take lunches together?

G: Just in bits and pieces. There's just time, you get talking [about] something and you'll bring it up – "And what do you think about that?" – and then someone else will come in and put their two cents in. We're all pretty close, and if a problem comes up, "How the heck is this going to work?" And they try to relate it to what they do. We'll have a golf tournament a couple times a year, and a Christmas party, and we get together. There's one girl I'd say is really a friend, but I like everybody. There's nine of us there in our cubicles. (W13a)

She describes not just the control and discipline capabilities of the company's computer system, but the way that features such as workplace design affect work (arrangements of cubicles so that horizontal contact with coworkers is difficult, whereas surveillance by the manager whose office is directly behind her is not). Christmas parties and golf tournaments aside, despite this tight control/surveillance, Gwen and her coworkers find (indeed, create) "bits and pieces" of time in order to talk, exchange information, and learn. It can also be noted that the PO Number field, although it appears as a regular user input field on the screen, is in fact a vital input field usable only by Oracle. The Status and Dialogue fields act as direct but temporary links between Oracle's requirements and the worker's actions, and it's through these fields that direct orders can be issued by Oracle to the worker.

Besides those fields that are the strict domain of Oracle, however, another category of fields are those that Oracle leaves unmonitored and unrestricted, and that are the domain of the clerical worker. The most important field of this kind is the Description field. This field is closely aligned with the needs of the local production plant, if not those of the clerical workers themselves. Although it is not a key field in Oracle's terms, it is key from Gwen's standpoint. It is the field that allows localized, informal variations of the organizational sequence to be created and organized spontaneously by the workers. It is the Description field that allows Gwen (not Oracle) to track the order. In the following dialogue, Gwen outlines how she uses the Description field, all the while insisting that her role in the accomplishment of the sequence is relatively insignificant.

G: I put in the requisition number [into the Description field]. That would be to track it back to a person. I'd put the requisitioner's name, say, "Bob from engineering is ordering this and the date." And very often, I know it's not supposed to work this way, but we'll receive a packing slip and it might not have a purchase order number on it, but they're supposed to and we're working on that, but you could bring up all the orders from, say, X vendor and match it and track it back to all the information. . . . Or, say you get a package with a purchase order number and you key in that purchase order number and it'll say down in here [pointing to the Status field] "incomplete." I have nothing from them [the person requesting the item]. The day I gave out that purchase order number [initiating an informal variation of the PO organizational sequence of action], I never received anything to allow me to enter it into the system [causing a bomb-out]. So then I'll say, "Oh, yeah, but that was Bob who asked me to enter this!" So then I can phone them [the local requisitioner] and say, "Hey, where's that req?"

I: I'm interested because it seems like such a key field when things don't go right.

G: Yeah, well but really, it's of no use to getting the paperwork processed and to allow you to receive. It's just [pause] that [the informal variation[11]] would be the main reason that we would use it.

I: No, but if something comes in and things aren't matching up, then you can go to that Description field and you can make things match up right?

G: Well, if somehow I can get a requisition number, or say the packing slip came in saying "Attention: Bob." And that's all I had. I could go into the Vendor field. Query on the vendor. Like say if it's company X, and bring them up [a list of all the PO electronic records involving X company] and then say, "Yeah, that was Bob," and then eventually figure it all out. It's just for us. For ourselves [clerical workers]. (W13a)

The computer system plays a major role in the reproduction of capitalist relations of production in the local office, the plant, and indeed across

---

[11] Recall that the informal variation in the organizational sequence of action accounts for "about 80% of the POs," according to Gwen.

the multinational corporation, but it also provides a contested interactive context within which Gwen and her coworkers learn to get the job done. Instead of direct managerial discipline, Gwen's work day is shaped by the corporate logic embodied in specific fields, screen texts, and design features of Oracle. Key fields, then, are the actual sites in which competing interests clash and formal versus informal organizational sequences of action meet. Before concluding, let me briefly put this into perspective using a comparative example. If these production relations were reproduced on a traditional auto assembly line, our imaginary autoworkers would be removing over 80% of the cars, fixing them manually (contacting suppliers for missing parts, establishing their own relations with suppliers, etc.), and then returning the cars to the line so that they roll off the back end in what appears to be a technically controlled and rationalized process. Driven by specific local/extralocal contradictions within the context of the multinational firm and mediated by the computer software, Gwen and her coworkers create their own systems of information flow, knowledge and skill. To do this, they generate interactive space in which they exercise their own form of collective discretion. Finding time within the underlife of the organization to work informally with other clerical staff, as well as with the engineering and maintenance departments, in order to bypass Oracle is the "space" in which the majority of their computer learning takes place.

Summary

In this chapter I've looked at two case studies for the purpose of microcontextualizing the computer learning processes while also suggesting the linkages between these processes and the broader political-economic situation. These case studies provide important suggestions about how class may be involved in the accomplishment of local practice, but they also offer background for the interpretation of interview and survey materials that cannot provide meaningful access to the tacit interactive dimensions of learning in the same way. These are nevertheless only "specimens" (Smith, 1999) that can sensitize given the fact that neither case deals with industrial workers learning throughout the full range of their everyday activity. Despite these limits, however, the model of tacit learning interaction that the cases outline, the specific problematization of expert–novice relations they demonstrate, and the class-based structures they make explicit have notable relevance to the conceptualization of computer learning described elsewhere in the book.

Although the analytic approaches I've used are obviously not the only useful ways to approach the concept of learning, the micro and specifically the sequential analyses offer powerful ways of taking a close look at, and generating warrantable claims about, the nature of computer learning. Furthermore, in keeping with a sociocultural approach to working-class learning, both methods resist a collapse at the microlevel toward internalized psychophysical explanations. Both methods make explicit how the individual agent is an active, skilled decision maker situated within a broader tool-mediated, political-economic, and historically specific activity system.

This chapter presented computer learning that helped make visible particular class dimensions of computer-mediated activity. For example, the notion of distal influences was suggested as a way of seeing that people's relationship to the labor market as wage earners (rather than as owners of capital) plays a role in microinteraction by producing what was in fact the very first action in the sequence: the copresence of participants at a certain place and time. Likewise, Gwen's relationship to the Oracle software illuminates certain class dimensions of human–computer–organization interaction in terms of the control exerted over clerical workers and their collective response in the context of a multinational corporation. This analysis demonstrated how historical relations of design and development of software are translated into activity in the workplace vis-à-vis tool-mediated labor. This tool mediation prefigures particular uses and social relations as well as particular class standpoints. Oracle clearly does not stand over the work of senior managers, particularly those at the pinnacle of the corporate structure in the same way it supervises Gwen and her coworkers. More specifically, Gwen's experience with Oracle is largely constituted by differential access to information fields that, likewise, runs along class lines. The informal organizational sequences of Gwen and her coworkers are not only essential for the profitable functioning of Oracle and the purchasing department, but allow her to learn in the course of work despite Oracle. This marks a contradiction in the systems of activity rooted in the capitalist labor process that must somehow enforce discipline and intensify work while maintaining the creative commitment of workers themselves.

5   Working-Class Computer Learning Networks

Exploring the Elements of Collectivity and Class Habitus

In the open-ended interviews for this research, when people talked about computer learning, they usually described practices that took place outside of the classroom. In most instances, they said their participation in formal course-based learning was a (rare) chore to be dreaded: a process of "getting your brain sucked out," as one person said. In the context of informal learning, even the notion of a "lesson," that is, a discrete situation in which an expert teaches a novice, was largely inapplicable. In the few cases where classroom-based learning was undertaken, which I'll discuss in Chapter 6, it was placed at the periphery of broader computer-based learning practice. Instead, the picture of computer learning that emerged from the interviews was one of multiple purposes and overlapping spheres of activity in which there were only isolated moments in the ongoing stream of doing that could be pinned down as instances of learning in the conventional sense. And, as I indicated in Chapter 2, it is all of this and more that calls into question the usefulness of conventional models of adult learning. Having outlined the two main sociocultural alternatives to these conventional models, in this chapter I apply several of their key concepts in order to better understand the class dimensions of computer learning. Specific to the application of activity theory concepts, it perhaps bears repeating that for the founder of the approach, A. N. Leont'ev, individual actions could never be understood independently of the entire system of activity, and that what people self-consciously recognize as the goal of their practice, on its own, does not provide a meaningful account of the practice as a whole.

We will see that these sociocultural theories of learning are important tools for making visible the otherwise invisible, denigrated, or denied learning practices of working-class people. In my analysis, I focus on detailed examples from particular interviews in order to explore fully the significance of their experiences in terms of the class dimensions of computer learning. Specifically, I draw on the concepts of activity, goal, motive, and overlapping spheres of activity. We will see the unique class character of solidaristic networks; we will see how these networks emerge and function; and we will see how working-class learning is often oriented to the "interstitial" spaces in dominant institutions. I also show how these networks are rooted in working-class life more broadly, and how differences and similarities contribute to the collective practice within networks. In the second half of the chapter, interviewees outline integrated networks of computer learning. Although it is impossible to learn in the absence of social relationships of some kind (whether they are the living relationships among people or social relations solidified in an artifact such as a book, language, etc.), interviewees described particular patterns of social relationships and cultural networks that I argue are unique to a working-class standpoint. I have described these networks as solidaristic because they were not simply group-based but also group-oriented and cooperative. Participants oriented to one another in mutualistic, supportive and collective ways that sometimes called for mundane forms of individual sacrifice. In these networks, although shared experiences were important, we also see the important role of difference. As Lave and Wenger (1991) have argued, for learning in *communities of practice*, difference is a resource to be drawn upon rather than a problem to be avoided. In the working-class computer learning networks examined here, we see that differences between group members were resources for collective learning that worked hand in hand with members' social standpoint and experiences.

Finally, although people from all social groups engage in informal learning in the everyday, for subordinate groups the relationship between informal learning, formalized learning, and participation in dominant institutions is unique. From a working-class perspective, the relationship between informal and formalized learning emerges from the standpoint of a "cultural outsider" that partially defines the subordinate position within class society. For most of the people in this research, this resulted in a more or less self-conscious oppositional perspective on formalized learning. Furthermore, there is a pressure to exclude from influence in the legitimated social spaces of work, the classroom, the marketplace, and so forth human practice that begins with and expresses a working-class standpoint. The result in this regard is that creative and transformative working-class practice tends to appear in the crevices – or interstitial spaces – of institutional life, and this too helps produce a unique class character to the learning that people do.

From Social Position to Disposition: Habitus in Working-Class Learning

To connect descriptions of class life to a workable class analysis of adult learning, it is important to recognize the patterns of expertise, preferences, and dispositions that this life produces. I argue that patterned forms of participation, such as engagement in solidaristic networks, are evidence of a working-class learning habitus in that these patterns or dispositions can be shown to emerge from a specific class position in the social world. Indeed, the dialectic of class position and class disposition that writers like Bourdieu (e.g., 1984) and Charlesworth (2000) describe so well is perhaps best understood – if it is to avoid the appearance of predetermination – as a process of social learning. These patterns of social learning, as Willis (1979) and others have shown so vividly, begin in school, the home, and community life as people grow up, and are further ratified by the types of regulation and resistance that working-class people experience into adulthood. Dispositions toward the creation of solidaristic networks and action in interstitial space, for example, are a response to these basic conditions and act not as a set of rules that determine behavior but, as Bourdieu says, as a strategy generation mechanism. Working-class people must actively rely on each other, whether formally (e.g., in trade unions, cooperative associations) or informally (e.g., buddy systems, informal networks) if they are to achieve significant levels of control in their lives, particularly in times of accelerated social change. In this way, although each of the chapters in this book contributes to our understanding of a class analysis of adult computer learning, this chapter makes the most direct contribution to the notion of working-class learning habitus. Thus, before proceeding, I want to introduce briefly the concept of *habitus* and provide some discussion of debates and implications that surround it.

The concept of class-based habitus has been most fully developed in the work of French sociologist Pierre Bourdieu. He defines habitus as follows:

[a] generative and unifying principle which retranslates the intrinsic and the relational characteristics of a position into a unitary lifestyle, that is, a unitary set of choices of persons, goods, practices. Like the positions of which they are a product,

habitus are differentiated, but they are also differentiating. Being distinct and distinguished, they are also distinction operators, implementing different principles of differentiation or using differently the common principles of differentiation. (Bourdieu, 1998:8)

The habitus, then, is a durable feature of human practice that, as an embodied disposition, can travel through space and time. At the same time, habitus, like any feature of cultural life, though durable, is not static. It can be partially reinvented in the course of its use, particularly in the context of changing material scenarios. The habitus undergoes change or elaboration in a sociocultural process that can be described as learning. It uses "differently the common principles of differentiation" by virtue of the differing standpoints from which people engage in a shared process. As I'll discuss later, working-class people generate a distinctive pattern of engagement in learning, though it is one that is ultimately rooted in shared principles of and a dominant discourse on what it means to "do learning." To be crystal clear, however, individual, conscious, goal-directed action has never played a major role in Bourdieu's formulations. Indeed, he believed that it was (unintended, collectively generated, and/or tacit) social practices and mechanisms, not self-conscious behavior, that explained how the world works in the ways it does (e.g., Bourdieu and Eagleton, 1992).

In Bourdieu's work, the habitus is closely connected to its realization in a specific field of activity. The concept of *field* refers to a system of relevance complete with specific roles, logic of operation, history, and, according to Bourdieu, forms of capital. *Capital* in the context of Bourdieu's work is a metaphor with only loose connections to the original Marxist concept. The field is semiautonomous, but with an underlying and unifying foundation in broader fields of institutional power and, specifically, class relations. Bourdieu's discussion and application of the concepts of capital and field, however, have been the target of considerable criticism. Even while endorsing the importance of the concept of habitus, many have noted that Bourdieu's notion of field – and its associated theory of symbolic capital – is too narrow, overly determined, and one-sided (e.g., Calhoun, 1993, 1995; Butler, 1999; Dreyfus and Rabinow, 1993, 1999; Livingstone, 1999). Seeing both the positive and negative dimensions of Bourdieu's work, Dreyfus and Rabinow, for example, explain it this way:

We want, however, to distinguish two components in Bourdieu's work: an ontologically informed research program, which we call "existential analytics," and the scientific theory of social meaning – Bourdieu's theory of symbolic capital – which we argue is a specific and contestable interpretation of who we are and what we are always up to. We think that these two components are analytically separable.... (Dreyfus and Rabinow, 1999:84–85)

Likewise, in his review of Bourdieu's work, Calhoun (1993, 1995) suggests that the concept of field can and should be abandoned while retaining the core of Bourdieu's theory of practice, that is, the habitus. Once it is released from its negative association with the theory of symbolic capital, we are free to make productive use of Bourdieu's otherwise important perspective and conceptual tool.

Examined more broadly, much of Bourdieu's empirical work demonstrates the links between the material and the economic on the one hand and the cultural on the other, and in his master work *Distinction* (1984), his goal is to demonstrate how it is that an apparently universal cultural aesthetic (taste) is in fact differentiated by class processes. Similarly, as I explain more fully later, I'm concerned with exploring how another apparently universal human process, adult learning and the generation of *learning capacity*, is also a class process. A mechanism whereby certain features of practice, including the material contexts from which they arise, are naturalized to produce a hierarchical order of ability and class differentiation. If in Bourdieu the class processes that produce the *pure cultural aesthetic* can be summed up in the term *distinction*, here in an analysis of universalized human learning we could apply the term *learning capacity* in a similar vein.

To summarize and close these introductory comments, in this work I take the concept of habitus to be an important way to explain the physically and culturally embodied set of dispositions that shape, but do not determine, forms of participation and hence learning. The habitus describes the sensibilities, interests, and expertise that allow people to take up specific participatory roles, and through this the habitus plays an important part in the types of learning that people undertake. The concept of habitus is not part of the conventional activity theory or situated learning framework. However, in the following sections, through the use of key concepts from these frameworks, I begin to identify core elements of a working-class habitus in relation to learning processes specifically.

Goals, Motives, and Overlapping Activity Systems in Working-Class Computer Learning

The development of discretionary time to engage in activity, the pooling of resources, and the collective development of knowledge and

skill that recognizes and expresses working-class standpoints are important needs that are met by informal learning networks. They offer a powerful antidote to the dominant and dominating beliefs and discourses
that surround people's ideas about learning. However, the exclusion that
subordinate groups experience within dominant institutions and public
space resists the development of such networks. Therefore, establishing
and maintaining relations among members of a network become key tasks
that cannot be taken for granted. In terms of the possibility of informal
learning, gaining or creating "membership" is the metaphorical equivalent of being allowed "on school property": One's education cannot begin
without it. The interactive relationships that define the bulk of informal
learning in the everyday life of working-class people are well described by
the concept of *peripheral participation in communities of practice* (Lave and
Wenger, 1991). However, more specifically, membership in working-class
networks produces the potential for a field of legitimate participation that
is denied elsewhere. In the learning life-history interviews I conducted,
the challenge of establishing alternative forms of legitimate peripherality
in the context of class relations played a major role in the production
of the distinctive patterns of practice and working-class learning habitus. In terms of computer learning networks specifically, people began
with shared physical space, as well as a shared position in cultural and
political-economic processes. From these shared meanings, specific interests in computer technology (Chapter 3), as well as specific tactics for
responding to these interests, evolved.

In Chapter 2 I indicated that activity theory defines goal-directed actions as conscious, whereas both operations (related to local conditions
of practice) and the motive of activity (related to broader institutional
and political-economic spheres) are typically beyond the self-conscious
attention of participants. These three different levels of activity are important for understanding working-class learning, but as contemporary
activity theory researchers have recognized, activity systems are not necessarily as stable or as self-contained as early writers suggested. Leont'ev's
basic approach, for example, must be expanded, it is thought, to develop
what has been called the *third generation* of activity theory. This expansion would include, among other things, the recognition of overlapping
spheres of activity that I argue is particularly important for understanding
the complexity of discretionary learning among subordinate groups.

What do overlapping systems of activity look like in relation to social
class and people's everyday learning? As a means of introducing several
themes, I draw an introductory excerpt from the following interview with
a woman who works in a chemical factory (formerly, she worked at a

steel mill). She describes an important overlap that is typical in this research: important to the working class specifically because it is the primary means of pooling scarce resources, integrating positive experiences that appear to be spread across different times and places of day-to-day life. Although elite and professional groups, of course, combine experiences across spheres of activity as well, in working-class households the premises, purposes, and patterns of this overlap have a unique social significance because they offer an important opportunity for forms of choice and agency in the learning process. This person illustrates distinctive class perspectives through her comments on the intersection of schooling experiences, family life, paid-work experiences, concerns about future labor market participation (for herself and her family), and computer learning.

R: I used the computer a lot at the steel mill when I worked certain departments.... So the kids wanted to know what I wanted for Christmas one year, so the kids bought [a computer] for me. So I worked at it a little bit and [my daughter] had this word processor on it. And my daughter's got the booklet and she showed me how to do it because she knows how to do it. [My partner] has to do it on his job too, and he has things to do at home too, so he said, "We've *got* to sit down and we've got to learn how to do it, more often than what we do."... [Learning] is not like one person teaches all the time – it's a group of people. It's not like the way school sets things up. You're doing it with a group of people.

I: And that's different than how you learn things in the school system?

R1:   I think so, yeah. Because when you're in the school system, I mean, you sit in the classroom and the teacher teaches you things, like you know, after that you're sort of on your own to do your own work. You can't say, "These four kids get together and do our homework" or "Let's get our answers together." I don't know, back when I went to school they didn't do it. You did your own homework. You didn't come in and say, "Can I copy your homework?" You know? That type of thing. So I more or less worked on my own when I went to school. I did my own thing. But when I've had a job like, you work with people. (W12)

This woman expresses concerns about job security for herself and her family members, and we see how it infuses computer learning in the home, across different family households, and across different workplaces (past and present). As we begin to reconstruct the concrete practices she is describing, we see that they cannot be understood without recognizing the overlap that occurs between different spheres of activity – some of which are tightly regulated and others that open space for discretionary practice. Economic imperatives infuse the relevance of computer learning for this woman, as they do for many working people. She highlights how both she and her partner feel the urgent need to learn about computers, and their response is to look toward a group task: "*We've* got to learn how to do it, more often than what we do." This description was common among the people I spoke with. It highlights how resources, experience, and expertise are combined across spheres, and that it is through the co-operative pooling of resources that knowledge and skill are produced. In the second half of the excerpt, she highlights the oppositional perspective that also informed many of the interviewees' dispositions toward learning practice. As discussed earlier in the book, working-class children experience the cultural and material context of schooling differently than other children (Willis, 1979; Giroux, 1981; Curtis et al., 1992; Bernstein, 2000), and it is these experiences – the perspectives, dispositions, and strategies that find their early development in this context – that follow them into adulthood. Though it was not always expressed this clearly, we see a description of schooling's culture of individualism and, more importantly, how this informs practice by running against the experience of working-class life in the home, in the neighborhood, and on the job. In these spheres people work together, rely on each other, orient to a more or less dependable collectivity, experience discretion, express standpoints that are relevant to them within the learning process, and develop forms of working-class skill and knowledge in the mundane, everyday ways that the woman in the preceding interview describes.

The preceding excerpt introduces the basic themes of an analysis of working-class learning. However, in order to look at overlapping activity systems in more depth, I want to focus on an interview with an autoworker I'll call Sean. Several key theoretical points can be grounded when we look at the description of everyday practice that Sean provides. The following excerpt outlines the articulation of multiple networks of relationships, each with its own system of conditions, goal direction, and broader motive. As Sean describes how he has learned about computers and how he would go about learning more, we see an example of a fabric of everyday life that contains only narrow patches of discretionary control. Understanding the significance of this fragmentation allows us to see, even in the most mundane description, how class processes are expressed in everyday computer-based learning. This description outlines the opening stages and foundational experiences of a computer learning novice. As we explore other examples of more expert working-class computer learners, we can nevertheless see how developed networks emerge from the modes of participation Sean outlines.

I: Do you get any information from TV or/

R: Yeah, actually a radio program about the e-line or what do they call it, e-mail and all that stuff, all through your computer now, how you go about it and you sort of, as you're driving along, say, "Oh, yeah. Well, I'll write that down." That's how I pick it up.

I: So if you happen to hear something on, you'll sort of perk your ears up?

R: Even the television has that, I'll be flicking through just trying to relax, especially when that new system came out for Windows, I was taping it off the television and it was like "Oh geeze! I didn't realize computers could do that. That would be really neat." They all offer learning programs on television and TV Ontario. . . . [But] it's something that probably in the next two years I'll get [a computer] depending how far my little boy is into it, because and I think the wife has a little bit of knowledge about it so, because she has to work a little bit with computers because she's in banking. And we'll probably use friends, because we have close friends who have just gotten into it so.

I: So how will you use friends?

R: Well they'll come over and give us an idea on how to use it, and I would think that one of us would eventually maybe take some kind of little course to learn how to run the thing. Because I have no knowledge of them at all.

I: Are these neighbors or/

R: Our best friends.

I: Probably get them to help you pick out a system too?

R: Yeah.

I: Anybody else you would ask about stuff?

R: Probably mostly friends who are into it, because all of our friends actually have them now, my brother just got into it this year. . . . Oh yeah, actually whats-his-name, that guy at work, Smith. I would definitely talk to him. And he just went into it not that long ago, I can remember him talking about it at work. . . . What I think is for myself, I have to get over the fear of them, and then I, they're probably easy I think, well look it, there is so much here and what do I do? See, I haven't attempted it, just those things at work, I've tried to avoid it because I don't want to ah, actually, I think I'm hoping that [my son] learns it and he can teach me. (W19)

While, driving his truck, listening to his radio, or flicking through the television stations trying to relax, Sean happens across information to which he may attend but that is not part of his goal-directed practices at the time. For a novice like Sean, these experiences become part of a coherent "computer learning project" largely in the context of the interview encounter itself, partly due to the positive recognition of his standpoint as a worker, indeed the recognition of his standpoint as a creative human being rather than a cog in a machine. Sean also outlines a network of separate relationships ranging from extended family to friends, his partner's workplace experiences, "little courses" in the local school, and his own coworkers. This network of relationships forms the skeleton of the informal learning process. He describes diverse sets of people whose roles, goals, or framing of activity are very different from each other, yet that all seem to provide a useful component to Sean's computer learning practice as a whole. In the majority of these different activity systems, computer learning is embedded at the operational level of activity (i.e., relating to local conditions of practice). In other words, the computer-based practice is a necessary condition of participation but not the focus of what's consciously going on as the goal of the activity. In activity theory, although several researchers have explored how practice takes place across multiple spheres of activity with reference to terms such as *polycontextually* (Engeström, Engeström, and Kärkkäinen, 1995), these types of analysis remain relatively rare, and few have sought to link their analysis explicitly to the production and reproduction of social divisions such as class.[1] The concepts of *activity* and *communities of practice* nonetheless bring into view a vast array of factors and expand our understanding of what learning as a practice really is.

Sean's practices, fragmentary as they are at this point, are closely connected to his job as a manufacturing worker, his relationship to the labor market, and his concern about his son's ability to get a job. Sean in fact began our set of interviews by telling me that at 40 years of age he had already spent half of his life working in a factory. At another point in the interview it becomes quite clear that Sean is extremely concerned about his ability to get another job if he is laid off or transferred. In these segments, as in the interviews that Richard Sennett and Jonathan Cobb (1972) did with American working-class people over three decades ago, the "hidden injuries of class" play an important role. All of these issues

---

[1] The work of Holland, Lachicotte, Skinner, and Cain (1998) on *identities in practice*, the work of Engeström et al. (1995), and Engeström, Engeström, and Vähääho (1999), as well as the work of Lave (1988) on mathematics, are examples of social learning theory research that extend across multiple sites of activity or multiple communities of practice. Examples of work that have, in various ways, sought to deal with social divisions and cultural diversity include Luria (1976), Cole and Griffin (1980), and Cole (1988).

point to a strong connection between learning, specifically how and under what cultural and material conditions it is done, and what we could call the *objective class relationship*. The issues confirm the distinctive concerns and insecurities that capitalist labor markets visit upon the working class specifically, and how these concerns frame ongoing life and even people's interests in technology and computer learning. For Sean, these issues merge to produce the specific forms of energy and anxiety that fueled his emerging interest in computer learning.

Drawing on Sean's account but focusing more deeply on the character of peripheral participation for working-class learners, we can recognize how this participation is accented by the many unplanned moments of learning not recognized by people as learning at the time they occurred. To use the language of activity theory, these unplanned practices were not recognized as learning because they were not situated within an activity system that had learning as its goal. As such, one of the keys to recognizing and developing these practices as a learning experience is entering them into the logic of a new activity system. In general terms, this is done through a process that Engeström describes as the cocreation of a collectively meaningful object of activity. However, this cocreation of learning as a meaningful object of activity on an ongoing basis (beyond the framework of the interview encounter) is highly influenced by material resources, namely, the distribution of discretionary time and energy. Furthermore, it entails a set of cultural practices and dispositions that involve the creation of *mental distance* from one's own practice that allows one to reflect on it as learning per se.[2] Drawing on the work of Bourdieu (also see Charlesworth, 2000), we could say that engagement in learning activity requires the ability to objectify one's own practice in a way that typically marks the practices of dominant rather than subordinate groups. Indeed, one of the facts I found most puzzling initially in this research was the ease with which interviewees from the elite and executive class groups could simply use the term learning and, by contrast, the paraphrasing, the clarification, the lack of fit, and the struggle involved in many working people's descriptions. In all of these ways, what becomes clear is that the

---

[2] This notion of creating mental distance is drawn directly from Bourdieu, but the general significance of the concept can also be found in the work of Engeström on research interventions in the medical system of Finland. Here Engeström outlines techniques that encourage isolated forms of this mental distance in the same way that sympathetic, open-ended interviewing did in my own research. Importantly, however, Engeström does not discuss the concept in terms of the particular social or political economic significance, as I do here.

social production of one's activity as a learning activity is a culturally and materially class-differentiated process.

In the first few chapters of *Distinction* (1984) Bourdieu discusses the idea of mental distance and its role in the development of the dominant aesthetic judgment or distinction within the *art of living*. In his opening analysis of photography, for example, we see how various class groups demonstrate vastly different forms of appreciation for various images. This empirical example provides one of the most direct analyses of how the concept of mental distance works in class terms. The development of one's judgment of one's own learning capacity parallels this process. In other words, the development of mental distance from one's own practice is fundamental to the ability to name and, in turn, to organize one's practice as learning and hence as part of one's capacity to learn. But what is it that allows this mental distance to be created? According to Bourdieu, the creation of mental distance is linked with the ability or inability to separate one's practice from the immediacy of its accomplishment. In my own interview research, for example, working-class people more often describe their learning as indistinguishable from doing, that is, as the functional achievement of a particular end or as simply a product of ongoing practice. The dominant class groups, on the other hand, could define a great deal of their participation in activity as learning and thus as part of the capacity-building or capacity-exhibition process. Closely related to the development of mental distance was the tendency to presuppose alternative characterizations of the activity. In terms of learning practice, this involves a discretionary command over the space in which learning takes place in such a way as to allow one to imagine the possibility of different forms of practice. Thus the identification of one's activity as learning, like the ability to generate dominant characterizations of art, varies with the ability to at least implicitly presuppose (as well as shape) alternative purposes or goals within activity. This suggests the important role that the organized representation of subordinate group interests, for example through trade unions, can play in building "learning capacity." Returning again to the theme of material conditions of practice, Bourdieu also discusses the role of one's *distance from necessity*, the ability to foreground form rather than content, and one's competence in using legitimate linguistic codes (also associated with advanced schooling). In terms of the learning practice of working-class people, there is a persistent linkage of learning to function and the inability to presuppose alternative goals and motives of activity (a reflection of power relationships). Together, these militate against the generation of the mental distance necessary to be able to think of one's life as a lifelong learning process.

If there is a particularly novel finding to be expressed here, however, it is that these barriers to learning are not absolute. As informal class networks emerge, a significant countervailing tendency is introduced. In these contexts, the cocreation of learning as a collectively meaningful object of activity reorganizes consciousness, and when expressing subordinate standpoints, it is, in a sense, a political act of resistance as well. Stable cultural networks that recognize, sustain, and develop working-class standpoints offer the greatest potential for the reinterpretation and reorganization of what would otherwise remain dispersed and fragmented experience, knowledge, and skill. In other words, as people come together in stable patterns of community life, their shared standpoints are allowed to emerge, thus becoming legitimized. This forms an alternative basis for the generation of mental distance, an alternative system of naming the world, one's activity, and through these one's capacities, which in turn provides the bases for collective strategies of development and social action, not to mention facilitating the pooling of scarce material resources.

This process of reinterpreting experience and finding new ways to understand and mediate experience through the use of cultural networks, none of which depend upon conscious, goal-directed actions, counters the fragmentation of discretionary control that subordinate people experience. An activity theory perspective allows us to better understand the relationship between computer-mediated adult learning and experience that is broken up and dispersed across systems of activity where working people exercise limited discretion. It is this arrangement of overlapping activity systems, which shapes and structures working-class learning throughout its full range of variation (formal, informal, experiential, incidental, tacit, etc.), that gives rise to particular responses and, over time, elaborates a patterned set of dispositions that define a working-class learning habitus.

To my mind, the majority of adult learning theories do not adequately grasp the significance and structure of the practices that Sean and others described. Yet these practices point to some of the foundational features of the vast majority of everyday learning in which interviewees engaged. At the same time, the broad system of incidental computer learning alluded to earlier, in all of its complexity, is different from the examples used in Leont'ev work. Indeed, his famous example of the primeval hunters occurs in a social world devoid of the complexities underlying the accounts of working people. For Leont'ev's hunters, all other frames or goals of activity cease while the hunters collectively hunt. In contrast, real-world examples must grapple with greater complexity, and it is here that we are able to discern important class dimension of practice. Practices embedded in one activity system affect those in another; conditions, goals, and motives can vary drastically across these systems, depending on both cultural and material resources and discretionary control.

Solidaristic Networks of Computer Learning

In some of his earliest work in the area of working-class culture, one of the foundational authors in the field, Raymond Williams, stated:

> [Working-class culture] is not proletarian art, or council houses, or a particular use of language; it is, rather, the basic collective idea, and the institutions, manners, habits of thought and intentions which proceed from this. Bourgeois culture, similarly, is the basic individualist idea and the institutions, manners, habits of thought and intentions which proceed from that.... [Bourgeois culture] is [an] area which can properly be described as common to or underlying both. (Williams, 1963: 313)

Williams understood both the general character of culture in the lives of the British working class and the contradictory experience it expresses in capitalist society. In later work, he was more specific about the content of working-class culture in comments that reflect back on his own life.

> There is a distinct working-class way of life, which I for one value – not only because I was bred in it, for I now, in certain respects, live differently. I think this way of life, with its emphases of neighbourhood, mutual obligation, and common betterment, as expressed in the great working-class political and industrial institutions, is in fact the best basis for any future [society].... A dying culture, and ignorant masses, are not what I have known and see. (Williams, 1993:93, in McIlroy and Westwood)

Class cultures, of course, are not static. Their content is a perpetually moving target and reflects a dynamic process of class reproduction as well as resistance. Critical cultural studies with myriad examples have shown this time and time again. However, much of what I discuss in this section deals with the same forms, not content, of working-class culture described by Williams. Later in the book, I discuss the ways in which the process of commodification of one's skills and knowledge run counter to these apparently traditional cultural ideals, but here I want to demonstrate the way they run through the computer learning process and the conditions on which its development depends. I want to direct attention to how people in interviews expressed, either directly or indirectly, these same orientations, concerns, and interests, though I want to emphasize the fact that these dispositions seem to depend significantly on the stability and coherence of working-class institutions and communities. Specifically, I want to show how computer learning is rooted in elements of mutuality and group orientations within stable working-class communities today.

The preceding exerpt from the interview with Sean described a fragmented computer learning landscape. Learning under these conditions was emergent, though in fostering relationships with coworkers, family, and friends in the way Sean describes, we see an outline of a working-class learning community. In fact, in many of the interviews I conducted, people spoke about this type of relationship, which, in turn, is linked with the description that Williams provided. Computer learners in these cases reflected the feeling captured in brief asides like this one.

> I had people coming in, wanting to have a look at it, eh? Like a couple of guys wanted to come over. They say, "Well, I was thinking about buyin' one." I says, "Instead of buying it, just come over!" (W5)

This autoworker describes how he relates to fellow workers who are trying to learn about computers. It is a description that runs counter to a model of competitive individualism and material self-interest, and it is practices linked to such attitudes that provide the opportunity to learn in conditions of scarce resources. It emphasizes the sharing of resources as well as a belief in mutual progression. The same autoworker goes on to introduce the group orientation that is necessary, for example, in buying a computer, a process that many interviewees found difficult, anxiety-ridden, and costly. Indeed, the speed with which home-computer products become obsolete offers another example of how the artifact and the conditions of its production, distribution, and consumption can cause shifts in knowledge and tool-mediated practice in people's lives. Under such conditions, purchasing the wrong home computer was a deep concern for working-class people. At the same time, as these computer learners tended to rely on their own networks of friends, coworkers, and neighbors, it inevitably meant learning from mistakes, which in turn occasionally meant that the mistakes of one served as fodder for the learning of others.

> R: You need to do your homework before you even go into a [a computer store] because they will try to sell you everything. The salesmen will try to sell you something that's either outdated or whatever, or something's that really low end, okay? Like I went in knowing what I want because I read about it, I talked to guys about it, and everything. Joe had bought his machine, my buddy there Joe, he had bought his machine just before I did, so he let me know an awful lot about it, see?

So that way, when I went to the store, if they're trying to tell me, you know, "Well, you should get this." No, no. Because I know this. You know what I mean? Yeah. And I think anybody goes in there blind, you're gonna get taken.

I: You're gonna have to upgrade in a little while. And that's happened, especially the first guy in the group?

R: The first guy in the group is usually gonna have to change. He's gonna have to be taken, so that everybody else can be okay [laughter]. Basically, he's a sacrifice. (W5)

A correlate of the mutualism that Williams described is a willingness to engage in self-sacrifice; this can be seen as part of the learning network described. It should be no surprise that when learners think in group-oriented ways, knowledge and experiences are collectivized and developed more quickly. The workers in the preceding excerpt express a group orientation and a division of labor within activity that, though not always benefiting single individuals at any one time, seem to serve the group as a whole quite well. As I conducted the interviews, it became clear that group members who made the sacrifice were compensated through membership in the group, specifically through their involvement in the sharing of resources, equipment, software, and information.

In order to look more closely at how these networks are initiated and developed, I want to focus on another interviewee. "Steve" is 36 years old and, like many of the industrial workers I interviewed, has become a computer enthusiast. He is married and has two young boys who use the computer frequently. After receiving his high school diploma, Steve went to work at a large auto assembly plant and has worked there for 17 years. He has changed jobs within the plant a number of times, and this process of being moved from job to job has provided much of the motivation for his interest in computers. The first time I visited Steve was at his house in the late afternoon just after his two boys had returned from school, but before his partner, herself in the process of retraining in computers, had come home for dinner. We sat down at his kitchen table for our interview, with the children running in and out between turns at the computer in the next room. The interview situation itself served as a demonstration of how forms of computer activity, family care, and so on can run together to form a complex system of activities when time and physical space are scarce. Steve supervised his children, yelled instructions about the computer into the next room, pointed the children toward a snack he'd picked up for them on his way home after his shift, made me some coffee, and answered my questions all at the same time.

After hearing about Steve's background in education and work, I turned the discussion toward his computer learning. The italicized portions in the following excerpts draw attention to relatively common forms of informal computer learning practice I encountered; however, clearly, they have developed beyond the fragmentary experiences of a novice, as described by Sean earlier. Steve's learning practice had become more organized as he became involved with a specific group of coworkers at the plant. The method he describes involves the constant interplay among participants in a computer learning network. It emphasizes the development of learning as an ongoing process of collective discovery. Indeed, it is this mode of social participation that in fact produces what is to be learned. Expert practice in this description is a moving target that no single member of the network of learners "possesses," and the practices and modes of participation described shift through a social process of talking, trying, and collective knowledge construction. The individual becomes more knowledgeable, and the network as a whole develops greater knowledge production capacity. There is a palpable intensity to Steve's engagement in the interview discussion that, to my mind, comes through even in the written text. It is a level of excitement that would be difficult to understand in isolation from the discussion of the formation of the working-class technological common sense: that intersection of the pleasure of learning with the desire, urgency, and sometimes fear that inform working people's experiences with technology. We see a group orientation or mutualism within network participation, and we also see a dynamic that can be described as a self–group dialectic. This self–group dialectic expresses a limit to the way of thinking and talking, that is, the discourse, of learning, which in turn makes it difficult for us to understand and express the relationship between individual and group action.

I: Okay, what are some of the other ways you solve problems? I mean, other than just by yourself, thinking it out, do you talk to people?

R: Coworkers. *Coworkers give you ideas, but they give ideas but you come home and try,* but you still have to answer those questions that they don't tell you, and you think, "Ah, geeze, what am I going to do here, what am I going to do here?" Basically, like for instance I have a problem right now, when I reloaded everything, my MS-backup in Windows isn't working but my MS-backup in DOS is working. Okay, so it comes up and it's telling me in the system, in e-file, I'm missing one line. Device equals MS-DOS path, it doesn't matter. But it's just one path that's missing, so I got in the system in e-file and I put the line in that I felt it was looking for, and then Windows wouldn't even start up. So, that's how I learn. I just try, I go in *I try and do what they say and it didn't work so I had to back into the system* and take the line out and I was able to go back into Windows, but in this case I haven't fixed the problem, so tonight I try and, I'll do it again, I'll try, like I think it's maybe the, when it comes to a path or something like that you're just guessing right, you try different paths to see if they work, but if I can't do it after an hour, I'll just phone 1-800-HELP because that's a software problem, I feel.

I: Yeah, like there is a user-friendly thing that should be involved in what they sell. Do some of these coworkers have anybody like an expert?

R: *Guys who we talk to at work we're all the same.* . . . Guys have *different interests*, though, one guy is real big on the Internet, one guy is real big on reading, he reads everything possible about computers, so you got a mixture of guys there. Guys who'll try anything. (W16)

Statements such as "we're all the same" but with "different interests" highlight the importance of both differences and similarities within learning networks. Steve's individual practice cannot be fully understood in isolation from the ongoing social process of talking to coworkers and trying out advice in a developmental mode of participation in activity. Steve's description highlights the computer-based learning that takes place across at least four more or less discrete spheres of activity: the workplace, the home, the consumer help line, and courses offered by a local school. The knitting together of experience from different spheres of activity was standard across descriptions of learning in informal networks. Like many of the factory workers I interviewed, Steve relies heavily on the existing relationships of the workplace to generate opportunities for participation in learning networks, yet only a small proportion of the computer skills developed were applied to production processes. As we'll see more explicitly in Chapter 9, these collective capacities were far more likely to be funneled toward fighting boredom, self-entertainment, or resisting management control. In effect, the hierarchical organization of work necessary for the effective appropriation of surplus value by capital through the labor process is a barrier to the full use of workers' knowledge production.

Steve goes on to outline other features of participatory networks that were common. Here he provides a clear picture of the skills and knowledge that many interviewees valued, and we also see the importance of fluid, open access to a durable network of relationships for working-class computer learning. Reflecting on this and other previous interview excerpts, we can begin to see how learning networks are closely related but not limited to patterns that characterize the strongly collective, and unionized, shop floor culture at Steve's workplace.

I: Do you have any general observations about how you learn the computer? Like, do you favor one kind of way of solving problems, just in a general?

R: Myself, if I was to talk from the way the group is, myself I'm rough: I go in; I go deep; I get myself into trouble a lot; I cause a lot of problems, but I don't mind it, I like trying to fix it. I like trying to fool with the configuration and system programs or the batch files or the autoexecbat or all that stuff. That doesn't bother me, but it has caused a lot of problems too, so, but I don't mind doing it. There's another guy at work, if you were to interview him, he reads and reads and reads everything before he'll do one thing, *and even after as a group we talk about what just happened*, he would be very leery of trying anything or doing it, like when we installed the autoexecbat that'd give you either games or normal, our way was the same as his but *we had to convince him* and he had to go home and *read* about it. You know it's one of those things where he eventually did it but it took him six times as long as everyone else. Then we have other guys who, they won't do anything unless they've *talked to some computer genius*. You know, they'll go out and find someone who's a real computer genius.

I: Like a buddy or/

R: Usually there's someone at work who really knows his stuff, and they'll go and say well, this is what *we plan on* doing, what do you think? And they'll get the idea. There's a couple of us who are willing to go muck around and but it's cost us a few times. (W16)

Related to the individual–group dialectic introduced earlier, there is a significant degree to which individual and collective dimensions of activity simply cannot be distinguished from one another. As sociocultural approaches to learning would have it, learners participate as individuals in a process that is nevertheless definitively social. However, this dialectic can even be seen in discussions of individual differences among group members such as a preference for learning by reading or the need to consult someone outside the group who was considered a "computer genius." Each of these is framed in the context of a group practice. Like so many of the descriptions of informal learning that interviewees provided, this overall frame of collective action is marked by such phrases as "*we* had to convince...," "*we* plan on...," and so on. The "computer genius" referred to is discussed as a collective resource rather than an individual pedagogue or leader. The patterns that emerge from this practice are based largely on specific forms of coworker relations that arise as a response to the barriers, constraints, patterns of association, and general conditions in which industrial workers live within and beyond the workplace every day.

Difference and Similarity as Resources in Learning: Realizing Peripherality in Working-Class Computer Learning Networks

The preceding discussions provide a glimpse of the basic patterns through which working people come to be interested in computer learning, create a participatory network, and establish their own modes of peripherality. The discussions also introduce the way in which similarities and differences function in working-class computer networks. In this section, I focus on how these similarities and differences relate to the establishment and structuring of the learning networks. Generally speaking, similarities among group members related to a general interest in computers shaped by their class-based experiences at work and in the labor market. For almost everyone I interviewed, computer technology was felt to be a powerful force in their lives requiring urgent attention in one form or another. As we saw in Chapter 3, the sphere of paid work was important in establishing this shared class perspective on technology particularly, but not exclusively, for working-class men and for those working in a unionized workplace.[3] However, according to Lave and Wenger (1991), difference plays an important role as a resource for the development of communities of practice. The differences between people within the computer learning networks seen in this research typically involved interests in specific subtopics (e.g., hardware, communications software, educational software) as well as preferred methods of accessing information (e.g., reading, talking). Each of these sets of similarities and differences was affected by activity within other spheres that, in turn, affected the distribution of the time, space, and energy people had to engage in discretionary learning.

As in previous sections, I discuss these and other issues by focusing on a particular interviewee, in this case a 44-year-old auto parts factory worker whom I'll call James. Like Steve, James was involved in a computer learning network that was connected to both his workplace and his neighborhood. While visiting James at his home for interviews, it was clear that

---

[3] See Chapters 6 and 8 for further discussion on the effects of gender and unionization, respectively, on working-class learning.

he was deeply engaged in computer-based learning. Downstairs, among makeshift shelves of home-preserved vegetables from the garden, the home renovation supplies from past do-it-yourself projects, the furniture, and the tools, there were scattered spare computers, spare computer parts, and sets of disks. James describes the type of solidaristic learning network that we have previously encountered. In the following series of extended excerpts, James presents examples of how differences function in these learning networks, and how many of these differences involve a response to life changes and the development of new relationships: the frequent and unexpected effects of many different overlapping spheres of activity. Perhaps more than in the preceding discussion, however, we see how working-class computer learning operates outside of formal training and even, in a sense, outside of the consumer market, in that materials and expertise are freely shared among group members rather than sold. Participants of the informal network shared software, exchanged hardware, and helped each other with system repairs. Although the social network is partially rooted in the workplace, when computer-based learning is not taking place during the breaks in the work day at the factory, it takes place in the spaces where working-class people exercise the most discretion, principally in their homes and neighborhoods. Differences within the group are used as a resource for all members, and as we saw earlier, the mistakes of some are collectivized and treated as particularly valuable learning experiences for the network as a whole. I interviewed James together with his partner (R2 in the following excerpt). We pick up the conversation as James answered questions about how he had become so involved in computer learning in the first place.

R: Like one of the other guys I work with, Gerry, "Well," he says, "I'm looking to buy a new one. What should I buy?"

I: So he came to you?

R: Yeah. And like all these guys at work. Well, I bought a computer and I say, "If you ever buy a computer, come to me before you buy one." Because *here I am, I got a unit that's not expandable.*

R2:   And *we learned too*, like/

R: So I learned right off the bat what to and what not to buy. Because here I am, I want to put a particular card in. Not available. I can only go with so many megs of RAM because one's on the motherboard permanent, and one's in a clip.... I had my ex-wife's computer a couple of days [trying to fix it], and then I end up I couldn't straighten it out, so I took it to Gerry, and he straightened it out. So he fixed it all up.

I: *But he kind of learned from you, though, I thought.*

R: Yeah.

R2:   *But he went by because you were saying he started after, but you'd be going to him about stuff after while too.*

R: Yeah.

R2:   Like he started to learn.

R: Within six months to a year. But, see, *he's a reader.*

R2:   He's teaching himself.

I: Yeah.

R: He's a reader. He loves to read. I don't like to read.

I: Oh. So he has that as an extra resource?

R2:   Like the manuals and that to learn.

I: Okay.

R: See, that's the difference among a lot of people. Some read and some don't. I'm not a reader.

I: So this Gerry guy has taken to some of these books, like he kind of looks through them?

R: Oh, he's passed me like a hundred miles an hour because I'll go in here and I'll go to work and I'll say, "Gerry, I couldn't get this to run." "Alright. Well, you gotta go in and you gotta do this and this and this and change your config sys file so that this'll run, okay? Or else, you gotta. Oh here! Here's a disk." Like we go through all this stuff together at work. I've got disks in my locker and so does he. And then there's Ross.

I: Ross?

R: He's self-taught, too. And his is like a computer that started out like yours.

I: Yeah?

R: His brother got him a panel and the next thing you know, he's got three hard drives in it and/

I: Oh. So he's really/

R: It's got plenty of megs, stacked hard drive and then the other one isn't stacked and another one's only for games and it's all just bits and pieces that they've put together over the years. He's totally self-taught. He bought a IBM. It's IBM clone or something like that.... Here he is, he's sittin' here and he's got nothing to do. He's bored. He sittin' – he lives alone, eh? So he buys another one. But he didn't just buy a whole computer. He went and well, gotta have a board first. Then he bought a box. And then he bought a sound card, and he built it all himself with no computer knowledge before at all.

I: And would he be over here a lot kind of just askin' stuff?

R: He did a lot of the, like, the programming and that, he got a lot of it from me, and he got a lot of it from guys where he works. But then, there's like twenty-five guys that he works with that are all into computers, too. So they say, "Go buy this one here or take a look at this one here." And then, "Come on over to my place tonight and look at this and look at that." And so on. He started right from scratch and did everything right up to the total program of everything worked perfectly. (W4a/b)

James outlines how his work relations overlap with his home and neighborhood-based computer learning, and how through this overlapping of different spheres he is linked into the learning networks of a wide variety of other learners in the neighborhood as well as those who work elsewhere. As in other excerpts, the dialectic of self–group is at play in this account. James makes claims about being self-taught, but as he explains further, we see that self-teaching is a dimension of participation in a social network. Exchange of hardware repairs and peripheral involvement with a neighbour who works at a different factory (and who builds his own computers) is part of the mutual exchange process. James also describes how the teacher and learner (as with James and his coworker Gerry) often switch roles. Many of the previous observations about working-class informal computer networks apply here as well. We see the connection to Raymond Williams's description of working class culture; we see the importance of pooling resources in the face of scarcity endemic to even the employed working class; we see the dispositions and pleasures surrounding being self-taught outside of schooling, and so on. As I commented earlier, we also see that coworkers in the factory find and make time within the routines of the shift to talk about computers, share the disks stored in their lockers, and learn about computers informally together.

Both previously and in the excerpt that follows, James describes how differences in expertise, interests, and resources such as free time help drive changing personal knowledgeabilty and patterns of participation. In the most basic terms, James moves from novice to more expert patterns of participation; yet this is a living set of relationships, and the ebb and flow of complex intersections of activities, different information access methods, and so on alter these forms of participation. Thus, what Lave and Wenger refer to as a *centripetal* force (1991:122) by which newcomers become old-timers is neither linear nor absolute in these informal (system of) working-class learning networks. In the following excerpt, James provides a relatively clear description of how a typical working-class computer learning network develops. He begins by explaining why it is important to share software – itself a statement that emerges from a specific class position – and then explains the process of exchange and social connection.

R: They want a couple hundred bucks for a program? No way!

I: Yeah?

R: Okay. If they want to sell that program, bring the price down and sell a million of them.

I: If it's gonna be up so high, yeah.

R: You know. See, because there are companies out here, they throw this old stuff out . . .

I: So you just keep your ears open and everybody else keeps ears open, pass things around, copy, work things out?

R: Yeah.

I: A network. Is it a fairly small group of people?

R: It's monstrous.

I: And it's all kind of between people, and somebody else would have some buddies/

R: Alright, here's an example, okay, since I bought computer, I got a lot of help from Robert. So you start at the top of the tree. Robert got me into it, alright? Then Kevin's got one. Alright. Well, Kevin's illiterate, alright? But he bought a computer anyway, so that his wife and kids could use it. So Kevin. Then Gerry, okay? And Chuck. It's all at the same time. And then, who else? Ross, alright? So there's five. . . . Well, they've all spurred one or two. Let's say, Gerry says, "Well, my brother was gonna look for a computer." Well [we help him out]. They're Internet surfing all the time eh? And they're into this stuff and they're on the modems every day, and they're still working with Bulletin Boards and that.

I: So it just grows and everybody probably will have a buddy in the next couple of years that's gonna want something?

R: That's right. Like now, Paul around the corner, he's got one and that. So there's another one there. (W4a)

The working-class computer learning network that James describes is expansive and provides a key forum for the interconnection of different computer-mediated activity systems among these working people. It is a type of network that is not unique to James. It is a living, treelike structure that is rooted in specific sensibilities, preferences, and dispositions, that is, a habitus, of working-class life.

Finally, it becomes clear that it is only by access to a set of stable cultural and material relationships that, according to interviewees like James and others, errors and potentially costly mistakes that render equipment unusable can become a correctable/learnable practice. Levels of stability are rooted in the distribution of material resources in society and thus, under capitalism, must be understood as heavily influenced by class processes. Equally important, beyond the material barriers that these networks help to surmount, they produce a mini-public sphere where learners find their forms of learning habitus, their past experiences of schooling, and the difficulties they sometimes have experienced accepted and even celebrated. In this way, we see how cultural and material stability is a key mediating factor in understanding patterns of social learning among adults. As a basic activity theory tenet rooted in the original observations of Vygotsky, the sustenance of the interconnections between people and their cultural-material practices drives the possibility for internalization or learning transfer that takes place on an individual level. Among other things, it suggests that the keys to the full development of a knowledge society and/or a knowledge economy are open systems of participation rooted in materially stable, culturally rich class-based communities.

Summary

In *Practical Reason: On the Theory of Action* (1998), Pierre Bourdieu poses several questions that relate to and help extend the preceding discussion. These questions help us see the linkage between working-class habitus and the social-relational approach to learning expressed in theories of activity (Leont'ev, 1981) and legitimate peripheral participation (Lave and Wenger, 1991).

Does a human behaviour really always have as an end, that is, as a goal, the result which is the end, in the sense of conclusion, or term, of that behaviour? I think not. What is, therefore, this very strange relationship to the social or natural world in which agents aim at certain ends without posing them as such?.... Ordinary analyses of temporal experience confuse two relationships to the future or the past which Husserl clearly distinguishes with Ideen: the relationship to the future that might be called a project, and which poses the future as future, that is, as a possible constituted as such, thus as possibly happening or not, is opposed to the relationship to the future that he calls protension or pre-perceptive anticipation, a relationship to a future that is not a future, to a future that is almost present.... In fact, these

pre-perceptive anticipations, a sort of practical induction based on previous experience, are not given to a pure subject, a universal transcendental consciousness.
They are the fact of the habitus as a feel for the game. (Bourdieu, 1998:80–82)

In many interview excerpts presented in this chapter, we see how working-
class computer learning is often embedded in activities that do not have
the goal of learning per se. Learning, in this sense, remains hidden from
the consciousness of the learner. Under these conditions, it is as if learning practice is governed by a "feel for the game" rather than a conscious cognitive choice, and as I've suggested, the uneven distribution of
projected versus *protensional* learning can be seen as an important indicator
of a class-differentiated process of distinction. Activity theory describes
learning as social practice that includes goal-directed "projects" but that
also involves operational elements that roughly describes what Bourdieu
calls *practical induction*. Bourdieu goes on to describe the relationship
that these forms of patterned practice have with differentiated previous
experience.

In this chapter, I discussed several ways in which specific patterns
of practice and participation are rooted in class relations, working-class
standpoints in activities, and a class habitus. People engaged in solidaristic networks of computer learning that depended on a group orientation
to function effectively. In these networks, people drew on differences in
skills, interests, resources, and methods in a fluid set of roles and relations
that were frequently rearranged according to influences related to their
broader social lives. Teachers became learners, novices surpassed experts
in some areas but remained novices in others, and activity was governed
by the ebbs and flows of class life in a variety of different spheres of activity. People drew on differences between members as a shared group
resource. One person's preference for reading was a resource for others
who preferred hands-on practice and vice versa. Within these processes
there was what I referred to as a dialectic of self and group in which
individual practice construed as "self-teaching" transformed group participation and vice versa. Reflecting the character of class life generally,
particularly in periods of accelerated change, the learning habitus is seen
to be both contradictory and subject to change.

At a general level, the activity theory and situated learning analyses
helped reveal the class dimension of computer learning by bringing coherence and visibility to what would otherwise remain dispersed and fragmentary forms of practice. As I noted in Chapter 2, in analyses of this
kind we are in fact destabilizing the class processes within (popular and

academic) discourses of adult learning by revealing learning capacities where before they were hidden. I claim that it is when learning is seen as a sociocultural concept in which specific individuals' practices are embedded in more general societal relations that we can begin to make relevant claims of differentiated and differentiating forms of class-based learning.

Finally, the analysis specifically drew our attention to the complexity and significance of working-class computer learning across a variety of overlapping activities. For subordinate groups such as a diverse working class, overlapping systems of activity expressed the fragmentation of their limited discretionary control. Necessarily, it seems, this structure of learning involved a patchwork of opportunities, many of which appear in the home (where people exercise the most discretionary control), but which also appear in interstitial spaces of the workplace and neighborhood. Interstitial spaces in dominant institutions were the places where interviewees could have their class standpoint positively recognized and expressed in terms of the development of specific skills and knowledge. In these spaces, people could most easily realize greater discretion and greater possibility for creative agency. The development of working-class learning networks, in fact, has the distinct potential to overturn the principles and processes that produce learning capacity as a naturalized, hierarchically distributed cultural feature of the dominant class group. Though in more specific terms, together with dispositions toward solidaristic networking, these skills, abilities, and dispositions toward interstitial learning and the collective construction of legitimate participation in communities of practice offer an opening approximation of the relations between habitus, adult learning, computer technology, and working-class life.

6   Understanding Working-Class
Standpoints in Computer Learning

Issues of social standpoint inform virtually every aspect of the discussion in this book, beginning with the definition of social class I provided in Chapter 1. However, in this chapter I focus on the most conscious and formally developed expressions of class standpoints in computer learning. In the following sections, I examine the way working-class standpoints in the industrial workplace influence habitus and specific computer learning projects both within and beyond the factory gates. Next, I examine how the most formally organized expression of the working-class standpoint, the trade union, affects computer learning processes in terms of the relationship between informal learning and formalized, course-based learning. Finally, I look at the experiences with computers and computer learning among a mini-sample of elites and corporate executives in Toronto, Canada. However, first, I want to elaborate on my introductory comments on social class and class standpoints in Chapter 1 by drawing on selected Marxist and Marxist-feminist literature.

One of the first writers to offer an explicit and sustained examination of the proletarian standpoint was Georg Lukács. Lukács's work was controversial amongst Marxists in part because of his complex political relationship with the Hungarian Communist movement and the emerging Stalinism of the period. His seminal work, *History and Class Consciousness* (1971), however, was vitally important to Western Marxism and, in terms of this book, helps us to understand how different class standpoints coexist within the production of concrete social activity. Lukács's work outlines how participation in *specific categories of mediation* produced a fundamentally different *objective reality* for bourgeois and proletarian subjects by virtue of the different class positions that they occupied in the process. Emphatically, the notion of *objective* was not used in the sense of a positivist account of reality, but rather referred to an account

124

rooted in conditions experienced from a particular standpoint. Following this, class processes could be understood as occurring within an entire range of practices. Computer-based activity, for example, could be understood as a specific category of mediation within which class processes and thus class standpoints are embedded. For Lukács, as for Marx, it was the underlying sets of social relations that gave concrete activity – what he referred to as *merely immediate reality* – its specific meaning and structure. At the same time, however, Lukács's work (1971) does have limitations. Those familiar with it will know that Lukács often referred to standpoints in generalized ways that obscured the fact that class is always a mediated process actively produced by living human agents. His work in these instances takes on a determined and mechanistic feel despite the persistent rhetorical flourishes regarding the "free action of the proletariat itself."

Nevertheless, Lukács's essay "Reification and the Consciousness of the Proletariat" (1971) has provided inspiration for a range of contemporary theories that deal critically with the idea of social standpoints. Most notable among these are the writings of Marxist-feminist standpoint theorists. Generally recognized to have begun in the 1970s and early 1980s with several key essays by Dorothy Smith, as well as Nancy Hartsock, Marxist-feminist theory is not monolithic (Smith, 1997a). Rather, it is an approach that represents a diverse collection of writers, foci, and intellectual traditions revolving around several shared theoretical commitments. These shared commitments, according to Harding (1986), are based on historical materialist analysis and, adds Smith (1987), the influence of the women's movement. At its core, each perspective in the tradition offers an explicitly politicized, counterhegemonic analysis with an appreciation for the relevance of social constructivism and the importance of people's everyday experience. As Collins describes it, theories of standpoint refer to "a common location within hierarchical power relations that creates groups" (1997:376). In her work, Smith emphasizes that the concept of standpoint focuses on how concrete experience can be used as a "method of discovering the social" from particular perspectives or standpoints.

[The] ruling relations become visible from a standpoint located in an embodied subject situated in the everyday/everynight actualities of her own life and engaged in the particularlizing work that organizes her consciousness. It is from here that the extra-local organization of the ruling relations becomes visible; it is from here that the project of investigating them and their characteristic forms of objectification and standardization as people's local practices can be conceived. (Smith, 1997b:128)

For Smith, then, a theory of standpoint is not primarily a *device*, nor is it the basis for knowledge claims in conventional sociological terms. Rather, it provides the starting point for a program of inquiry that draws on everyday experience in order to bring to the fore the means by which the patterns of social life are created. Both the work of Lukács and Marxist-feminist standpoint theory, as noted from the start, are central to the conceptualization of social class in this book. Each offers a refinement of the concept of social class that includes instructions on how we can explore class differences in everyday life and adult learning practice.

Within the tradition of activity theory, one of the basic ways in which social standpoint is discussed borrows the term *multivoicedness* from the work of the Russian philospher of language and literary scholar Mikhail Bahktin (e.g., Engeström, 1987, 1999; Wertsch, 1991). An activity system, according to this perspective, is a multivoiced formation. In Engeström's discussion of *learning by expansion*, for example, he points out that expansive learning requires a sense of the history of the emergence of divergent voices and *reorchestration* of the different perspectives that these voices represent. Through this type of analysis, multiple points of view, traditions, and interests within activity systems can be examined. However, one of the best examples of sociocultural analysis that details the role of standpoints in social practice can be found in the work of Dorothy Holland and collaborators (e.g., Holland and Reeves, 1996; Holland et al., 1998). In this work, issues of social standpoint or perspective are definitive not simply of one's view of activity but also of one's current and ongoing possibilities for participation in it.

A person engaged in social life, a person involved in an activity or practice, is presumed to have a perspective. One looks at the world from the angle of what one is trying to do. Postmodernists and feminists also attend to perspective, especially to the perspectives that come from being treated according to broad social divisions such as gender, race, class, ethnicity, and sexual orientation. Persons look at the world from the positions into which they are persistently cast. Another type of placement is at least as important as narrativized or discursive placement: positioning by access to space, to associates, to activities and to genres.... Perspectives are tied to a sense of entitlement or disentitlement to the particular spaces, relationships, activities, and forms of expression that together make up indices of identity. (Holland et al., 1998:44)

To my mind, this analysis parallels the Bourdieuian conception of position/disposition discussed earlier in the book, but more important, it offers an empirically grounded example of the way that different standpoints play such important role in differentiated and differentiating forms of participation in activity. Specific to the focus of this book, it is through the identification of differentiated standpoints in social practices that we can see how the local production of everyday computer-mediated activity is part of the broader social, political, and economic world. In Holland et al. (1998), there is also an important recognition that people bring a coherent set of basic dispositions, preferences, comportment, skills, tastes and knowledges, that is, habitus, to bear in the course of their participation with others. Simply put, although people can participate in a wide range of activities, they cannot participate in these activities in any way they choose.

To summarize and move to the following sections, I argue that Lukács's work sensitizes us to the historical relations that inform different class experiences of specific categories of mediation, among which we can include practices such as computer-based learning. Marxist-feminist standpoint theory, partially emerging from the work of Lukács, offers an important elaboration of the theme, emphasizing how the entire complement of social standpoints, including those based on gender and race as well as social class, is involved in the active accomplishment of what Smith calls the *relations of ruling*. Finally, Holland and colleagues offer a sensitive empirical analysis of how standpoints are implicated in the analysis of activity specifically. Taken together, and beginning with some of the earliest Marxist approaches to the issue of social standpoints, these perspectives combine to provide a powerful tool to make visible learning throughout its full range of variation and its relationship to class standpoints.

The Linkage between Computers and Class Standpoints in the Workplace

Interviews offer a chance to identify the class standpoints from which people experience their lives when they connect with concrete events such as receiving a paychek, receiving orders and explanations from supervisors, and coping creatively with specific forms of dumbed-down technological change. Social standpoints can be identified through a close examination of how people select their words, the active voice that is ascribed to certain things or people and not others, and so forth. Social standpoints become particularly easy to identify in class terms when there is a fundamental contrast between people's concrete experience and dominant discourses that are used to make sense of and that partially order that experience.

Now let's briefly consider a few extended excerpts from the interviews, where we can begin to see both a dominant, class-based discourse of computer technology and the transitions that interviewees make beyond it when they draw on concrete descriptions of their own lives. The following autoworker outlines a number of central points observed from his position in a batch-process production system. I had worked with him several years earlier, and made arrangements to meet with him again one day after his shift at the factory. At age 35 he has been working at the plant for 10 years, over which time he has seen various changes to machinery and work organization.

I: Would you say that the technology in the workplace has made things better, worse, or hasn't changed things all that much?

R: I'd probably say its' changed things for the better. It makes them stay competitive, it makes them competitive with other companies, because I think Ford and Chrysler like to see the new machines with the computer control, like CNC program-type machines brought into the plant. It takes away that human error.

I: Is there any downside to it that you can see?

R: Not that I can see. [lengthy pause] Well, I don't know if you've noticed the one line this week, they've just put in a new robot on that line, they have a new robot on the roll threader . . . like where I work there's one guy on the hollow mill, one guy on the threader, on the other line one guy runs the hollow mill, and the robot takes it up and runs it on the threader, so they have one guy basically running two machines . . . [and] the operators aren't doing, they're doing maybe minor adjustments, they're not doing any programming, basically they bring a job in, they proof it all out for a month or so, and set the program up so basically it runs itself. . . .

I: How would you define *technology* then?

R: First thing that comes to mind is probably computers, computers and control, probably new ideas, advanced ideas type of thing, new ways of thinking maybe. Technology is changing things and I would say not just industry but the world in general, things are changing so fast these days now with the information highway they're talking about, things are changing so fast. And a lot of the newer machines seem to have glass enclosures, it seems just the machines they build nowadays seem to be more thought out than years ago, with the way they made machines. Like on the valve line oil used to be dripping from the ceiling because of all the oil in the air, or if you ever get a chance to walk by the big drill-press machine look above that. . . . I wouldn't say it's getting rid of the drudgery, and leaving us with more time, the company doesn't want to hear about that. They like to see the guys work all shift type of thing, they don't want to see you with more time on your hands in the plant. (W1)

What this man's extended description provides is an opportunity to map a system of interests, relevancies, and key contexts of experience. It provides insight into the nature of technological common sense, but more important for our discussion here, it highlights the intersection of discourse and concrete experience. Specifically, it allows us to chart the contradictory moments of work and computers from a specific working-class standpoint. As I've said, one way to understand the interweaving of dominant discourse and subordinate standpoints is to pay close attention to the syntactic and semantic variations, specifically the use of *I* and *we* as opposed to *them* and *they* in accounts. As Harold Garfinkel has commented, "[t]he activities whereby members produce and manage settings of organized everyday affairs are identical with members' procedures for making those settings 'accountable'" (1967:1). Or rather, in interview situations, although "the original setting is not operative, [it] registers as an underlying determinant of how the informant talks of the setting because it is the only way in which it makes sense to talk" (Smith, 1987:189). In this sense, the selective assignment of active and passive voices by interviewees in their descriptions takes on important social significance. W1's opening line, for example, indicates how the *I* takes on the interests and concerns of the *them* and how CNC machines are granted active voice as a subject in the sentence ("*It* takes away that human error"). This description outlines how his own actions are both objectified and denigrated (as "human error"). In this case, we can also see that positive notions of computers in the context of both profit and progress are interwoven with more critical observations when comments turn to concrete arrangements, job descriptions, and software programming on the shopfloor. More generally, we might reflect on the fact that it is the conflict of interests between company and worker that are reflected inherently in the interviewee's description of computers at work.

Another example, however, provides a slightly more direct contrast between the standpoint of the person and the dominant discourse of computers in the context of learning and work. The following excerpt was taken from an interview with a 50-year-old woman who works as a machine operator in a electronics manufacturing plant. Because computer-based technological changes had begun to sweep through her workplace, much of this interview focused on the role that these new computerized machines would play on her shopfloor. She was a lead hand and one of the most senior workers in her department; as such, it was not unusual for coworkers to come to her with their questions on how the new machines would affect their workplace. She explained that with the coming changes, coworkers often asked her whether work would become more strenuous, whether it would become more safe, or whether these new machines might help them to obtain the bonus they sometimes received (free lunch for a day) when weekly production quotas exceeded targets. By far the most frequent question she was asked, however, was whether people would lose their jobs with the introduction of the new technology. In the interview, I asked her about her general impressions of the new technology and whether these new machines had brought about changes for the better or for the worse. Her answers help to show some of the ways that manufacturing workers experience computer technology in the workplace and, in turn, help us to better understand the possible class dimensions of computer-based activity. These experiences can be understood as class processes by beginning with people's own standpoint in activity, where, for example, we can see how concrete practice produces both technological common sense and the foundation for its critique.

The electronics plant is a nonunion shop, and importantly, the woman herself did not openly articulate her experience in class terms. She told me that she actually wasn't very interested in what went on in her workplace, but nevertheless, even under these conditions where class relations are so far out of focus, we can begin to trace a coherent and distinctive class standpoint in her talk. After beginning with a claim about the overall positive effects that computer technology has on work, as the exchange continued she slowly problematized these effects. The resources for this critique are her own experiences of a wage freeze, the experience of little or no influence over decision making at work, the experience of friends and neighbors who've been downsized, and so forth.

R: [Technology has changed things] for the *better*, like we talk about *more product* going out the door and *less people* doing it.

I: Now why's that for the better then?

R: Well it's not for the better of the people, but it is I guess for the company. [pause]

I: It must be better for the people somehow. How do you think it might be better? How's it all connect? I'm just trying to get your own words on it. How is it better or how's it worse?

R: Well, like I said, I think it's better for the *dollars for the company*.

I: But you say not so much for the people?

R: Well no, not if they're *losing they're job*.

I: Well, you guys have kept employment pretty stable eh?

R: Yeah, we have, we're lucky.

I: But you sense that other places aren't so lucky?

R: No, I don't think they are. [long pause] I guess when you think about it in the plant, technology is taking away jobs. [pause] Man's outsmarting himself, losing his own jobs because of it....

I: Do you think computers and technology offer a chance to create new wealth?

R: Yes I think so because you can put more product out again.

I: And so the *wages would go up* with your company doing better?

R: Well it should but *not at our place*, we haven't had a raise in a while.

I: The wages have been frozen for a little while then?

R: Yes, a wage freeze, but like I said, we're lucky, we never had a layoff, so that says something.

I: So, when you say it does create more wealth you mean ...

R: Well, if you can be more efficient, it has to create new wealth.

I: For the company?

R: Yes it has to.

I: But not as much for the workers?

R: Well, like right now with the wage freeze on and like [the manager] says the money that they're making they're putting back into the plant to buy these new machines, so I would think they must be making money to have a credit line to get the new equipment.

I: So do you sense that it will come around to higher wages then if the company gains a competitive edge?

R: I would think it would, yes.

I: Do you have good faith in that?

R: Well, I think May is the end of our fiscal year and they're going to look at that and see what [pause] everyone's hoping.

I: Do you have a pretty strong workplace association or union then?

R: No.

I: Who does the negotiating for you then?

R: Nobody, they just give it to us. (W6)

It was in the movement of the discussion toward the realm of concrete practice, often brought to the fore through the interviews, that the actualities of people's experience became visible, revealing the powerful class processes and class differences involved in people's everyday lives. We can see how the woman's standpoint in these types of activity provides the means of generating a working-class perspective on technology and the labor process. Indeed, in many ways the industrial workplace offers perhaps one of the most tangible and best developed expressions of class processes and class standpoints in daily activity available.

The features of work life in manufacturing plants involving the technical design of jobs and computers in order to maximize managerial control also play an important role in structuring goal-directed learning practices. Braverman's (1974) classic deskilling thesis can be applied generally to help explain how the separation of conception and execution is rooted in the fundamental dynamics of the capitalist labor process. In the following interview with a chemical worker, for example, there is a description of how the social organization of the labor process shapes practice. In contrast to the preceding excerpts, we see that one's standpoint in relation to work design and control more generally can direct learning to actually encourage non-work-related computing. Common and powerful forces in the work life of manufacturing workers are issues such as routinization and alienation, accentuated by what they describe as "idiot-proof" computer technologies. These particular forms of mediated practice are ones that working people engage in regularly, and they represent an important dimension of the social processes through which class standpoints are actively produced in the context of work, computers, and learning. In other words, routinization and the pronounced alienation that workers experience penetrate and shape their learning practices, directing attention and motivating efforts to engage in alternative practices, in general setting the stage for rule making, rule breaking, and mundane conflict.

R: I didn't really get any formal training in it at all.

I: So where did you do most of your learning?

R: Well, *back corners* [laughs], midnight shift, that sort of thing, just playing around with it.

I: So there's a computer sitting there and you just sort of

R: Yeah, *it's either that or do work, it's a little more interesting* so

I: It's a change then?

R: Yeah, yeah

I: Other guys do the same thing, I hear.

R: But like I say, I don't get into the operating system or anything, but some of the guys are just phenomenal, but like the light at the end of the tunnel is a better game, you know what I mean. The games don't interest me at all. . . . But it's actually a big problem because like I have guys complaining to me [as a shop steward] about these guys playing the games, and I'll tell them mind your own fucking business, but you know what do you do you can't go to management, it's a difficult position to be in . . . [but] as soon as management sees us playing around on our spare time with these computers and games and stuff, we're going to have supervisors start to crack down.

I: So you'd sit down and eventually over the course of each day you'd learn. Can you put a time estimate on that then?

R: [laughing and putting his hand over the tape recorder] The company's not going to find out about this?

I: [laughing] No, no, it's anonymous

R: No, I'm only joking.

I: It's that much then eh?

R: Yeah, I would say eighty hours over the last year maybe, at the terminal.

I: Split up into little ten- and fifteen-minute chunks

R: Or hours, depending what shift you're on, if you're on midnights you can sort of hide a way for a few hours, yeah.

I: That's a good amount of time, eh, it's better than any course?
        (W18a)

Computer learning practices of workers take place within capitalist relations of production experienced from a particular standpoint. The tour of the plant that managers occasionally take versus the experience of the workers who inhabit the shopfloor every day and night give proof to Lukács's notion that experience (i.e., the experience of the shopfloor) can be split into fundamentally different objective class realities. And, more to the point, computer learning can be a component of this experience that is tightly interwoven with workplace attitudes and class practices generally. At the most basic level, alienated and distracted workers spending their time playing computer games provide greater justification for management to remove even more control and creative functions from workers, resulting in even greater alienation. It is this type of practice that contributes to the further entrenchment of class perspectives, resulting in the formation of more or less stable patterns of a creative working-class culture.[1]

These class experiences are not limited to the workplace. Instead, vis-à-vis general material conditions and the production of a working-class learning habitus, they spill over into the full range of computer-based learning practices. The following autoworker, for example, describes how the need to find creative outlets at work translates directly into broader computer-based interests and activities.

I: Did you buy a computer before you had any knowledge of it or/

R: No, no, I had limited knowledge at work so.

I: Tell me about that.

R: Okay, so at work we have, not particular to my job, but we have a computer which runs a machine and of course it's just a basic, it has its own program, the computer has its own program, but in the background it has Windows. So that was my first experience. You could get out of the program that ran the machine, and you could go and you could get into Windows and there was just a basic Windows program, and at work with that, well we got ourselves in trouble a few times. And with that, you know, guys would come around and different guys would have different limited experience in trying to fix the computer whenever we screwed it up, and basically that's how I got interested in it. Of course, you talk more and more with the guys because you fool around with it more, and the next thing you know I bought one. (W19)

One of the unique features of contemporary computer technology is the convergence (Greenbaum, 1998) between home and workplace computers that the preceding excerpt describes. Practices such as this one reiterate the importance that experience in the workplace has for learning generally and vice versa. Equally important is the fact that the work-based learning that this worker alludes to expresses an alternative class standpoint.

Using activity theory to direct us to a series of questions on the way class is implicated in the learning process, we could begin by asking how the tools involved express differing class standpoints. The cultural tools that working people draw on to participate together (e.g., discourse, comportment, self-presentation) are the most obvious expressions of class

---

[1] This oppositional class culture is the subject of an entire arm of sociology of work, anthropology of work, and particularly labor process theory analyses. See Thompson (1989) for a relevant introduction to academic work in the area. For the most intelligent, direct account of shop floor life in North America, see Hamper (1991).

experience. Once again, this speaks to the relation of position and disposition, as expressed in Bourdieu's concept of the habitus. It is just as obvious that machinery in the workplace takes on a fundamentally different character for the workers who use it versus the manager who supervises its work and the owners who collect the lion's share of the reward for its use. In short, for capital, computers are a "money machine"; for workers they embody, among other things, the threat of drudgery and potential unemployment on the one hand, and the risk of a penalty if they try to use computers creatively on the other. Extending the question of the meaning of tools, it is important to inquire into the object and outcome of the activity. Likewise, the class dimensions are clear. For capital, the outcome is the appropriation of surplus value and profit. For the worker, it is a wage. Building on the basic object–tool–person triangle of activity theory (review Figure 1.1), we could consider broader elements of the activity system including rules, community relations, and division of labor. In each of these elements we can trace similar class dimensions (respectively): in the hidden codes of shopfloor culture versus the formal authority and rules of management; in the connections workers have to the broader labor community versus the connection management has to the parent company and the corporate world; in the division of labor that sees the separation of planning and execution; and so on. In all cases, we can see how class dimensions of activity emerge when we begin from distinctive class standpoints.

Here, another autoworker describes how he first came to be introduced to computers and the important effect these origins had on his future learning. As in the previous excerpts, we see how the language of the experience expresses a particular standpoint in activity. In this case, we see a standpoint in which computer technology forms the basis of vast and important changes in one's day-to-day life.

I: Did you go to school to pick up any of this computer knowledge?

R: No. I'm just grade 11 education.... The biggest effect [on my computer learning] was the robot on number five press came in and it had a computer.

I: What year was that?

R: It's been seven years, six or seven years. And so every time we walked down there, it was all "*Geez! This is the way it's going. Everything is going this way,*" you know, and so when I got there I said, "I don't know nothing about computers. I don't know nothing about robots." So there was always one guy that was there permanent anyways and then, the one day I'm there all by myself, there's no other person there, so I had to learn it. So the electrician says, "Okay. You gotta do this to do this to do that to do that." And he wrote everything down on a piece of paper, and he says, "You keep it." It's still in my locker, you know. . . . [But] I look at the amazement of the stuff in the factory. Like I walk up there and I'm like, "Oh, yeah! Geez! That's simple. When you think about it, it's simple." If you go look at it. Okay, take for example, my robot complex that I worked down there, the number fourteen. When it first came in, the first week it came in, I'm lookin' at it and, "Glory geez! What am I gettin' into? Just give me my job!" You know, and then I started, "Well, how's this work?" And then, pushing the buttons and, "Oh! Okay! Boy, that's easy." And then, I move on to the next one: ka-choo, ka-choo, ka-choo, "Oh, yeah! Oh, that's really easy!" You know? And then move on to the next one. The next robot setup, because there's like your loader, your roll, the reducer roll that makes the steel thinner, then a robot picks it up and bends it and puts it in the thing and puts it in the press and then the press forges it and the robot picks it up and moves it over and so each process all the way along, there's basically seven robots that do the work there. (W4a)

The idea that "[t]his is the way it's going," in this context, is itself an example of the interiorization, in the Vygotskian sense, of concrete practice reflecting class relationships. Specifically, it is an expression of the social terrain one experiences as a working person on a daily basis and comes to more or less govern the way learning life is accomplished. In other words, the pull for this worker to get involved in computer learning generally is related to the pull of the activity systems of the workplace in which involvement with computer technologies is not a choice freely made. It figures an essentially passive role. It is in this context that computer technologies seem to condition strong, specific, goal-directed behaviors in and out of the workplace. Indeed, this describes the production of a specific cultural tool shaped by one's standpoint in class relations. A form of technological common sense – that mix of fantasy, desire, and fear discussed in Chapter 3 – is develops that workers carry with them through the many spheres of their lives, which in turn acts to bind and integrate their learning, via overlapping activity systems, in the home, community, and workplace. This same worker continues. He describes how this has affected his views about child rearing. Speaking about his daughter, making a powerful statement that was by no means unusual he tells us:

I took Tammy into the plant one day at work, and I says, "See this? *It's all computers." I says, "You gotta have it."* Well, Tammy says, "Well, I don't really like doing computer stuff." And I said, "Tammy, here you are." She's ten years old, and I says, "There it is. *You've gotta know this stuff!*" (W4a)

Organized Expressions of Working-Class Standpoints in Computer Learning: The Role of Trade Unions

Focusing on the relationship between computers, learning, and the labor process is only one way to highlight class standpoints in computer learning. Another way involves taking a close look at the role of trade unions. As a social institution, unions represent a countervailing force to raw business imperatives and are established on the basis of their direct representation of the interests of waged labor. This representation is translated into many practical activities including collective bargaining, education of members, the policing of contracts and relevant laws, engagement in electoral politics, and so forth. Unions are, in effect, an organized expression of a working-class standpoint. Activities connected to such organizations reflect a class standpoint in terms of the planning and organization of practice that they implicitly or explicitly support. Thus, examining computer-mediated activity interwoven with trade union life is another way of exploring how class relations and working-class standpoints specifically are interwoven with computer learning. In this section, I briefly examine the possible effect that trade union culture has on people's learning methods and preferences.

Probably the easiest way to investigate the role of trade union culture on people's learning practice is to look at activity among unionized and nonunionized industrial workers described in the interviews. Before I do this, however, it is important to situate the comparison by drawing on large-scale survey findings from Ontario. Some important differences in learning practices of unionized versus nonunionized industrial workers can be seen by looking at a special run on the survey data provided in Livingstone, Hart, and Davie's *Eleventh OISE/UT Survey* (1997).[2] Among both groups of workers – and in stark contrast to elite and executive groups – computer learning is rated as the top personal learning interest. Perhaps more important to us here, however, is the fact that unionization among industrial workers correlates with statistically significant differences in rates of computer literacy. If computer literacy is defined as the ability to use standard computer software and communications, unionized workers have a computer literacy rate of 41% compared to

[2] Permission to access to these data was provided by D. W. Livingstone.

just 28% among nonunionized workers. Earlier I made the point that informal learning that occurs outside of formal educational institutions is particularly important for working people. In connecting with this issue when we compare unionized and nonunionized industrial workers, we again see an important difference. If informal learning is understood as total weekly hours spent on learning outside of organized courses, unionized workers reported an average of 13.6 hours per week of informal learning, whereas nonunionized workers reported only 11.6 hours per week. Another important point relates to the differences between unionized and nonunionized industrial workers in terms of access to material resources to support their learning and the overall organization of their learning. The survey indicates that unionized workers were almost twice as likely to have taken part in an adult/continuing education course. Twenty-seven percent of unionized industrial workers participated in a formalized course of some kind versus only 16% of nonunionized workers – a statistically significant difference. This is a remarkable finding given the almost century-long history of research highlighting workers' general aversion to organized courses. What's more, when continuing education was undertaken, unionized workers attended a much broader range of courses (including for-credit and noncredit school-based courses as well as trade union–based courses and company-provided training). Finally, the survey data made it clear that unionized workers were far less likely to bear the financial burden of course-based learning themselves. All of these findings suggest important ways in which the organized expression of working-class standpoints in the form of trade unionism affects the broad patterns of learning practice among workers.

However, in spite of these aggregate data, it is still difficult to be sure what practicess are being undertaken. Is it sensible to conclude that unionization has such broad effects on adult learning, or do the preceding findings simply show statistical correlation with no real connection? To understand the survey data more clearly, I decided to look at two subsets of interviews and examined unionized versus nonunionized computer learning directly. I focused on learning networks and compared the experience of workers in unionized and nonunionized factories. To help control for some obvious sources of variance, I selected workers who worked in the same economic sector (automotive) and who lived in the same city.

The unionized workplace was organized under one of Canada's most progressive trade unions, the Canadian Auto Workers (CAW). The CAW is arguably one of the country's most advanced labor unions in regard to its interest in membership learning/education broadly conceived. Indeed, one of Canada's leading labor educators, D'Arcy Martin, describes the CAW's commitment to education and training as the "most developed" of all the unions in Canada (Martin, 1998). This is demonstrated in a number of identifiable ways ranging from the union's leadership in the area of paid education leave (PEL) bargaining to the intensive development of its Family Education Centre and its partnerships with postsecondary educational institutions. At the local level, the union consistently attempts to attain greater influence over education and training initiatives at work, along with increased general support of education outside the workplace. The nonunionized plant manufactures autoparts and includes none of the broad educational provisions and no direct influence by workers over training. Beyond these differences, the operations are comparable in size, have similar levels and types of computerization on the shopfloor, and are both part of multinational corporations.

The comparative look at the workers in each plant is rooted in interviews and ethnographic work on the lives and learning networks of interviewees we heard from earlier (W16 and W4a). However, here, I try to draw out the ways that their experience of trade union culture affects the learning they do in their respective informal networks. Like so many of the interviewees, each of these men claims that his computer learning interests were closely associated with experiences at work, specifically the introduction of computer technology on the shopfloor. Clearly, changes in the workplace provide some of the most powerful compulsions to participate and learn. Second, in both cases, informal activity and unsanctioned computer use in the plants were central to starting and maintaining their learning. However, in the nonunionized plant, these forms of everyday learning represented a greater challenge because workers were more isolated from one another and experienced less freedom of movement, tighter discipline, stiffer penalties for leaving their work station, and, of course, no mechanisms to legally appeal unfair treatment by supervisors for doing so. Thus, as a basic activity theory analysis would have it, work rules and the mediating structure of the collective agreement and the union played an important role in the structure of work-based computer learning. In addition, the physical layout of the plant shaped learning by affecting the patterns of movement and surveillance among workers. In the unionized workplace, though there was significant variation, in general workers found it easier to make space to learn by engaging in informal conversation simply by hanging around each other's work areas. In Chapter 5, this unionized worker described how, in exploring the company's software with coworkers, "we got ourselves in trouble a few times [but] guys would come around and different guys would have limited experience . . . and basically that's how I got interested. . . ." In contrast, for the workers in the nonunionized workplace, learning began in greater isolation: "I'm there all by myself, there's no other person there, so I had to learn it" (W4a). In short, the unionized workplace had different rules, appeal processes, and work design, all resulting in a slightly different balance of power between management and workers and different learning experiences. Nevertheless, in both cases, informal learning networks became established and evolved into the formations described in Chapter 5.

For learners in both of these networks, sets of computer activities were absorbing and rooted primarily in everyday participation and collective problem solving with people within and beyond the workplace. However, the unionized workers, with their experience of union-run educational programs, did what factory workers usually don't do: They decided to take a local college course on computers. By contrast, paralleling the statistical findings from the provincial survey outlined earlier, the nonunion workers continued to avoid formal courses altogether. These workers commented that such courses were a "waste of time" and "wouldn't give them what they wanted," "sucked their brains out," and so forth. Of particular interest in regard to understanding the working-class learning habitus, when the unionized workers decided to attend courses, they did so as a group. Partially based on their experience of actively influencing training in the workplace and actively choosing to bargain for access to educational programs outside the workplace, these unionized workers incorporated formalized courses into their computer learning network. Attending the courses together allowed the experience gained and the information presented there to be more easily shared and, in a sense, given meaning vis-à-vis the learners' common social standpoint. As such, formal course attendance didn't govern the overall pattern of learning but instead was incorporated into the informal network.

Between these brief discussions of both survey data and comparative analysis of the two learning networks, we see the interrelations of people's economic lives and their interest in organized learning. Martin (1998) notes the importance of informal traditions of learning among the organized working class.

The lessons of collective action by workers have traditionally been learned on the job and in the streets. By contesting management rights in the workplace, by withdrawing labour power in a strike, by joining allies in political action, union activists continue to develop their knowledge, confidence and skills. Any non-formal, structured education programs remain, even today, secondary to the learning that members gain through voluntary engagement in action. (Martin, 1998:72)

The author directs our attention to the fact that for subordinate groups such as the working class, learning that begins from their own standpoint – indeed, the learning that contributes most to what Marx called the transformation of a *class in itself* to a *class for itself* – tends to take place informally, in the interstitial spaces of dominant institutions and within the stream of doing rather than in structured educational programs. In the comparative examples such as the previous one, we see that unionized factory workers seem to experience work-based computer learning differently, which in turn translates into slightly different approaches to learning in their lives more broadly. Unionized worker experience a different form of industrial relations, participate with each other differently as a result, and generate an alternative perspective on formalized learning. It is these workers who actively bargain with employers on matters relating to learning, and they often come to allocate significant resources to learning within their own unions. Through this, it seems that unionized workers more often come to see certain forms of formalized learning as potentially useful. Together with the more straightforward effect that collective bargaining produces in regard to resources for learning efforts, these cultural and material dimensions of class life help us understand the *unionization effect* on working-class computer learning.

Class Differences and Computer Learning

Working-class people's computer learning, particularly under conditions of stable workplace and community lives, tended to occur in group-oriented solidaristic networks. Their learning habitus seemed, in fact, to encourage learning in spaces where people could exercise the greatest control and creativity in participation. Learning in the home, the neighborhood, and the union hall was important in this regard, as was the learning that went on in the interstitial spaces of the workplace. We've seen basic descriptions of these activities. However, it is important to ask how these practices compare to those of elite and corporate executive groups, people who experience social processes from a fundamentally different class standpoint. I will take a brief look at some illustrations from a large-scale survey in Canada and again compare these data with

Table 6.1. *Preference for Methods of Learning Across Class Groups*

Class Group	Work Out on Own	Professional Paid Expert	Friend/Family or Coworker	Network Group-Led
Elite and executive class group	75%	10%	9%	7%
Working-class group	60%	7%	15%	18%

Note: All class comparison scores are significant: Pearson chi-square .002; likelihood ratio .001.
Source: NALL (1999). $N = 728$.

information based on interviews, this time with a small sample of people from the dominant class group.

Survey data are sometimes difficult to interpret because of the ambiguous connection between people's description of their activity and the activity itself. At the root of this difficulty is the fact that in most survey research there is no opportunity to assess the differential use of language. Still, survey research has unique powers of its own, and in looking at the NALL Canadian Survey of Informal Learning survey introduced briefly in Chapter 1, we see several important class differences in the area of learning.

Table 6.1 suggests that the methods by which working-class respondents learn are statistically different from those of elite and executive class groups (at least as they describe their own practice). We see some important differences that, particularly when combined with the interview data, help us to better situate the ways that class affects people's learning. To be clear, as I've said, the dominant ways of thinking and talking about learning, particularly as assessed within most survey methodologies, overwhelmingly privilege the individual dimensions of the process, and Table 6.1 and all subsequent tables should be read with this in mind. Nevertheless, in Table 6.1 we see some interesting things. In moving from left to right across the column headings, for example, we move from individualized and/or formalized accounts of learning practice (the first two columns) to accounts of more informal and collectively organized practice (the second two colums). The findings suggest a trend in which the class deficit grows smaller as learning becomes less formalized and more collective. The survey also indicates that whereas corporate executives are about 40 times more likely than workers to have a university degree, in the places where working-class groups exercise greatest discretionary control (i.e. in their own homes), estimates of time spent learning were almost double that of the elite and executive class group (6.1 versus 3.5 hours per week).[3]

To help answer some of the questions that findings like these raise, we can take a look at a series of interviews with a small sample of elites and corporate executives (see Appendix 1 for the characteristics of these interviewees). Although small samples like this one have less explanatory power than large samples, they can be useful in the context of research triangulation. The mini-sample itself is a rough cross section of a dominant group that, like the working-class group, is hardly uniform. Consistent with a process-based approach to social class, this sample is composed of people who are all engaged in different forms of class processes (cultural as well as economic), though from the dominant rather than the subordinate class position. For example, each person either holds a top management position in a large corporation, in most cases with significant ownership interests, and/or has been brought up in an upper-class household (where the household head had significant corporate ownership) and still identifies his life as rooted in this social group generally.

These interviewees provided descriptions of extensive learning that was not done in any classroom. Importantly, this refutes potential oversimplifications that might suggest a necessary relationship between class position and informal learning generally; that is, informal learning is obviously not the strict domain of working-class people. At the same time, however, the descriptions of informal learning provided by people in the dominant class group were hardly interstitial or fragmented, as we saw among the working-class interviewees. People from the elite and executive group entered into everyday learning with very different experiences of formal schooling (see the educational levels in Appendix 1), a very different command of resources, and very different abilities to create the mental distance necessary to conceptualize and discuss their practice as learning. But at a more basic level, these people also experienced informal learning that was positively embedded in the various spheres in which it occurred. In short, informal learning for the dominant group took place in culturally and materially supportive contexts rather than ones that tended to obscure, denigrate, or deny the practice. Along with

---

[3] Question on survey: "Thinking about all the informal learning you did in the last year that is related to all your household tasks or house work type activities, how many hours did this amount to in a typical week?" ($N = 491$).

their greater "distance from necessity" that comes with command over material resources, the ability of dominant groups to exert greater discretionary control over their environment supported the opportunity to see and engage in a mode of participation that constantly revealed their apparent learning capacity. Take, for example, the case of an owner/partner in a large corporate law firm. In an interview, he describes how he schedules time to meet with fellow partners during limousine rides.[4] Not even the need to travel from place to place hampers his learning, learning he finds directly applicable to his work and, indeed, what he sees as his life's work as a lawyer, top executive, and owner of the firm. The practice is a form of consciously organized, goal-oriented activity situated in a set of social/material relationships that are fundamentally different from the myriad unrecognized practices that go on in the back corners of the factory, in the neighborhood, and in the family rooms of working-class interviewees. For elites, these activities are immediately aligned with (rather than tangential or in opposition to) the related activity systems and overall purposes of the organizations, venues, and clubs in which they operate. They represent a scheduled and supported informal learning that rests on a foundation of control over resources rather than accommodation to an already existing distribution of resources. In terms of computer learning specifically, among interviewees in the elite and executive mini-sample, we do not see the sense of urgency to learn that we saw among the working-class interviewees. Interviewee C4 describes himself with amusement as a computer "virgin" and adds that perhaps his interest in learning to use computers may emerge when he retires and can turn his attention to better organizing his stamp collection.

Now let's take a closer look at the comments of a senior vice president of a large insurance company. When asked about the learning he does in the course of his day, his response is as follows:

R: I mean, a lot of it has to be during the day because that's when *the resources are available*, but a lot of it, we'll *rely on reports that are done [by employees]*. As I say, we've got a *very cooperative network*, so what can happen is, I may contact somebody in Tennessee who's worked on an account similar. Maybe they've looked at a smoke detector account before, or can point me in the direction of somebody that has. And

---

[4] How different this experience might be if, like industrial workers we've heard from already, this learning were forced to take place on a crowded bus or on the shopfloor, with earplugs, fumes, heat, and the threat of discipline by a supervisor if the worker was caught during working hours.

that's a case of saying, "Okay. *Send me the information you've got.*" So, obviously, there're not enough hours in the day, so a lot of it is bring it home, read it, underline what's important, develop it yourself, and then all of a sudden, you're the authority.... And, as I say, *I've got a staff here*, so everybody's got a specialty, so they share that information, and then when somethin' comes up, I'll go to that person and say, "Okay, where's the stuff on this?"

I: And, okay. Are there any other types of learning activities that have helped you? Perhaps by working with, you've already talked about networking with your staff. I'm just thinking in terms of learning with other people, perhaps friends or neighbors or?

R: *Not to any great degree.* I mean, you know, the people that I know are in business for themselves, I'm always asking them what kind of, how they handle certain things. Like, you know, if somebody is fired from a job, they can either accept the terms of departure or they can sue you, so I'm working on the account that's had a problem with employees being terminated and suing employers. So if I'm working on something like that, I might pick the brains of, you know, some people I know who are in business for themselves and ask them, "How do you terminate people if you have to do that?" I've got friends who are lawyers and I'll ask them from their side, do they get involved in this very often? You know, so, I mean, I'm always, you don't just talk about the weather and going on holidays, you know, like you tend to talk business with these people.... (C3)

A remarkably different landscape of learning is being described here, one fundamentally different from the alienation, routinization, discipline, and class antagonisms that manufacturing workers experience. There is instead a ready staff (termed a "cooperative network") to support the interviewee in his work and learning. Discretionary work-based learning is a process that is incorporated positively into the corporate organization, as well as the economic system as a whole, as surplus value flows to rather than away from his field of influence. At the most basic level, the interviewee's pattern of learning is supported by vast resources and paid assistants. Beyond the office there are communities of business people, consultants, and lawyers, each with something to add to the learning process in the course of talking, learning, and doing business. Similar to other interviewees in the mini-sample, for C3 there is both minimal expertise and minimal interest in computer technology as a persona learning goal:

I: How about your computer? Do you spend any time/

R: Don't touch it. I'm computer illiterate.

I: Are you?

R: Yeah.

I: I'm surprised.

R: ... Well we did away with telephone messages, the little pink slips, your messages and everything were put on the screen. In the States, we have a number of the major computer companies, like Microsoft is a client of ours, IBM is a client of ours, and they've won awards for programming and this sort of thing and we have a network that we built in the States.... I'm sure I'll be rolling into computer stuff and learning that sometime. (C3)

The lack of urgency about understanding computers is clear, and this form of technological common sense is unique to a dominant standpoint in relation to work and learning. In fact, the only meaningful connection to computers for C3 comes through his company's business with another company. How are we to make sense of the discrepancies between this dominant form of technological common sense and the calls by working-class interviewees for computer literacy as a mandatory "master literacy" for the 21st century? No one in the elite and executive class group sample, although obviously a limited sample of the class as a whole, described themselves as computer literate.[5] Indeed, as in the remarks of C4 quoted earlier, computer technology in relation to their own practice took on a trivial character, with none of the strong emotional orientations we saw among working-class learners.

Returning to the general view that people had of themselves as learners, among working-class interviewees the descriptions suggested unused potential, disconnection from schooling, and in some cases strongly negative feelings toward institutionalized learning. In contrast, elite and executive interviewees not only experienced success in school (see the column fifth of Appendix 1) but went on to suggest that they were in fact above the need for formal schooling. In each case these interviewees described realized potential (e.g. "I've achieved a level [of success] where I think I have maximized my talents" [C5]) in a field of vast, perhaps even limitless, opportunity for learning and reward. As with the other interviewees quoted earlier, C5's informal learning flows in an unbroken web of connections to employees and typically spreads to golf courses, tennis courts and restaurants. Each sphere of activity is woven into a well-articulated network of connections with other corporate lawyers and business leaders.

---

[5] Noting that the mini-sample did not include representatives of all types of the elite and executive groups.

I: So you find in your life you're constantly networking with folks, whether it be over your meals or/

R: Playing golf.

I: Playing golf, playing tennis.

R: Yeah. I think an integral part of a lawyer's life is constantly networking, calling people.

I: And, I guess/

R: Discussing different things, initiating things, helping the clients discover opportunities. . . . Next Wednesday, I'm having lunch with the owner of a good-size printing company, and we're meeting to discuss possible acquisitions to build up his business, looking for smaller companies where perhaps the owner is ready to retire. That's frequently the sort of thing I do. And it may or may not result in further activity. (C5)

These processes are comparable to the activities of working-class respondents to the extent that important learning practices occur outside of a formalized classroom setting. There is also considerable overlap of activity systems, though importantly, this overlap represents a coordinated rather than a fragmented and contested terrain of activity systems. Interviewees in the executive/elite mini-sample showed a very different level of discretionary learning throughout their spheres of activity that translates, vis-à-vis the dialectic of position/dis-position, into a different learning habitus. Their way of talking about learning is characterized by a certain distance from practice that allows not only its ready identification, but also its highly positive valuation as well as its conscious development. These people do not sneak away from their duties in order to learn in the workplace, nor do they find themselves seeking out unsanctioned activity out of boredom, routinization, alienation, or idiot-proof workplace technologies. The informal learning of elites and executives cannot be characterized as interstitial; rather, it reflects integration within the legitimated, even celebrated, strategies of business leadership. Learning takes place as a strategic part of the legitimated participation in business life. There is little need for the solidaristic, group-oriented practices we saw among working-class interviewees in Chapter 5 when dependable networks can be purchased directly (vis-à-vis paid staff).

Summary

The property-owning class and the class of the proletariat represent the same human self-alienation. But the former feels at home in this self-alienation and feels itself confirmed by it; it recognizes alienation as its own instrument and in it possesses the semblance of a human existence. The latter feels itself destroyed by this alienation and sees in it its own impotence and the reality of a inhuman existence. (Marx, *Capital*, Vol. 3, 1867–1868/1990:324)

As this quote suggests, at the most basic level, alienation is a function of capitalist life for all concerned (workers as well as elites). At the same time, however, the dynamic ensures that elite and executive groups feel at home within this alienation, in many ways culturally and materially strengthened in the process as their efforts ultimately return to their own control. In other words, these practices "necessarily appears as an activity (albeit this activity is objectively an illusion), in which effects emanate from himself [*sic*]" (Lukács, 1971:166). The working class, on the other hand, generally cannot sustain this illusion. Their learning emerges from and, despite its character as solidaristic and collective is frequently destined for reinsertion and incorporation into, the system that works against them, reproducing their subordination. In this chapter I used several separate but related analyses to provide a sustained exploration of class standpoints surrounding practices associated with computers and learning.

I began with a discussion of the importance of several specific pieces of work (Lukács, Marxist-feminists standpoint theory principally) in order to provide some theoretical depth to the empirical analyses that began with examples of how computer-mediated practices were affected by activity related to the industrial workplace. The concrete experience of working people was the starting point for further understanding the technological common sense discussed in Chapter 3, but it also offered a critique of this common sense from a working-class standpoint. Also discussed in this section was the relationship of the basic technical design of work and the division of labor under capitalism to the routinization and alienation of computer-mediated practice. In turn, this was seen as an important feature shaping the range of practices associated with working-class computer learning in and around the workplace. One worker's message to his young daughter was an explicit reminder of the power of these experiences to organize emotions and consciousness as well as activity. The second section of the chapter explored the role of trade unionism in shaping learning practice. Trade unionism was understood as an organized expression of working-class standpoints. The interests, organizational needs, and participatory structure of the trade unions mediated what, why, and, more important, how people learn to use computers. I showed how participation in trade unions affects the way people organize their computer learning more broadly. Together with the use of some survey materials, illustrations from the interview data showed how unions help to expand the scope and foci of informal learning networks. One of the most interesting findings related to an alteration of the basic class dynamic of participation in formal education. The cultural and material dimensions of the "unionization effect" seemed to encourage a form of collective participation in formalized courses. In the final section of the chapter, I turned my attention to class difference through a brief but informative comparative analysis of a mini-sample of elite and corporate executive learners. This group talked about a variety of learning processes but generally downplayed the importance of computer literacy skills in their own lives. The important difference, however, was the relationship of their learning to discretionary control of material resources and the general relationship of these practices to the political-economic context in which their learning took place.

7 Oral Culture, Computer Learning, and Social Class

In approaching learning as a socially constituted participatory form of practice, we should reserve, as Vygotsky originally did, a special place for the role of sign-mediated activity. Language, specifically oral communication, is an important means of producing shared understanding and the possibility for transmission and innovation in ordinary, everyday situations (Middleton, 1996). The focus of this chapter is the role of oral communication and, slightly more broadly than this, oral culture in the production of working-class computer learning practice. I will explore how talk grounds group membership and specific *identities-in-practice* (Holland et al. 1998), and how it offers an important means by which people establish meaningful interaction, shift their patterns of participation with one another, and hence learn. Oral artifacts are seen as knowledge storage and transmission tools. I explain how technical languages associated with computer use are partially appropriated by working-class learners who use what Jean Lave has called *gap-closing* procedures. In each case, I examine ways in which these dimensions of oral communication bear traces of their origins in a variety of class processes. In order to do this, however, I want to provide a brief introduction to a work by Julian Orr that serves as a conceptual starting point for the discussion.

One of the most provocative studies on the relationship between oral culture, learning, and technology that I've encountered is Orr's *Talking about Machines: An Ethnography of a Modern Job* (1996). Developing the tradition of situated learning, Orr analyzes the collective, mostly informal, constitution of working knowledge in occupation-based, technologically mediated activity, claiming that this knowledge is a collectively produced and diffuse resource that depends on the operation of oral traditions within a specific cultural group. The claim of particular relevance here is that workers produce oral *texts* for themselves that, in turn, serve to organize, produce, and transform practice largely outside of the formal organizational structures and training programs of paid work. Orr analyzes the working and learning lives of photocopy repair people through participation in key institutional spaces such as repair school, field visits, and formal meetings. Throughout the study, close attention is paid to the less formal interactions of downtime in repair people's lives including lunchhours, coffee breaks and so forth. As I did in Chapter 4, Orr also spends some time reflecting on the work of Lucy Suchman and draws on her argument that plans and other cognitive features of human behavior are rooted in social practice that is accomplished moment by moment. Although it's not central to the analysis, Orr also deals with the conflictual relations of the workplace, drawing on the argument made by Kusterer in his classic study of know-how on the job (1978). For Orr, the generation of resistance to things like management-led workplace reorganization is an important component of the oral culture. Orr details how photocopier repair work must respond to characteristics of the organization of the labor process such as isolation (i.e., repair people typically go on site to do repairs alone) and discusses how narratives, stories, sayings, and oral culture maintain a community within and sometimes despite the organizational structures. In relations to my interests, the limitations of the study concern the representation of the factors that structure participation among these workers. Specifically, the full range of effects that political-economic limits and pressures impose, including those related to the life histories of the repair people, are not fully explored.

Orr's work, nevertheless, is one of the most engaged and engaging looks at workers' learning practice at the level of interaction and as such can be instructive. The analysis problematizes conventional accounts of learning and knowledge production to construct a detailed empirical analysis that does not separate learning from the ongoing production of frames of activity. Orr's analysis builds on the notions of *talking within* and *talking about* practices as distinct but essential features of the learning process (e.g., Lave and Wenger, 1991). Briefly, talking within includes operations such as the exchange of information necessary for the progress of a strip of interaction. Talking about, on the other hand, includes sign-mediated activities such as storytelling, the production of *community lore*, and so on, which seem to connect with and partially define broader and more durable dimensions of activity. Lave and Wenger (1991) describe these two types of verbal interaction as follows:

Inside the shared practice, both forms of talk fulfil specific functions: engaging, focussing, and shifting attention, bring about co-ordination, etc., on the one hand; and supporting communal forms of memory and reflection, as well as signalling membership on the other. (1991:109)

Working from this perspective, we might say that talking within is part of the ongoing machinery of coordinated practice, whereas talking about relates to the broader social context including the forms of rules, community involvement, and the divisions of labor that give it meaning vis-à-vis particular social standpoints. In general, analysis of these forms of talk provides a window into the interactive, creative, and contingent as well as the cultural historical nature of learning.

In this chapter, I discuss how these issues relate to the oral communication and oral culture of working-class learning. I analyze talking within, talking about, and gap-closing procedures along with several specific oral artifacts or devices. As in other chapters, I demonstrate how class standpoints are involved. My interest is not simply to demonstrate the applicability of these concepts but also to show the relationship of oral culture to class processes in capitalist society. Thus, the backdrop to the discussion deals with broader dynamics, specifically the relationship of oral culture to written culture, to working-class and trade union culture, and to the possibility of a proletarian public sphere.

Oral Culture and Social Class

To better understand how social class and oral communication are related, we need to situate practice in its historical and political-economic contexts. A relevant starting point is the important relationship of oral culture to written literacy. It is this relationship that, in particular, helps to define the historical role of oral culture and its relationship to class processes. There is a range of works that can aid us in this regard. Focusing on the early development of capitalism, for example, Ong (1982) notes the connection between the emergence of clock time and the expansion of written culture as a definitive element of the period. Lash and Urry (1994) outline the close connection between the emergence of dominant forms of 19th-century culture and the emerging dominance of written literacy in Western Europe. These authors, like others, document the enormous growth in the publication of inexpensive books and the number of daily newspapers (doubling every 15 years or so in this period), the general growth of time-keeping records, and the widespread documentation of citizens (registration of births, deaths, marriages, travel, and later the use of the passport) that seemed to go hand in hand with the development of modern society and capitalism specifically. These analyses provide important evidence of the growth of what has been called the *scriptural* society (e.g., Fiske, 1993), and it is the emergence and eventual dominance of this society that provides the basic context for understanding the relationship between oral culture, capitalism, and class processes.

At the same time however, it would be a mistake to overestimate the influence of the written text on everyday life. In relation to culturally and materially stable working-class life, as E. P. Thompson (1963) demonstrated in the context of 18th- and 19th-century England, oral culture coexisted, as it does today, with written culture through the persistence of cultural practices such as song, storytelling as well as the cooperative impulses of those within subordinate groups such as the working class who, literate enough, served as a resource for other members of the community. Describing working-class community life in West Riding, for example, Thompson states that although most working people were not literate as such, as community members they could listen to the broadsheets read aloud at the blacksmith's, the barber's, and public houses. Beyond this, as Thompson indicates, there were always street singers and everyday discussion that served to mediate the class distribution of reading skill. Indeed, despite the higher levels of literacy within the working class in countries like Canada today, more contemporary versions of the same practices are common. These practices were, in fact, important features of computer learning among the people in this research. Most generally, those who preferred and had the ability to use written texts served as a resource for those who preferred practical exploration, and vice versa.

Further useful entry points to a discussion of the relationship between oral culture and social class are the works of writers such as Negt and Kluge (1993). Influenced by the work of the Frankfurt school in *Public Sphere and Experience: Toward an Analysis of the Bourgeois and Proletarian Public Sphere*, these authors link the production of experience with the need for a public sphere that makes proletarian experience comprehensible. They go on to implicate oral and written communication in the development of the a coherent proletarian standpoint in the 20th century. Specifically, Negt and Kluge suggest that "[g]enuine experience is torn into two parts that are, in class terms, opposed to one another" (p. 18). This tearing apart of experience, in fact, properly describes the phenomena explored in the previous chapter, where people's talk displayed a clear break between dominant discourses of learning and technology and their own concrete experiences. Thinking, Negt and Kluge emphasize, is social. It is a "discussion carried out not only in the imagination, but on a social scale" (p. 23). In sum, they argue that a public sphere rooted in stable forms of class community that at the same time express and develop from a working-class standpoint is a fundamental resource for making the fragmentary character of class life coherent for members.

In the field of cultural studies writers such as Fiske (1993) discuss the power relationships that infuse oral culture. According to Fiske, people operating from subordinate standpoints can and do exercise a type of countervailing control unique to oral expression, though he is quick to indicate that linguistic practice in itself does not guarantee an open opportunity from the standpoint of subordinate groups.

[P]articular expressions evade the power of language to "speak" its subjects and are instances of people's ability to speak for and of themselves. It is tempting to suggest that the most materially deprived social formations, who materially possess fewest things accord proportionately greater significance to linguistic practice and creativity, for language is always available to everyone. [However] it is not, of course, equally available.... The language that a society develops is always inscribed with the interests of that society's power-bloc.... [D]ominant culture is scriptural, for scripture is where the power to represent is most effective, and popular culture is oral, for orality is the means by which subordinate histories and identities are maintained and circulated. Orality participates in ways of knowing that are different from those of literacy. (Fiske, 1993:211–212)

The relationship between oral and written culture is therefore a nexus: a key intersection for understanding the reproduction of social class as well as other major social divisions.

As I stated earlier, while helping to distribute significant material support, trade unions offer an organized expression of working-class standpoints. In Negt and Kluge's terms, the labor movement offers a public sphere that contributes to participants' collective understanding of the class dimensions of their own lives. Investigating oral culture in the context of the labor movement, then, suggests yet another important way of situating the relationship between oral culture and social class. Writing on life in the labor movement in Canada, for example, Martin (1995) outlines practice that relates union culture to oral culture. As a trade union educator, Martin presents one anecdote that helps us reflect on the importance of gaining acceptance in the types of networks that I've described as informal, group-oriented, and solidaristic. Within the context of delivering trade union training at one workplace, Martin talks about his relationship with a local union member named Jim:

Jim was respected among his fellow workers and he had afterwards spoken positively about me and the union on the floor of the plant. In the informal logic of that local union, my word was now good. I was inside the network of trust. This meant I had room to be fully myself and that I could call for a certain openness among the people I dealt with. Mistakes could be forgiven, misunderstandings straightened out. . . . (1995:36)

He goes on to outline the traditional relationship between written and oral culture in trade unions.

Part of the reason that the wider public knows so little about unions is that so little of the internal wisdom is written down. . . . On paper, union input tends to be precise and defensive; in verbal communications, off the record, unionists are more eloquent and spontaneous. (1995:39–40)

As Martin indicates, oral culture in the context of subordinate groups such as the working class offers a means to judge authenticity and to communicate openly. Notions of membership and the processes through which membership are produced become defining features of both the group and the processes of communication, learning, and knowledge production in that group. It is through controls such as these that subordinate groups have the potential to exert some control over their own discourse and social practices. In general, we could say that oral communication is *repeatable*, whereas textual communication is *retrievable* (Feenberg, 1989). In other words, whereas written texts are retrievable forms of discourse that can be accessed individually, oral communication is, text "stored" in human memory and as such must be accessed through repetition and more often than not performance, social events, and ritual. The significance is that under the latter, control is regulated socially, emphasizing the importance of membership through participation in public functions mediated by community rules and roles. Textual communication, on the other hand, is far more open to individual regulation, beyond the forms of collective regulation available to subordinate groups.

  This brief review merely scratches the surface of the deep relationships between social class and oral culture. However, if we reflect on the range of approaches to oral culture and the historical and political-economic dimensions of practice, it should become clear that analysis of talk is an important window into the way major divisions within society are produced and reproduced. As I explore the everyday features of talk in computer learning and class life, the elements of this subsection will, I hope, provide a meaningful backdrop.

Oral Culture and Working-Class Computer Learning

In one encounter with the community of photocopier repair people, Orr (1996) outlines the interaction within repair teams and identifies the importance of understanding the role of talk in the situated production of knowledge. Following is a discussion of the experience of a particular repair person. It points to the difficulties experienced in exchanging and developing knowledge when participants lack an ongoing foundation of shared daily experiences that come from engagement with one another in the course of work. When workers are limited to contact with fellow repair people in meetings and classrooms, for example, learning is seen as a difficult if not an impossible task.

> It is particularly striking that he feels the lack of comparable experience makes it difficult for the other teams to understand what his team has learned, so they cannot take advantage of his team's experience. Implicit in this are the technicians' assumptions that their skills are not learned in school but from each other, and that the meaning of their talk about their skills is not obvious outside the context in which they were developed. (Orr, 1996:60)

Orr's point is that the situation is not problematic from the standpoint of the repair person because of lack information. Rather, what's missing is the opportunity to participate with other repair people on an ongoing basis. This participation with others sharing the same occupational standpoint, is definitive of the learning process. Orr develops the concepts of narrative types (e.g., *celebration of identity and community, consultation among members, problem diagnoses, war stories*, etc.) that elaborate on the basic talking about and talking within concepts. He also develops the notion of *discourse groups* (e.g., *social* versus *experiential and existential*) as a means of sorting out the different elements of activity. Together these concepts explain the basic knowledge storage and transmission mechanisms, and they are useful for analyzing the talk necessary for learning among the computer learners in this research as well.

The computer learning practices that working-class interviewees described were also shaped by the arrangement of their opportunities to participate with one another, though this participation involved practice across many different spheres of activity. Access to talk with others experiencing the same concerns, interests, and perspectives was crucial. In the following interview, the comments of a chemical worker, for example, were typical of those I recorded. This man works on the night shift, where, he says, supervision is more relaxed and coworkers find it easier to get together and talk. These basic freedoms were essential to the learning process, and being on the night shift is in fact a learning strategy, though it is not identified by the learner as such. He outlines the community of computer learning practice closely associated with but not limited to the workplace. His interest in computers emerges from both his home life, where he is concerned about his son's education, his future schooling success, and his future ability to compete in the job market, and his own life, where he is concerned about his future job prospects. In multiple ways, the basic class conditions of needing to sell one's labor power to survive provide an overall motive for the system of activity he describes. For him, the most important computer learning comes through a group of coworkers who meet on breaks.

R: [my son] takes computers in school so that's why I feel I gotta get one at home. . . .

I: Do you do any talking to anybody about it?

R: Oh yeah, *that's the natural conversation every night in the smoke shack* [a storage building in the back of the shipping yard where workers take their breaks]. Because so many guys have gotten them and every night, *they just talk about computers, talk about computers*. I pretty well got everything listed that I want in a computer. I'm still not up on all my *terminology* and everything, but my biggest thing about is it's good for my little boy. He'll have his games on it but, you know the unfortunate thing about it at work is all they do talk about it are the games.

I: These guys sound like they're pretty into it, they know all the ins and outs.

R: Surprisingly, yeah. We got one guy there man, you look at him and you would never say he was good at computers but he's probably one of the best guys there. He's got this long hair. He drives a Harley. It's great!

I: So how do they learn this stuff? They don't seem to go to school for it?

R: I don't know. We got one guy there, started the same time as me at the plant and he's really crack on the computer. But far as I know, *no training, just picking up from each other* type of thing you know. Lending out and all this stuff. I had an older computer here and a couple of weeks ago I brought it over to my buddy from work to see if we could get some stuff into it, so far not much.

I: But for you, do you think you might be able to pick up some skills in case you need to change jobs?

R: Definitely. (W50)

We get a view of the world of learning that many factory workers depend upon most, as well as the broader class context in which this learning makes sense. From this description, we can begin to figure out the routines, discussed in depth in the following chapters, through which this man and other workers make time for their computer learning. His account reveals the social organization of the learning, shaped by the need to earn a wage and the specific contours of workplace rules and conventions (i.e., formal and informal break times). As in the account Orr provides, the structure of participation is the structure of learning and knowledge production. At the same time, however, the computer learning I investigated is not related to the workplace in the same way as it is in photocopier repair work.[1] Computer learning is largely incidental to though integrated with the labor process. Because the length of break times and the informal achievement of discretionary time for coworkers to talk in the plant are formally and informally contested, learning can be seen as shaped by the conflicting interests of labor and capital. In addition to the contested regulation of how much time workers can spend together, the industrial workplace is noisy and hot, full of grime and fumes, and physically dangerous for workers. These too are features of a major component of the working-class learning process.

Perhaps more important for this chapter, however, is this worker's description of activity at the physical center of the workplace-based community of practice, the smoke shack. It is the primary site for free exchange of ideas and an important location of learning in working-class life, and through excerpts like the preceding one, we can get a sense of how the process works. Workers can sit on the sidelines of conversation (as beginners) and listen in, perhaps make a connection with a coworker to have a computer repaired, as this fellow is doing, pick up information on the latest technology, and gain exposure to basic technical language. W50's description goes on to show how coworkers solve ongoing

---

[1] The role of computers in the lives of clerical workers is different again. Most clerical workers, unlike the manufacturing workers (male and female), had very little interest in pursuing computer learning for its own sake. If there is a gendered structure to a technological perspective, as, for example, Hacker (1990) and Cockburn and Ormrod (1993) suggest (and there seems to be though it is not highlighted in this research), it appears to be mediated by occupation.

technical problems, share resources, and exchange stories about these activities. Drawing on Orr's terms, we can reference several of the different narrative types through careful consideration of the excerpt:

1. *Expressions of identities and community*, for example, the discussion of the "Harley" man[2] and the depiction of the "surprising" liveliness of the smoke shack as a positive expression of an active working-class culture; indeed, the interviewee seemed to find delight ("It's great!") in the inversion of class-based stereotypes in this regard.
2. *Consultation among members and problem diagnoses*, for example, sharing information on hardware software, upgrading of the computer, and so on.
3. *War stories*, the basis of many stories about computers, the use of games within and outside of work, and the sharing of stories about good and bad home computer purchases.

This analysis also highlights the relevance of the distinction between talking within and talking about practice. It's of particular significance that no computers are physically involved in the interaction despite the fact that a great deal of computer learning is obviously going on. This is an important dimension of computer learning that makes identification of the digital divide difficult for current survey-based computer access/use research: Some of the most significant and lengthy sessions of computer learning take place without a computer. An interviewee like W50, for example, might have difficulty determining how much time he has spent learning computers, because this learning is so diffuse and doesn't always involve an actual machine. In this research, talking about computers (as opposed to reading a magazine, watching television, listening to the radio, etc.) was the most important means of learning. Indeed, talking about computers, based purely on the time people spend, rivaled actual computer use as a feature of computer learning broadly conceived.

Solving the Problem of Technical Languages

Orr's work (1996) demonstrates that narratives form an important element of the knowledge production process amongst photocopier

---

[2] The "Harley" man refers to the coworker with long hair who drives a Harley Davidson motorcyle. For those unfamiliar with the cultural reference, it points toward involvement, whether actual or not, in "biker" culture defined by rejection of mainstream society and economic life, with its origins in working-class disillusionment in North America following the Second World War.

repair people, and the preceding section extended the basic analysis to the practices of computer learning among manufacturing workers. Orr shows how the preservation of knowledge among the photocopy repair people rests on the way they share stories of "new fixes" or "strange new problems." However, for computer learners, language, specifically the technical language of computer hardware and software, can be important for participation. This presented a problem for most working-class learners because the majority can't, won't, or don't access courses and other materials where these languages could be directly deciphered. Developing a shared understanding of technical language is a key element of the problem-solving process for these people. As a general introduction to the dilemma, we can examine a brief excerpt from a discussion with an autoworker. Here he outlines, even in his attempt to describe the problem to me, the difficulty of coming to grips with a new language in order to continue to engage in active group learning process.

R: I knew I was on the right track, but, you see, I didn't know what the system actually used to retrieve the mail, so that's where I was making my mistake. *I just didn't know the words that they used.* And the guys they would tell me, "Yeah, they're keeping it simple. Just put 'mail.' "

I: So it's almost learning a little language, eh?

R: Well, basically. Yeah, you have to know what the, like if I would have actually either e-mailed somebody and told him, "What's your, you know, *whatever the thing is called?*" He could have told me right off the bat, but I was trying without asking him, plus *I didn't know what to say.* And I did try it without asking him. And I couldn't get it and I was trying this and trying. . . . We figured it out before because, again, he's the one that told me about it. And that's how we figured it out, we're playing like that. So, actually, I sent a message to myself to see if it worked.

I: Oh, yeah. Sure. So to see if it comes back.

R: Yeah, you see. So that's one thing that we figured out. There's still a lot of things I haven't figured out, because, you know, *no manuals or nothing,* so it's kind of hard. (W5)

Throughout the excerpt we see allusions to the collective character of the learning process, such as "that's how *we* figured it out, *we're* playing like that," but specific forms of language proved to be a barrier, which slowed the learning process (and the description of the learning process) because a workable terminology for the problems experienced was not available.

A common technique for collectively solving the problems of technical language involved the conversion of a technical problem into one more easily understood through the use of analogy or metaphor. These were bridging devices that aided what Lave (1988) has referred to as gap-closing procedures. Lave's discussion of how grocery shoppers use a gap-closing procedure to transform arithmetic problems into ones that can be more easily solved parallels the practices interviewees used in this research. People indicated that such procedures were required to continue to talk about issues even though only one participant (sometimes neither) had functional command over the necessary technical language. These gap-closing procedures allowed participants to continue learning despite the language barriers to interaction. One example of this can be seen in the way that interviewees discussed aspects of the computer system by drawing on descriptions of how different software programs ran on different machines. They used the performance of software (immediately available to one's senses in terms of timing, detail of graphics, movement, colors, sound, etc.) on particular computers as an important means of discussing more abstract technical issues of processor speed, frequencies, RAM, monitor type, video cards, and so on.

> For me to describe it to you, well, okay, uhhhh. Do you know "Links Golf Course" [a computer game]? For me to run it on my computer takes a while to draw the picture. Jack's runs Faster. These computers are perfectly graphic, eh? They're much faster and better. So that's a better video card than I had. (W4a)

The example describes a gap-closing procedure. Understanding the meaning of a video card is accomplished with reference to the performance of a computer game. This comparative process occurred among group members who shared software often and continually engaged with one another to talk about computers in places like the smoke shack. Without the help of formal training, technical problems were converted into a form available directly to the senses and/or available to existing shared understandings within the group.

Crashes, Blueprints, and Rip-Offs: Connecting Oral Artifacts and Social Class in Computer Learning

Lave and Wenger draw on research on the collaborative knowledge production process in midwifery to discuss the relationship between oral culture and learning. They draw attention to the functions of oral artifacts such as stories as an essential mediating tool.

What happens is that as difficulties of one kind or another develop, stories of similar cases are offered up by the attendants [at the birthing], all of whom, it should be remembered, are experts, having themselves given birth. In the ways in which these stories are treated, elaborated, ignored, taken up, characterized as typical and so on, the collaborative work of deciding on the present case is done.... These stories, then, are packages of situated knowledge.... To acquire a store of appropriate stories and, even more importantly, to know what are appropriate occasions for telling them, is then part of what it means to become a midwife. (Lave and Wenger, 1991:108)

Similarly, in Orr's work the notion of a war story and the creation of a coherent description of a troubled photocopier are important elements of the collectively produced discourse of practice. Such stories provide the means through which knowledge can be seen as a socially stored and distributed resource. These oral artifacts are, in Orr's words, "the medium through which [worker/learners] preserve their hard-won knowledge" (p. 148). Storytelling is a means of amusement; however, it is also the primary means by which the technicians in Orr's account organize membership in learning networks and, more fundamentally, construct positive identities-in-practice through which to enter into activity. The stories that are told, and the forms of argumentation that surround them, define and redefine the values and norms of the group and play an important role in the distribution of attention, recognition, and access to particular social roles as well as material resources.

Each episode of machine repair is built on shared knowledge of earlier successes and failures, and the stories that the technicians tell circulate that knowledge. The stories also celebrate the technicians' mastery of the complex and sometimes obscure interaction between technicians, customers, and machines, while acknowledging the contingent and temporary nature of their success. (Orr, 1996:2)

Oral culture and specific oral artifacts make up the machinery through which individual forms of participation and overall patterns of participation in activity shift. However, stories can play a broader role beyond the generation, storage, and transmission of knowledge. They can generate, store, and transmit a broader tacit understanding of one's standpoint in complex social and political-economic processes as well. Several stories that interviewees shared with me could be seen to work this way. They were a means of learning about computers and generating coherence and meaning about working-class life.

To introduce the way that oral artifacts can make visible and in turn help to produce class life, let's take a look at a story told by an autoworker. It is a story that, as it happens, I encountered in the course of several different interviews. It seems to express a particular form of shared, tacit understanding of a workplace reorganization scheme that swept across North American manufacturing in the 1990s called *lean production*.[3] In this managerial strategy, work is intensified in a coordinated, ever-increasing process of incremental adjustment. Indeed, as countless workers have discovered, this approach can end up jeopardizing the very companies it is supposed to help by removing important human infrastructure. In any case, in the course of interviews, several people relayed a similar story in response to my questions about the role of computers in the workplace. My own interpretation of the meaning of the story is that it attempts to explain the limits of production (under capitalism), as well as the fact that those who are in control do not know what is really going on and that workers who are employed are overworked while others remain unemployed.

> The only way I can tell you to honestly understand that whole concept [of how work is changing is to look back] on Saturday mornings there used to be this fucking cartoon, and it was about a shoe factory, and the cobbler was cobbling away but it was the mice who would actually come in and make the fucking shoes, and then they go through the whole thing. It's a cartoon you must have seen, but it's saying exactly what is happening today, and so the little cobbler has to move out of his little corner store, no bigger than a barber shop, and he's got the big building and the car and everybody's making money, but sooner or later that all has to crash. . . . (W17a)

The story goes on at length. It presents information about the contradictory relationships, perspectives, and feelings that describe the production process from a working-class standpoint. As a device, the story expresses a form of identity within a context that the worker finds difficult to describe. A chemical worker (W48a) remarking on the same cartoon, however, used it in a slightly different way, to dispute management's wish to view workers and management as a team. Just as any tool can be used in a variety of ways while retaining its basic properties, this oral artifact was used to respond to a localized context while expressing participation in a contradictory class process.

---

[3] See Moody (1997) for a recent discussion of this process from the standpoint of workers.

Turning to examples of computer learning specifically, another basic oral device, related to but distinct from storytelling, was the use of analogy. One that was popular among interviewees in several different locations was the comparison of computer programming language and computer architecture to the blueprints and physical layout of a house. In this context, analogy served, once again, as a gap-closing procedure, but one used to establish a shared account of the problem at hand. Analogies such as the blueprint drew on shared understanding in one domain and transferred it to another domain that may not be shared. I asked the following interviewee, for example, how he first learned about computer programming language, which seems too difficult to understand without taking a course or at least using a manual. He proceeded to tell me how he learned.

R: The way I was taught was: There's a computer; now you turn it on. That's like just coming in your back door of your house and you turn the key to come in your back door. First of all, you have to open it. Alright, so you turn it on. Alright. Now the doors open and you're there. There's the room, alright? Now if you want to proceed into that room, okay, well, you want to go in the kitchen – that's through your BIOS into your operating system, okay? So you want to go into your operating system, say. Then from there you want to go into the bathroom, but the bathroom is, say, a spreadsheet like Quicken. For an example, okay? So the door's locked. You can't get in there, so you gotta know the key to Quicken. Okay? And then you come back out, you have to close the door behind you and exit that to go to the dining room, to the living room, to the bedroom. Okay? Then to come downstairs to the basement, to go to the laundry room, to whatever. Like that's the way I was taught. Like you said, "Now, hey, but you gotta know the key to get in."

I: You solve the problems as they come up that way?

R: Yeah. But now the key is no good, so you have to make a new key, right? Or something like that. And it just keep adding to it, alright? And then you've moved into a new neighborhood. It's just a road map and that. That's how Rick told me, "Okay. That's the easiest terminology.". . . That's how I learn. (W4a)

We see an analogy that allows use of the technology despite the existence of technical language that may not be shared among participants in the learning network. Like stories, these analogies are expandable (e.g., "then you've moved into a new neighborhood"). As the preceding interviewee remarked, "you just keep adding to it," but the analogies can also be tailored to generate specific accounts of various problems at hand.

Sustained scholarship on the use of analogy within "naturalistic" forms of knowledge production dates at least to the 1970s (e.g., Sternberg, 1977; Ortony, 1979). Supported by an eclectic mix of research from cognitive psychology, anthropology, and linguistics as well as the study of artificial intelligence, the research supported the idea that such devices allow the transfer of knowledge from one domain to another because key relations of interest remain the same in the two domains (see Gentner and Stevens, 1983). The use of analogies in this way was common among interviewees. However, although recognition of the use of analogies within learning is not a particularly startling finding, the contextualization of analogy use as a particularly vital form of working-class practice does have a certain novelty. Along these lines, I note that the use of analogy emerges as a response to the distribution of a specific form of knowledge, namely, an exclusive technical language of computer programming. The working-class learning habitus, specifically the general resistance to formalized learning, makes this knowledge form scarce among working-class learners. Thus, the use of rough and ready analogies in informal learning relationships comes to be more than just a clever tool of communication. Rather, it and other oral devices become a significant resource for these learners. Analogy use, seen in this way, therefore has a specific social significance with relatively clear class dimensions.

In terms of other oral devices, in this research I found it striking that across different interviewees, different neighborhoods, and different workplaces, very similar stories emerged. Again as before, the form of the story was flexible. One story that had particular currency involved a computer that had crashed. As Orr and others have noted, the function and meaning of a particular oral device are found at least as much in the context of the telling, that is, its place in a specific exchange, as in the specific information it imparts. When I asked this autoworker what kind of computer learning he was engaged in and how he preferred to learn, like other interviewees he quickly launched into a story of battling a crash to explain his practice.

R: [T]his week, or I'd say the last month, I loaded my computer up so much, I kept on putting software in, software in, software in and I ran into a problem. It was running so slow because there was so much in there but I felt I could fix it. I installed some new software and the system got slower, then I installed the new version of Windows and then the system crashed. Actually, when you phoned, I had formatted my hard drive and I've now just installed the basics again and I'm right back to the beginning.

I: Did you lose some things?

R: I lost everything. Basically, I've got a hard drive that had no room. To get Windows in, I had to dump a whole bunch of stuff. Actually, I was just working on it. All I have in there is just Windows, Microsoft Works, Quicken.

I: So what are your plans?

R: Well I'm basically going to run on CD ROM now I think, like for the kids' games. Instead of loading them all into the computer on the hard drive I'm going to switch to just a CD ROM as a new method, keep them all stored on CD ROM. I actually have two CDs and they total about 40 games on the two CDs. Different ones, educational or little fun games you know, where you can shoot and blast everyone. Other than that I'm not going to bother loading this stuff on anymore. Because I made up a [new] boot system and they would go games and it would launch itself and it would boot itself up and it would come up with all the games and you would just pick from the games so, it ran good for a bit, but like I said, I almost crashed the system. (W16)

This story is designed to share specific technical information, but it serves a variety of other purposes as well. For example, it plays a role in establishing membership in the sense that pushing relatively inexpensive computers beyond their capabilities (causing a crash) and then having to fix the computer oneself signals a certain level of access to financial resources. Of course, these forms of experimentation are also important because, connected to the learning habitus, they must stand in place of access to formal courses and/or written sources. Finally, the story is one of the central means of talking about learning per se, which, again, is highly affected by one's ability to generate mental distance from one's practice. In interviews with another participant in W16's learning network, the story is repeated with yet another purpose in mind: to demonstrate an intrinsic enjoyment of problem-solving tasks. The following interviewee, for example, refers to W16's crash explicitly. I asked him if he enjoyed computers and why, and this was his explanation.

R: Oh, yeah. I enjoy it. I really enjoy it now. At the beginning I was very terrified of computers. But, you know, after a while you get more comfortable with it. That's how you learn. Talking with the guys, like I say. I talked a lot to Steve about it. Did you hear Steve crashed his machine.

I: Recently?...

R: Oh yeah, it was a real mess.... (W5)

The description of the crash that followed was used to explain this interviewee's fascination with computers. Drawing on Orr's terminology, the crash story is an example of the entire range of narrative types dealing with issues of identity, diagnosis of a problem, and the sharing of information. As an oral artifact it circulates through the learning network, to be used as a means of engaging attention, presenting information, and meeting a variety of other needs.

The preceding examples link the use of oral devices with particular applications that are in one way or another shaped by the experience of class life. However, an example that shows how class standpoints can also be embedded in an oral devices itself is the following war story, which deals with purchasing a home computer. I call it the *rip-off*, and it emerges from the intersection of working-class technological common sense, class learning habitus, the anxieties of keeping/getting a job, and limited financial resources. Although middle-class professionals may loosely identify with these feelings, we should remember that the feelings of interviewees in regard to buying a home computer, as I discussed in Chapter 3, are often heightened because of the symbolic as well as material presence of computers in their work lives. In this way, the rip-off story describes what happens when working-class concerns meet the logic of commissioned salespeople and technical language in the local home computer store. In virtually every interview, the need for networks and trusted informal information was discussed in the context of a future or past home computer purchase. This situation was often the core *goal orientation* (i.e., the object of activity) of computer learning in its earlier phases. This computer novice, whom we heard from earlier in the chapter, describes how the help of his friends and coworkers in the smoke shack would be needed to avoid being ripped off at a computer store.

I: So some guys would be able to steer you a little bit about buying a computer or/

R: Yeah, for my needs. Like we got one guy there who just got a computer, and what he got is way too much for me. He got his programmed in Austin, Texas somewhere. He went into it big time.

I: So they can get pretty pricey eh?

R: Yeah, he paid a lot for his. The one I'm looking at is about not quite that expensive.

I: I got a computer fairly cheap. You ever think of cost in terms of upgrading?

R: That's what I'm doing. I went to the Future Shop and I talked to guys, and you know they have to make a sale, that's their job, and we almost bought a certain one and got ripped off, but *then I said no, let's just buy what Ron told us.* So I said to the sales guy, write everything down that this computer can do, and I brought it back and went to work that night, and some different guys took a look at it. Now do I really need this, you know, what do I need a fax for? I don't need fax. You know stuff like that, you know. So I'm still pretty dense about computers but I'm learning. (W50)

Although people used these networks to save money, the activity involves more than this. When they are told, this and other stories are expressions of social connection and in fact reproduce a specific type of solidarity. These collective responses make sense in terms of the cultural and material conditions shared by working people. Closely associated with this process, the stories have embedded in them elements of the anxiety and desire that lie at the heart of working-class technological common sense. Each of these class themes, along with the specific information about computers, are circulated in the process of computer learning within working-class social networks.

Talking, Participation, and Membership in Working-Class Computer Learning Networks

Lave and Wenger (1991) claim that participation and "move-ment" toward more skilled practice includes one's "increasing sense of identity as master practitioner" (1991:111).[4] Indeed, they argue that

from the perspective we have developed here, learning and a sense of identity are inseparable: they are aspects of the same phenomenon.... This idea of iden-tity/membership is strongly tied to a conception of motivation. If the person is both member of a community and agent of activity, the concept of the person closely links meaning and action in the world. (Lave and Wenger, 1991:115, 122)

The empirical elaboration of this theme in both Lave and Wenger's (1991) and Holland et al.'s (1998) analyses of identity formation among non-drinking alcoholics grounds this claim well. For both sets of authors,

---

[4] The development of identity or personality was central to the original Vygotskian project in terms of child development. Leont'ev's discussion of personality is broader and, as such, more useful for in relation to notions of adult identity formation in the learning process.

identity is not primarily a conception of self but rather, paralleling the work of Erving Goffman (1959) in many ways, is something rooted in the active presentation and social construction of self in everyday life. Both sets of authors emphasize as well as demonstrate the dialectical relationship between shifting identities and the shifting forms of individual participation in communities of practice of the self-help group. Holland et al. specifically foreground the work of Vygotsky. Reviewing basic Vygotskian principles, they comment:

In the ordinary development sequence proposed by the socio-historical approach, the child first interacts the sign in concert with others. The interaction of the sign, for the child, is part of a behavioural sequence that may have no meaning in and of itself. It is likely that relations of identities are borne in a similar way, in what phenomenologists used to call the natural attitude, the uninterrupted flow of everyday life. The meaning of actions remains transparent or taken for granted in the natural attitude, and response follows as a matter of course. The formation of identity in this posture is a by-product of doing, of imitation and correction, and is profoundly embodied. (Holland et al, 1998:138)

They go on to say:

. . . [T]he cultural figurings of selves, identities, and the figured worlds that constitute the horizon of their meaning against which they operate, are collective products. One can significantly re-orient one's own behaviour, and can even participate in the creation of new figured worlds and their possibilities for new selves, but one can engage in such play only as part of a collective. One can never inhabit a world without at least the figural presence of others, of a social history in person. The space of authoring, of self-fashioning, remains a social and cultural space, no matter how intimately held it may become. And, it remains, more often than not, a contested space, a space of struggle. (Holland et al, 1998:282)

Thus, as both Holland et al. and Lave and Wenger conclude, learning and the production of identity are fundamental components of the same social process. Both are definitively social and cannot be meaningfully understood in individualistic or strictly cognitive terms. Understanding how people learn, then, must include an understanding of the process by which our identities vis-à-vis participation are formed and re-formed.

In my own interview data, the basic "learning identities" that people developed in the process of use and used to produce their activity have been described using the concept of working-class learning habitus. Linking these issues with a common story that circulated among manufacturing workers, we can look at stories that involved the company's support for employees' computer learning. People working for different companies, in different cities and within different sectors, shared a similar story in their interviews. The story demonstrates talking about computers and is a type of war story that celebrated a particular set of themes relating to working-class identity. These themes constructed workers as reasonable and as having practical solutions to the problems of the workplace. The same story also constructs management as unthinking, at best motivated by short-term economic gain rather than quality production. The story has as its backdrop the fact, taken as self-evident, that workers continue to be caught in hierarchical relations of power in the workplace in which management has ultimate control. This autoworker described the story this way:

> So this leads me back to the conversation me and you had back at the plant. Why don't the company, when they get rid of their computers upstairs, put them so the guys at work can bring them home, and I asked the supervisor about that and he said that what they do with those computers is send them to the shipping docks. Like that's where they go, because the environment is so bad there, with the dust and the dirt and the grime that they wear out very quickly, so when the get too worn out upstairs, they move them out there to save themselves a little bit of money. So he says to me, "No, they're not going to give the computers away for a ridiculous price to the employees." (W17a)

What this brief account makes clear is that in the context of computer learning and workers' desire to upgrade their skills, the company is portrayed as adversarial and shortsighted. A range of other interviewees told remarkably similar stories about workers who wish to become more computer literate by partnering with the company, yet the company refuses this partnership. In the case of each telling, different emphases were added: Sometimes the story began with a conversation with a supervisor encountered while shopping at a grocery store; at other times, it was rooted in collective bargaining; at still others, it began with an account of seeing computers thrown in a garbage dumpster behind the loading docks at the plant.

Regardless of the specifics, indeed regardless of the truth of the accounts, it is more the form and the representation of social relationships that make the story significant enough to circulate among computer learners. In all cases, the story expresses positive valuation of the working-class standpoint in the context of people's thoughts and feelings regarding the role of computer technology, learning, and work in their lives. The formation of identities-in-practice is a key outcome of the circulation of these oral artifacts and accounts for the horizon of meaning that the working people seemed to share, and against which a positive computer learning identity seems to emerge. Thus, as in previous sections of the chapter, the computer stories that circulate among learning networks can be seen to do more than deliver technical information. They can disseminate a shared sense of the social world and one's standpoint in it.

Summary

This chapter provided a brief look at the intersection of social class, computer use, and oral culture. I examined the unique role of several oral artifacts commonly used during computer learning among manufacturing workers. Julian Orr's work (1996) served as a point of departure from which I discussed the meaning and use of talk in and about computer learning. Following Orr, I presented an analysis of three types of narratives: those dealing with identity and community; those dealing with consultation, problem diagnosis, and the challenge offered to working-class computer learners by exclusive, technical language; and those dealing with the character and function of specific devices such as war stories and analogies. Each of these was seen to describe modes of oral culture in working-class life that were important components of computer-mediated activities.

We saw that computer learning in the everyday goes on in a variety of spheres of activity even – in fact, often – in the absence of an actual computer. I outlined the types of oral artifacts people produce and use in order to learn together. Specific oral devices such as the crash and the blueprint played a role in people's gap-closing procedures. However, talk and the use of oral devices were more than simply a means of transmitting information. They contributed to the formation of group membership and identities-in-practice that in several cases expressed and helped contribute to the development of class-based standpoints in practice through the circulation of class narratives of computers, work, and learning. The circulation of these artifacts aids in the development of computer learning networks as well as contributing to the ongoing elaboration of the learning habitus. To summarize, as the opening subsection claimed, oral culture is not socially neutral, but rather is always produced from particular social standpoints and reflects particular class experiences. The expression and development of working-class standpoints requires some form of proletarian public sphere where the otherwise fragmented experience of working-class life can be openly and constructively addressed. The learning networks discussed in earlier chapters and the elements of oral culture discussed in this one support this claim. Working-class and trade union cultures continue to rely on oral forms of communication, which in turn provide subordinate groups a modicum of social control over the production of meaning and knowledge from their own perspective.

8   Material Barriers in Working-Class Computer Learning

Vygotsky stated that learning practice occurs wherever there are forms of sociocultural participation. However, as we look more closely at what this means for specific social groups, we quickly recognize that not everyone participates in the same way, from the same social standpoint, or with the same degrees of discretionary control. Rather, cut along the lines of familiar social divisions including race, gender, and class, learning displays specific patterns. When we look closely, we see that all learning, within and beyond the classroom, has a way of corresponding to the structure of society, and that to a significant degree, this structure depends on the distribution of material resources. In this context, the notion of *learning opportunities*, seemingly everywhere under Vygotsky's claim, can be understood as a shaped, differentiated, and differentiating process.

In this chapter, I discuss the material structures that shape the computer learning that working people engage in. To begin to envision the factors I want to consider here, consider a scene I encountered often in the course of doing this research: people passing in and out of someone's basement in order to exchange software, repair hardware, and build customized computers by drawing on a loose social network of learners, some of whom are coworkers, some neighbors, some friends or family members. Supporting the encounters are the investment in computer equipment, the space to keep and work at it, the electricity to keep the computer running, and the time needed to pursue the activity when not engaged in paid or unpaid work. Each of these features expresses the distribution of time, money, space, and human energy, each patterned by relations of production, distribution, and consumption, wage levels and negotiation work, and finally, the division of labor in the home. Invoking such broad political-economic connections to the processes of everyday learning suggests that people's learning is a deeply structured activity.

173

In the literature, issues of material access to and use of computer technology have been linked to issues of class difference in a variety of ways. In Canada, Livingstone (1997a) has shown that there is now a significant danger of a "new technocratic elite being generated by the greater access to home computers by kids of affluent families" (p. 107). He notes that children from affluent households are about twice as likely to have home computers and computer literacy skills as those from the poorest families. More recently, in a major study of the distribution of computer access and use in Canada, Reddick, Bouche, and Grosiellier (2000) reported:

From 1997 through 1999, higher income households were three times more likely than lower-income households to have home access.... [B]arriers and obstacles to access are aggravated for those in the lower social classes who have less resources or skills available to overcome them. (Reddick et al., 2000:1–2)

At the same time, the picture of access and use is not quite as clear-cut as Reddick and others suggest. In the previous chapter, we learned how much computer learning goes on in the absence of a computer. A range of alternative sources such as the Nielsen/NetRatings (from the United States), for example, suggest that although web-based computer activity is still dominated by "upscale Americans," a mix of new working-class learners has emerged, a finding that parallels the dynamics seen among the people interviewed for this book.

True, the clusters with the greatest access to the Internet are still home to early-adopting, upscale Americans. But the cluster whose surfers spend the most time online at home left some analysts agog: Mid-City Mix, a working-class, African American lifestyle whose residents like to chat, exchange e-mail, and hang out at entertainment and sweepstakes sites. The other top clusters for online longevity include Norma Rae-ville and Back Country Folks, characterized by people with lower incomes, modest educations, and blue-collar jobs. (Weis, 2001:3)

Both the Reddick and Weis reports (as well as the more general Statistics Canada reports referenced in Chapter 1) provide descriptions of a powerful emerging interest in computer technology among working-class groups. Each references the role of material barriers, the Reddick report describing the barriers and the Weis report suggesting that they are being challenged in some ways. Each report, however, provides a description rather than an explanation of the role of material conditions in computer-based learning among working-class groups. Pairing them helps provide some depth to their description but, as usual, we cannot discern the actual practices involved. Understanding these practices requires a recognition of the way in which people's learning is a form of practice mediated by the materiality of social life. Moreover, it becomes clear that the *digital divide* may refer to differentiated opportunity to apply skills as much as it references access to equipment.

Although many of the forces that shape working-class computer activity are cultural-historical, it is the way activity is mediated by material structures that is the focus of this chapter. I deal with several different but related themes in this area. First, I examine the distribution of time, space, and human energies in terms of the political economy of the working-class household. Here the gendered patterns of activity are so deeply embedded in relations of social class that, unlike in other chapters, one cannot be meaningfully discussed without the other. The gendered distribution of household labor mixes with the class dynamics of declining wage levels and increasing numbers of dual-income households to play an important role in shaping the forms of computer-based activity that occur. Later, I examine issues of home computer ownership with a focus on a key Canadian analysis by Nakhaie and Pike (1998). Just as the statistics discussed in the Weis article add depth to the basic identification of the digital divide in the Reddick report, I use interview data to problematize certain aspects of the Nakhaie–Pike analysis. I do not deny that a digital divide exists; however, my conclusion is that the form of class reproduction these authors describe, drawing explicitly on Bourdieuian language, needs to be expanded to capture the real dynamics and creative human agency within the process. Closely connected to this expansion is the material presented in the final section, where I discuss human agency as the art of "making do" that seems to elude so much of the computer access/usage literature. This last area helps us understand how people continue to operate despite constraints within the structures of class society. Meaningful analysis of learning cannot take place in the absence of a clear appreciation of the materiality of social life. The aim of this chapter is to bring this dimension more clearly into focus.

"Especially for Women": Intersections of Home and Work and the Effect on Learning

As we've already seen, computer learning and the class processes that shape it are not confined to a single sphere but instead occur across overlapping activity systems. The realm of paid work plays a key role in this system of systems not merely because of its role in defining the technological common sense and providing a key meeting place for working people, but also because of its role in the distribution of material resources. However, the relations of production and the distribution of material resources in the household play an important role in the way working-class computer learning is carried out as well. The overlap between these two spheres is an essential point of departure for analysis of the materiality of computer learning practice.

In her studies of working-class households in the United States, Lillian Rubin (1976, 1994) draws a connection between the decline in real wages and the rise of the dual-income household with the distribution of discretionary time for women. Rubin's analysis highlights how the barriers and constraints imposed on working-class households, and working-class women specifically, emerged as a function of the development of capitalism at the close of the 20th century. In Canada, Vosko (2000) has recently provided one of the most extensive studies to date of the gendered dimensions of declining free time, falling wages, and the dual-income household in the context of the growing trend of temporary employment. According to Lowe (2000), the labor force participation rates of Canadian women have risen steadily over the past four decades. Dual-earner families comprise over 60% of all two-parent families. Lowe goes on to say that "these changes occurred at a time of declining real incomes and greater work intensity and insecurity [when] work–family conflicts and stresses have become major problems" (2000:166).

How does this ugly situation figure in the everyday learning lives of working-class women? In this research, it was working-class women who disproportionately bore the brunt of these increasingly challenging material conditions. It was very common, for example, for working women to describe how difficult it was to find space and time in the day for discretionary forms of activity. In the following interview, for example, an autoworker talks about the way a typical day in her life is structured: She battles with her partner at home for help with household work; she must squeeze in time late at night, when everyone else has gone to bed, to study for a course she's decided to take; if she wishes to do some extra reading, she fits it into the bus ride to and from the factory, and so on. When asked about her learning activities, she provided us with this description.

> I have a really *cramped time*, so many things I love to do, but *I have the children*, I get up at 5 a.m., don't get home until 5 p.m., so by the time supper's cooked, and I've played with kids, and get eight hours sleep, I'm really *squeezed for time*. I have to *read on the bus*. . . . [For women generally] to continue our education in the evening is such an inconvenience for everyone – *we're suffering with guilt, the children are*

sick, he's not a great caregiver. I'm wondering if he's looking after the little one with a fever. I'm *studying for exams. No cooperation* from my partner.... For a lot of women, they need that support from a partner, or if they have workplace training, especially workplace training, if workplaces would just squeeze some time in and allow the employees to learn, or *take a day off and allow them to learn*, or have more options for Saturday trainings, it would be a great help. Especially for women. (W58)

"Especially for women" is an important message that this and other women in this research sent loud and clear. It sums up a distinctive pattern of time use that has been well understood in the literature generally, but here it allows us to see the linkages between the division of labor in the home and the broad structure of everyday learning practice. Of course, gendered as well as racialized processes are woven with all of the class processes I've dealt with in this book, but the material structure of free time and discretionary learning vis-à-vis work and household responsibilities seems particularly dependent on the tight weave of class and gender processes.

In terms of computer learning specifically, these same issues (i.e., the structures of time and space imposed by the organization of work, wages, the household, and so on) are central. Like the other women interviewed, the following chemical worker describes the way that working-class life in and outside the factory overlaps. Her description exemplifies the overlapping character of activity occurring across multiple spheres, as well as the powerful role that gender–class interactions play. The distribution of the most basic material resources (time, space, and especially the human energy necessary to focus attention), rooted in her life as both a worker and a married woman in a patriarchal household, mediate the possibilities for discretionary learning. She describes how she cannot get involved in many extra workplace functions such as company training or trade union activities because of cramped home/work time. At 53 years of age, she also seems to suggests that one's life stage plays a role in the opportunities available to obtain more rewarding and more secure work. None of us are "getting any younger," of course, but from her standpoint as a working-class woman, this phrase signals an important link between opportunities for different types of waged work and discussions of computer learning.

Basically I just go to work and do my eight hours work, help out as much as I can, do my job and come home. I don't normally get involved in too much extra because I don't really have the time. Since I've been with the company I'm *not getting any younger*.... We're all going to have to do it [i.e., learn computers]. Maybe I'll have to update it, I don't know. I know I need to get a printer, but the rest of the stuff, I mean, I have the screen, I have the keyboard. Everything is there, it just depends on how much more I need to do. I should really sit down and do it, but then *I can't sit down and relax and do something if there's something more important that I have to do*. Like if I had a lot of *housework* to do or if I felt I had *bills to pay*, that's *more important to me than sitting at the computer* because once I get my bills paid up, my *mind is at ease*, I can go do it. (W12)

Clearly, descriptions such as this problematize simplistic models of computer access and use. Paying the bills, doing the housework, and having one's mind at ease are important components of discretionary participation in activity. For working-class women, they are also a function of specific gendered relations of the household and paid work, mediated by the distribution of material resources, that leave little opportunity for their participation in computer learning.

Another female worker states that she is very interested in computer courses at work in order to upgrade her skills and perhaps move into more secure work of some kind. Like the woman quoted in the previous interview, with primary responsibility for housework, her mind is not at ease until this is done, so learning about computers in the narrow gaps available in her day is made more difficult. She describes a hyperfragmentation of learning opportunities and goes on to outline how the need to structure work and home life in a working family keeps her and her husband apart.

I: Anything you'd be interested in taking courses in at your work?

R: Computer courses. Still thinking about it, but with the little one, and husband working every other weekend, it's difficult. An upgrade course or something. . . . [But] you're working to pay the bills. I look after the daughter in the day, then my husband comes home and looks after her. I don't see my husband except every other weekend. Talk to him on the phone. Maybe that's why it's lasted so long [laughs]! When you're busy, it's impossible. Like right now, for me, no way. I could probably do it, but then there's certain things in the house that wouldn't get done. And I'm the type of person that has to have everything just organized! I can't leave it. I'll go bananas. (W42)

The comments of both of these female workers reveal the degree to which gender, interwoven with the need for a double income in the context of class life, shapes learning vis-à-vis the distribution of scarce material resources, namely, time and money.

Among male interviewees, this tight weave of gender and class might not seem as strikingly apparent, though, of course, it is still obviously present. The description of women's learning lives forms a stark contrast to the working-class networks described by men, whose description of computer learning tends to leave invisible their gendered standpoint in activity. In the same way that the standpoint of the owner of capital limits understanding of the workings of capitalism, the standpoint of men limits understanding of the constraints of patriarchy. In this research, the men detailed activity in which material resources shaped learning as well, but in very different ways. For them, free time for computing in the neighborhood and at home was largely, though not exclusively, assumed. The rise in dual-income households, as Rubin (1994:78) anticipated, has encouraged some degree of consciousness raising around gender imbalances among working-class men. However, for the most part, among the men interviewed, free time seemed to appear out of thin air rather than being a product of a specific division of household labor. Overall, the implications of participation in working-class learning networks for women are clear. Difficulty in engaging in computer learning stems primarily from constraints on their discretionary time. This leaves little space to generate the types of networks described in earlier chapters. In their powerful and diverse examinations of the interlocking character of capitalism and patriarchy, Marxist-feminists (e.g., Firestone, 1971; Sargent, 1981; Smith, 1987) have outlined how gender and class life provide interlocking support for one another and cement a type of hyperexploitation that extends, vis-à-vis the ability to generate and engage in informal networks, to issues of adult learning.

Of course, as with the interrelation of gender and class, it is important to note that we might just as easily trace the effects of ethnic and racialized processes on adult learning as well. As mentioned, neither gender nor race is the focus of this book, but some discussion of how these issues are implicated is in order. For this, it is easiest to refer to earlier work. As in the preceding analysis, where we saw how relations of paid work overlap with adult learning more broadly, a similar dynamic helps approximate the role of race and ethnicity in shaping computer activity. Specifically, in Sawchuk (1999a; Livingstone and Sawchuk, in press), I outline how racialized standpoints play an important role in learning and the material structure of opportunity for discretionary practice. There I focused on relations of language in the workplace. Although relations of language provide, admittedly, a thin conceptual slice of the race/ethnicity–social class linkage, it was clear that workers' first language played a key role in the patterns of learning interaction, for example, at work. Language affected people's participation with one another, shaped the patterns of promotion in the industrial workplace, and in turn, contributed to a racially segmented internal labor market. The factory and the working-class learning I examined were often multilingual. On the shopfloor (Sawchuk, 1999a; Livingstone and Sawchuk, in press), for example, at least eight different languages were spoken. This was in sharp contrast to the English-only operations that dominated in the supervisory, managerial, and executive ranks, which extended to the company literature and official workplace communications. Workers often gained functional literacy in a variety of languages informally by working side by side with one another, against which English was imposed by management as the *language of production*. The relations of language at work, as well as the dual labor market effects by which linguistic minorities become concentrated in particular occupational enclaves, were shown to be important interrelated features of the material structure of working-class learning. These processes affected the distribution of resources, extending the effects of a linguistically and racially structured workplace into people's broader lives. This is at least one of the major ways in which race and class can be seen to interact. In the research on computer learning reported in this book, race was an underlying dimension of most of the accounts; the majority of interviewees of both genders tended to take for granted their standpoint as white working-class learners.

These brief references to the interaction of class processes with gendered and racialized ones, of course, are only minor illustrations. They point to the need for further investigation. As brief as they are, however, they point to a level of complexity within class analyses of adult learning and technology that has not been the focus of detailed discussion in any literature to date. Together, mediated by the distribution of material resources, the interlocking sets of class, gender, and race/ethnic relations produce a structure of opportunity for discretionary participation.

The Structuring Effects of Home Computer Ownership

In contrast to most analyses of social class and computer access and use, in this book home computer ownership is not viewed as the definitive determinant of computer activity. Nevertheless, issues surrounding private ownership of home computers are important. Building

on some of the works discussed in the Introduction, we can better understand that computer access and use are shaped by the material dimensions
of class life in Canada by taking a look at an article by Nakhaie and Pike
(1998). This article is important not simply for its detailed class analysis
but also for its contribution to research on technology and social class in
terms of the work of Pierre Bourdieu. Nakhaie and Pike note that along
with the general advantages of greater access to formal education that the
middle and upper classes enjoy,

> educational advantage translates into higher economic resources and cultural capital
> which ensures a higher rate of computer access and use. This finding is consistent
> with Bourdieu and his colleagues' view that education is a measure of cultural cap-
> ital and that those with higher cultural capital are more likely to adopt the new
> technology and to integrate it in their strategy of reproduction. (1998:443)

Nakhaie and Pike suggest a "them who has gets" dynamic. Following
Bourdieu's theory of symbolic capital, they go on to depict the constraints
on the computer learning experiences of the working class:

> [S]ome may have attended schools where computer facilities were limited; many
> would also not use computers on the job, and hence be less disposed to have them at
> home, especially since there would be no work-related connection. And of course,
> for those on limited incomes, there is always the question of the sheer cost barrier
> of buying and running a home computer. (1998:442–443)

Nakhaie and Pike (1998) report statistically significant correlations between computer access, class origins, and educational attainment, as well
as between home computer use, educational attainment, and occupation
type. They go on to suggest that these findings confirm Bourdieu's notion of class reproduction. However, there are a number of criticisms that
can be voiced. In Chapter 5, I identified the basic weaknesses of this dimension of Bourdieu's work (as opposed to his notion of habitus). The
same basic critique applies here, namely, that Bourdieu's metaphors of
capital and field are far too static to provide a meaningful description of
the contingency of social life. In addition, limited by the survey methodology itself, Nakhaie and Pike's depiction of the effects of social variables including educational attainment, occupation, and social origin offers only
a loose approximation of the way these variables actually function in concrete activity. Likewise, computer access and use is primarily understood
in terms of private ownership and home use. Thus, as we've seen in previous chapters, here too we miss important, even definitive, elements
of working-class computing. Although home computers are an important component of working-class computing, they are certainly not the

Table 8.1. *Informal/Formal Learning, Computing, Technology, and Learning at Home*

Survey Question	Elite and Executive Class Group	Working-Class Group	
Do you use a computer at home?*	71%	48%	(N = 610)
Do you use the Internet at home?*	66%	48%	(N = 354)
Have you learned anything about computers or computing unrelated to paid work?*	77%	55%	(N = 395)

* Significant at or above the .001 level.
Source: NALL (1999).

only way working people learn about computers. Indeed, home computer ownership is as much a symptom of the overall character of working-class computer learning as it is a determinant of it. Of course, as noted, even more novel to conventional computer access/use literature is the realization that a good deal of learning goes on without a computer being present at all. This occurs through a process of peripheral participation and through the use of oral artifacts in a variety of settings, only one of which is the home. Without even considering the tacit learning that conventional survey methods cannot typically assess, the analysis from previous chapters strongly suggests that huge numbers of working-class people would simply fall through the cracks if this method were used. One could even go so far as to argue that studies such as Nakhaie and Pike's express a private ownership bias that ignores the complexity of class practices in which people continue to make use of less formalized learning, unsanctioned as well as incidental, and diffuse contact with computer technologies.

At the same time, in my own analysis of the *NALL Canadian Survey of Informal Learning* database, I attempted to parallel some the basic class analyses provided by Nakhaie and Pike (1998).[1] Table 8.1 summarizes these comparisons. What we see confirms their basic observations. Although the groupings I use are somewhat different, there are some very clear class effects in computer practice, particularly those in which home computers are directly involved.[2] Looking beneath the surface of these

[1] The SPSS formula devised for this purpose was based primarily on occupational classification and ownership elements. See the discussion in Livingstone and Mangan (1996).
[2] See the explanation of how these groups were formed in Chapter 6 (following Table 6.1).

findings, however, we can see how different class practices help to shape these statistical differences. What becomes clear in the interviews is that working-class people who strictly attempt to act alone, through individual, self-directed learning or through conventional formal education and training in the workplace and schools, find it extremely difficult to engage in computer learning. For example, the following woman outlines exactly how effective individualized informal or formalized learning pathways are from a working-class standpoint. We see how, in conjunction with the effects of lower access to privately owned computers, other class differences in computer access and use are reproduced.

> More or less I was taking computer in a first basic course like, you know, and it was once a week. And they would just show us how the computer was run, how a disk is put in and things like that, you know. And then you would just go home and the next day, he would show you something else. Unless you had a computer at home, you couldn't really do much. So the most you could do was to look forward for the next time and learning something else. And I've done that for two years on the computer. So I figured that I needed the two years because the first year, you couldn't, like myself, I couldn't pick it up fast enough, you know. But then in the second year, it was okay. It's okay through the union to suggest courses but if the employer doesn't support it, they won't give the employee the hours to sign up for it. Because if the boss feels it's okay and will help me then, okay, it will help me. But if the boss says it's off limits, then that supervisor will say I can't do it. And you're not going to go after work, on the weekends, then you're stuck staying with the work you're doing. (W20)

This description focuses on the role of the home computer but reiterates a host of other themes already discussed, including the role of management rights to grant access, the effects of unionization, the material constraints of the gendered dimension of household labor, and even the role of job design in working-class computer learning. The woman indicates a need for a home computer she cannot afford, and she talks about how, on their own, the countervailing effects of unions cannot overcome the control that management exerts over course-based learning opportunities. Descriptions such as this help to make visible the complex sets of material constraints that shape working-class computer learning. What is key is that this woman's learning practice does *not* include access to a stable, collective, informal learning network. This is significant because it is by drawing on this type of network that many of the basic challenges posed by both management's control of work and course-based learning, as well as the distribution of time, space, and resources, can be effectively countered. In sum, it is those working people who don't have access to informal learning networks who are predominantly subject to the class differentials outlined in the statistical analyses discussed previously.

As we saw earlier, affording a home computer is also mediated by a concern over technological obsolescence, which, again, reflects the class dimensions of computer ownership in an additional way. Insecurity in the workplace, the fear of losing one's job, constant downward pressure on wages, lower pay than that of middle- and upper-class groups, and so on make the concern about the expense of replacing a computer more or less unique to working-class groups. Indeed, if working-class people are isolated from the informal learning networks we've seen earlier, this fear can immobilize all but a small number, increasing their already vulnerable position in the labor market. However, we saw that as people engaged with one another, articulated these issues, and shared knowledge, they began to progress. They found themselves drawn into greater contact with others and specifically into computer networks. Psychodynamic explanations aside, as we saw earlier, it is material access to working-class social groups that allows meaningful and constructive resolution of the anxieties of the basic class condition. In any case, at the outset, most workers took the idea of purchasing a home computer very seriously. It was an event that was planned for and extensively discussed at home, in the neighborhood, workplace, and union hall, and so on. These initial conversations were one of the key initial goal orientations of peripheral participation in computer learning that didn't involve a computer at all, and it was a concern for material resources, in particular, that drove these initial conversations. This autoworker outlines the basic issues involved.

I: You know that idea that you always have to upgrade? Does that worry you?

R: Yeah that's a *big worry* because, I think that well yeah I'm going to put out about three thousand dollars on a machine and will it be useful in one year? Like everything changes so drastically now, or has that big change finished because if I bought five years ago, that computer would be *useless for today's software*, that's what happened to so many people. They couldn't use it. Is that going to happen anymore?...
        That's where you have to ask so many people which one to buy.... If you screw up it's a real problem. (W19)

Technological obsolescence together with the material constraints of working-class life thus plays an important role in the computer learning process. Planning and action surrounding this issue were all shaped by the material conditions of people's lives.

Another important feature of the material structure of home-based computer learning activity that emerged from the analysis is an elaboration of the conceptualization that Lave and Wenger (1991) refer to as the *center* of communities of practice. Lave and Wenger spend a good deal of time discussing the notion of *mature practice* as the center around which learning is generated and through which *developmental* cycles of skill and knowledge are established.

Legitimate peripheral participation moves in a centripetal direction, motivated by its location in a field of mature practice. It is motivated by the growing use value of participation, and by newcomers' desires to become full practitioners. Communities of practice have histories and developmental cycles, and reproduce themselves in such a way that the transformation of newcomers into old-timers becomes unremarkably integral to the practice. (Lave and Wenger, 1991:122)

In Lave and Wenger's (1991) discussion of Navy quartermasters, for example, the distribution of resources is largely unproblematic. The motive level of activity in this setting may in fact be driven by the dynamics and emergence of mature practice largely because the social roles, rules, and division of labor are not contested but rather suspended in this context. However, when we move beyond discussions of occupational groups and specific institutional settings to discuss the complexity of skill and knowledge development across multiple spheres of activity in everyday life, we see that material factors, as an expression of important contradictions in the learning process for working people, play a significant role in driving and shaping learning. The context of class life compels people to make the organization of material resources one of the important features of the learning process. Thus, materiality comes to play a key role in constituting the center of communities of practice among working-class people.

For analysis of legitimate peripheral participation centered on the standpoints of subordinate groups such as the working class, the center of practice becomes as least as dependent on finding space, time, and energy as it is on developing specific knowledge forms, skills, and interests. In examining the computer learning among working-class participants in this research, it sometimes difficult to locate a center based upon the notion of mature practice alone. Activity takes place across several sites, involves varying levels of participant control, and incorporates multiple sets of interests as well as knowledge and skill. Never mind that the rapid change in home computer technologies and software ensures that "expertise" is unstable; it was the material resources, cycles in family life, and effective formal and informal negotiation of institutional life that became central to shifting participation in working-class communities of practice. In other words, if there are identifiable centers to these communities of practice, they coalesced around mature practice as well as the production of discretionary spaces, availability/time, energy, and other material resources.

Some of the most tangible centers of communities of practice, according to the interview data and ethnographic notes, were specific individuals and specific physical spaces in the working-class community. A particular person's basement or an area in the industrial workplace, the quiet corners or places where people went on their breaks – these were the places where mature practice and networked learning occurred, sometimes involving an expert practitioner, sometimes not. In terms of the computer learning centered in working-class homes, these spaces were not necessarily the basements of the most skilled, mature practitioners. Rather, they were the homes of key members of the activity system who had the time, space, and energy as well as the interest necessary to play a leading role in the continuity and coordination of the learning network. In my research, I came across several of these people and places. They necessarily served overlapping functions. In the basements of these working-class homes, for example, we discovered several more or less obsolete computers in various states of disassembly (e.g., one or two belonging to the resident, the others dropped off for examination), stacks of copied disks, a comfortable well-worn couch, and children busily searching the Internet or blasting space invaders, with the strong odor of hockey equipment mixed with the fresh moisture that hanging laundry adds to the air. It was also in these centers that we found some of the last vestiges of functioning Bulletin Board Systems (BBSs). In fact, my research found several local BBS's are up and running. All were run out of the basement/center of a "lead" computer learner and informal organizer within the community of practice.

To clarify briefly, BBS's are a pre-Internet communications forum, what we might call today an *Intranet*. It was used for discussion and online computer-based interaction. The key difference between these systems and today's Internet is that whereas the Internet depends on commercial computer servers, BBS's could be run very inexpensively from someone's home. Because the server was small-scale and local (and because long-distance telephone charges applied), the participants tended to be local, issues tended to be community-focused, and among manufacturing workers, trade union activities were often an important issue. Being rooted in a local physical community made a significant difference for users and the types of interaction that occurred. According to Jeff Taylor,[3] one of Canada's leading computer-based distance education/labor education specialists, the Canadian Union of Public Employees' world-renowned Solinet, one of the first trade union–based online forums, began as a cross between a community-based BBS and the system we now know as the Internet. Solinet's purpose and effect was to create a specifically union-based working-class-oriented electronic communications forum, and it was highly successful. Today, BBS's still exist in isolated pockets of activity and function as discussion groups or listserves, but clearly they are less central to computer-based communication than they once were. The fact that elements of these systems continue to exist among working-class groups, however, emphasizes the importance of paying close attention to the role that material resources play in the structure of computer learning and the use of specific forms of computer technology.

In general terms, more often than not, working people are forced to do things on the cheap. This is an important basic structural feature of capitalism – its constant downward pressure on wages; *however*, it is also a source of creativity in working-class life as a form of bricolage. It is an important force in shaping learning culture and the working-class habitus. Bourdieu's discussion of the working-class *taste for necessity* (1984:chapter 7) obviously has some relevance here and helps explain how material constraints become integrated into a range of cultural tendencies. Indeed, we can extend this to preferences concerning adult learning choices as well. In terms of home computer access and use, working people often need and, as a form of cultural value, prefer to find the most cost-effective and expandable computer available, and in interviews many said that it was not unusual for them to work with used parts and borrowed software. These needs, in turn, shaped the selection of interests within a great deal of working-class computer learning. This cultural-material dimension draws the center of computer learning activity systems to the sites where these material resources are most easily concerted and most stable. Subverting conventions of private consumption, for example, the autoworkers I interviewed tend to share resources in order to make do, although this presents additional difficulties. And in the end, although

---

[3] Personal communication (April 9, 1999).

the price of some software may still be too high, it opens up new learning opportunities. One autoworker explained it this way:

> Well we *exchange stuff*, like we bought SoftRam together, it was only forty dollars, so it ended up being ten dollars each, and we talk about buying different things but the problem is that, well, I find with the group, that you got guys who are scared to put some things in, some guys who want to put it in, no problem. Guys try things out and they say, "Here, you want to try it?" But as far as good, expensive software in our group, no one buys it in our group. We all buy all the cheap stuff. (W16)

As in the other ways that material resources shape working-class computer learning, home computer ownership is not simply a "force" acting on a passive subject. Many of the interviewees actively responded to the challenges posed by the relatively high price of software and hardware by sharing resources and finding new ways to use resources that were available. This defined making do in working-class computer learning.

In the Hawthorne Works research by Mayo (1945), and in analyses of quota restriction from Roy (1952) and Burawoy (1979) to Hamper (1991) and even workplace sabotage literature (e.g., Sprouse, 1995), there is an expansive literature on the art of making do among workers, though with the exception of Kusterer (1978), few have focused on issues of knowledge production and learning per se. In terms of computer learning practice and home computer ownership, the interviewees in this research described making use of a variety of techniques to respond to and partially overcome basic material constraints. As we've seen in many of the excerpts in previous chapters, one of the most popular techniques was unsanctioned use of workplace computers. Although computer-mediated work is structured to keep people on their work-related tasks, workers appropriated work time and equipment for their own use. The following chemical worker, for example, describes how this appropriation of workplace resources has in fact delayed his purchase of a home computer. On the shopfloor of the plant, the computer systems are designed for recording and regulating the production of resins. In the background of the company production software, however, is a general operating system (Windows) that allows workers to make alternative uses of the technology.

R: Well this is kind of the thing that I've *dragging my heels* about because, like, there's nothing at home that I could have that I don't *already have at work*, and I get paid to do it, you know what I mean, so and if I want to do anything I'll do it there instead of at home.

R: ... the *expense* of it that's one thing, though.

I: Yeah, the monthly charges.

R: Not only that but I'd *have to buy a decent system* to do it. Like [his partner] has been hounding me, that we have to get a decent system and get on the Internet. (W18a)

This example shows the intersection of different spheres of activity in which the material structures of home computing overlap with the activity (including rules and enforcement of discipline) of the industrial workplace. This computer activity is undertaken outside the bounds of the formal organization of production and contributes to computer learning in a very broad way.

Structure and Resistance within Computer Learning at Work

The last portion of the preceding section straddles the line between issues of material structures shaping home computer ownership and the creative activities that working people undertake in their workplace to use company computers. As we've seen, the workplace is an important part of the relationship between computer technology and learning in working-class life. In the workplace, access to computers is structured by management's legal rights to organize job descriptions, choose work station designs, select the forms of technology, define skill requirements, control advancement, and so on. Because these decisions structure the modes of participation in the workplace, they also go a long way toward defining the mode of learning and the material structure of computer learning more broadly. In turn, we could say that this arrangement of the labor/learning process is rooted in the dynamics of the historical development of capitalism and therefore in effect stamps learning with an important class character.

Informal everyday learning has particular importance to the analysis, as this is how the majority of working-class learning occurs, but we cannot ignore the role of formalized training in the workplace in working-class computer learning. Therefore, before going further, I want to discuss briefly the role of formalized technological training opportunities in the workplace. The development of formal training programs is obviously an expression of the organization of resources as well, and as these resources are not under the control of employees, training comes to represent another means by which learning is shaped by antagonistic, if not contested,

Table 8.2. *Course-Based Computer Learning and Class Differences in the Workplace*

Survey Question	Elite and Executive Class Group	Working-Class Group	
Have you taken any computer courses for paid work?*	48%	25%	(N = 596)
Have you taken any courses on new technologies for paid work?†	40%	28%	(N = 568)

* Between-group difference significant at the .001 level.
† Between-group difference significant at the .003 level.
Source: NALL (1999).

Table 8.3. *Reasons for Not Taking Formalized Courses Across Social Classes*

	Inconvenient Time/Places	No Affordable Child Care	Too Expensive
Elite and executive class group	33%	0%	22%
working-class group	58%	12%	47%

Note: All differences statistically significant at the .001 level.
Source: NALL (1999). *N* = 542.

material conditions. A general view of the class dimensions of formalized computer training in the workplace is presented in Table 8.2.

Again, drawing on the NALL survey database (1999), we can see that important class differences exist in terms of the access to formalized training by different groups. We see that the elite and executive group tends to get more opportunities to take computer courses in the workplace. The general description of the structure of workplace opportunities for course learning favors the dominant group. Expanding further on this theme, Table 8.3 shows how class affects access to courses within and beyond the workplace. These data confirm the powerful effects of class and point to specific material considerations. When we recognize that women still have primary responsibilities for home and child care, the scores in the second column reflect the extreme difficulties that working-class women face when attempting to access conventional course-based learning.

Taking a closer look at the structure of the workplace and the quality of the learning environment, we see that for the majority of workers interviewed, the commitment of companies to computer training is largely rhetorical. As people indicated, the inflated talk about new forms of training and the creation of a high-skill, high-value-added workplace for a competitive "knowledge economy" did not translate into new organizational forms, training, or work techniques. One autoworker's comment summed up the situation well: "They don't want to teach us too much, just enough" (W58). Indeed, people described their workplaces as dominated by old-fashioned management techniques including hierarchical distribution of knowledge and information. In terms of access to computer learning specifically, another autoworker outlines the relationship between formal training opportunities, the chances for career advancement in the workplace, and the fact that even when computer courses are available, they sometimes have little direct use when the functions of computer technology in the workplace are so narrowly defined.

I: Any other courses or learning opportunities?

R: There are a few computer courses. But there is no real need to follow it up and use it.

I: Can anyone take them?

R: We need permission forms from our supervisor. I took the courses because they wanted safety reps to generate work orders. That's how I got permission to take the course. But I never really used the training.... There is also computer training for using the terminals in your own department area. It shows the raw materials, what's been added already, and what's needed. It is an inventory. Most people do it, but it's set up in a very simple way. (W55)

The narrowly defined job category and the equally narrow functions of most shopfloor computer technology play an important role in shaping the learning potential in the workplace. Sanctioned computer access/use in the workplace is distributed and controlled by management through workplace rules. Although it seems reasonable that *knowledge workers* (e.g., Porter, 1971; Bell, 1973; Reich, 1991) need hands-on experience to develop their creative capacities, the imperatives of managerial control influence work in the opposite direction. Computers on the shopfloor are configured not to be knowledge-intensive but rather, as most workers said, idiot-proof.

The ideas of idiot-proof technology and dumbed-down work design remind us that the physical layout of the workplace plays a powerful role in shaping participation, experience, and learning. The shaping of communication patterns is key in this regard – what John Fiske (1993) refers to as restriction of the *horizontal interaction* among workers. Although he does not use a manufacturing setting, Fiske outlines the effects of job design that are equally applicable to the manufacturing shopfloor. His main argument is that work station design and workplace technology reproduce relations of class by controlling time and space.

The first operation of power is always to enclose its territory, within which to concentrate rather than to dissipate its energies. Enclosure entails separation, not just the separation of the enclosure from the rest of the system (which is actually an insertion into it), but, more importantly, the separation of the individuals who have been enclosed.... Individuated control requires stations which are open to monitoring from above and closed off horizontally. Each station is designed to encourage desired behaviour and discourage what is prohibited by making it visible. The more completely the body's behaviour is monitored, evaluated and recorded, the finer the control over it. But behaviour takes place in time as well as space. TWA's computer logs every moment of work and non-work between SIT and SOT (Sign In Time and Sign Out Time). The non-work times are categorized into the legitimate (meal breaks) and illegitimate (toilet breaks or a personal phone call) and each are computed precisely. At the end of the day, the human supervisor rates them against an unspecified norm.... (Fiske, 1993:71–72)

It's important to recognize that a basic activity theory approach allows us to link analyses of the labor process, including the control of movement and horizontal communications, as described by Fiske, with the notion of learning. However, people are not simply nodes in vertical and horizontal systems of communication, as Fiske knows. They think and act in these contexts, sometimes re-creating hierarchical relationships of power but at other times acting in ways that run tangential or in opposition to these relationships (as seen in the second part of Chapter 4). At the same time, however, identifying active human agency within the workplace can sometimes be difficult. Indeed, it is often only the most obvious deviations from normal patterns that confirm the existence of conscious social agents.

Identifying human agency among employees in the workplace requires an analysis of power and the way the less powerful operate in systems where the deck is stacked against them. One way of understanding the interplay between the practices of the powerful and the practices of subordinates in the everyday is outlined in the work of Michel de Certeau. Certeau, a historian by training, provides in *Culture in the Plural* (1997) and particularly in *The Practice of Everyday Life* (1984) a profound discussion of the different bottom-up and top-down practices of power. This analysis is useful for helping us to identify the ways that workers can sometimes take control of their own learning in the workplace. Certeau uses the concepts of *tactical* versus *strategic* practices, which are distinct in the ways they use time and space. According to Certeau, strategic practices are those of the strong. These practices allow the powerful to formally control space: They monitor, they exercise rights, they "produce, tabulate and impose" upon time and space. Tactical practices, on the other hand, are those of the weak and occur more or less within the basic parameters set by the powerful. In the context of work, the heart of tactical practice, according to Certeau, is *la perruque*.

La perruque [the wig] is the worker's own work disguised as work for his employer. It differs from pilfering in that nothing of material value is stolen. It differs from absenteeism in that the worker is officially on the job. La perruque may be as simple a matter as a secretary's writing a love letter on "company time" or as complex as a cabinetmaker's "borrowing" a lathe to make a piece of furniture for his living room.... Accused of stealing or turning material to his own ends and using the machines for his own profit, the worker who indulges in la perruque actually diverts time (not goods, since he uses only scraps) from the factory for work that is free, creative, and precisely not directed towards profit ... whose sole purpose is to signify his own capabilities through his work and to confirm this solidarity with other workers or his family through spending his time in this way.... The actual order of things is precisely what "popular" tactics turn to their own ends, without any illusion that it will change any time soon. (Certeau, 1984:25–26)

Interviews with people for this research revealed similar activities occurring within informal networks in the workplace. Time off one's job, for example to fiddle with the computer at another worker's station, often was disguised, had to occur in opposition to management work rules, and was relegated to the gaps in surveillance and workplace discipline. They were the types of practices described by Hamper (1991), and ones that I remember being taught on the shopfloor as well. These were very important elements of working-class computer learning more broadly, as well as the principal opportunity for participation with coworkers and creative engagement with the technology beyond simply waiting for the next meal break. These gaps were actively and creatively produced in response to workplace rules. One example is provided by an autoworker who outlines the collective efforts of coworkers to learn more about computers in the workplace. In this account, we again see the important features of working-class computer learning that sometimes do not involve computers directly. In these instances, computer-mediated practice is not the goal of the activity but rather takes place at the operational level. The excerpt begins with a discussion about the introduction of computers on the shopfloor and the potential for managerial control. The interviewee goes on to describe forms of subversion, collectively accomplished,

representing a countervailing effort at control that among other things
opens up opportunities in the workplace for greater exploration of computer systems by workers.

I: Pretty much computers are getting involved now at the plant, eh?

R: Oh, yeah, on the floor even now, well the ADM machine, you know
where they cut off the bars at the back of the plant? Well, you see, I've
got my own *PIN [identification] number*, if you're an operator you have
to learn how to enter the material, so you have to enter that into the
company computer that a bundle of steel has gone into production and
how many pieces you've cut off.

I: So it's automatic inventory?

R: Yeah, like when I cut it, I have to tell them it's been cut.

I: Pin number, eh, you can't just plug it in?

R: No.

I: Does that kind of strike you as/

R: So no one else can use it.

I: Oh, so nobody can screw around with it.

R: Yeah.

I: So they know exactly who's doing what, they can really get an overview
of what

R: Yeah and when I punch it in, the time comes up, like when I go in the
next day I come in, and it tells me the last time you used it was at 9:05
and what part number I entered and how much of it, so *it keeps track of
everything going through the plant*. Everything is done on computer now.
Where when I first started there, there was a ton of paperwork, now
it's just on the screen and that's it.

I: Boy, management can really know what's going on.

R: Oh, *they know everything now*.

I: Does that kind of strike you somehow?

R: Well, *like anything else, you get together and learn how to manipulate it* so
they can't find stuff. Somebody is always there to manipulate.

I: People will always figure something out.

R: Oh, yeah. Actually, some of the people on the floor that do have
[supervisors'] PIN numbers have been able to get into the computers and
have been able to get into the *forbidden* zones of the computer. See, our
numbers will only allow us so far if you don't know the *access codes*. So,
we've gone into the foreman's office and found codes and figured out where

they lead to, and so we can go in and look around.... We got one guy, I won't name names, and he can go right into personnel files, which is kind of shocking to me, our absenteeism reports, everything. He can pull it all out, and he has *no training at all* [laughing], he *doesn't even own a computer*, he just figured it out on his own at work. He fiddles around all the time between just punching away and *watching over the foreman's shoulder*.... (W19)

The types of control over time and space that Fiske (1993) outlined among the TWA call center workers can be identified through accounts like this one. These instances direct our attention to the fact that there is a dialectic of resistance and control in even the most electronically advanced labor process. We saw this among the clerical workers described in Chapter 4 and now here on the shopfloor of an auto parts plant. PIN numbers and requirements to log in and out offer management a means of monitoring workers, but workers continue to find ways to penetrate technological systems and disrupt this control. Workers' creative responses to these conditions, how they learn, why they learn, and what they're up against in learning provide a description of the material structure of working-class computer practice in the workplace as well as an example of how people creatively overcome material barriers in even the most disciplined contexts.

Another activity commonly revealed in the interviews was the workers' use of unsanctioned access to company computers to respond to the alienating dimensions of modern industrial work. Workers suffering from boredom, faced with computer systems that are supposed to be closed to them, hide their own computer programs in company system subfiles in order to carry out their own version of *la perruque*. In this interview, a chemical worker describes how he first learned this form of computing from coworkers in an earlier job at an aircraft manufacturing plant. He now applies this skill and knowledge and passes them on to his new work mates. Again, many of the themes from earlier chapter recur here, including how different spheres of activity overlap and how collective practice in interstitial space is often a central feature of working-class computer learning.

I: Do you have anybody you can talk to about it, a friend you can call?

R: Used to. I used to work with a guy at the plant where I worked before. We used to just kind of *talk all the time*.... He took a company course, so that's *how basically I got into it*, he showed me some stuff.... You know, the more you see the system and kind of *hack around*, you learn that way.

I: Have you learned any programming hacking around at work so far?

R: No, basically I was just reporting the batch and stuff and making the labels and stuff. It's pretty basic. Just follow certain procedures, you know, for a receipt you press F1.

I: But on your own, on your spare time.

R: Yeah, well, it's kinda like *you go in and out of the system, and see what's there, but sometimes they won't let you get access* to some of the stuff.

I: If it was a centralized system I bet it would be really interesting, eh?

R: Oh, yeah, well I was just fooling around, and [a coworker] said, "How long have you been here?" and I say, "Ah, four or six months." "And you know how to go in there? I've been here for five years and I don't know how to do that." I say, "Ah, it's pretty basic, you know."

I: So, do you show them anything?

R: Yeah. They say, "Well, how do you do this?" and I give a command, go to whatever, and then once you've gotten into the operating system it's pretty basic, you know. . . . *I tell them wherever all the games are hidden,* and then you get out of there, and usually once you're in there [a program or game], they tell you what to do so.

I: So you're showing other workers how to get into these games and things or whatever?

R: Yeah, yeah. You can't really harm anything unless you delete something and you can't really delete anything. You go in and out and you don't harm anything. (W8)

Making do is an expression of subordinate standpoints in local practice in the context of systems of power. It is described in general terms by Certeau (1984), but here we see the concept grounded in a discussion of class relations and computer learning practice specifically. Although *weak* (using Certeau's terms), these forms of subordinate learning and the local skills and knowledge they produce are an important dimension of computer learning in industrial working-class life. In response to boredom, routinization, and idiot-proof technology, workers learn how to hack into machines at the workplace, pass this knowledge on to coworkers, and in so doing contribute in a concrete way to learning cultures and the working-class learning habitus. At the same time, the workplace imposes disciplinary structures that have real consequences with important material effects. The workplace and the technology are physically designed with managerial control in mind. Electronic surveillance and work discipline, as well as narrow job design, are material structures of the workplace that workers collectively attempt to learn their way around.

Summary

This chapter focused on several key ways in which working-class people's computer learning is shaped by the distribution of material resources. I began by discussing some of the most obvious ways that working-class computer learning is shaped by material structures of practice in the home, community, and workplace. I briefly outlined the importance of time, space, and human energy in the home, with attention to the way gender is implicated in class processes. In considering the household division of labor we saw how important it was for working-class learners to generate informal learning networks, how these networks aided in meeting the challenges of scarce material resources, what happened when such networks were not available, and how these networks were gendered. The portrait of the isolated, usually female, working-class learner is not a positive one. It seems that it is only within a developed, solidaristic network that the typical class-based patterns of opportunity and resource distribution can be effectively countered in working-class life. It is through careful use of narrow openings and sharing of resources that the most organized segments of the working class can generate the material resources necessary to subvert these basic patterns of computer access and use.

I explored a large-scale survey analysis of computer access and use in Canada by Nakhaie and Pike (1998). Here I demonstrated both the importance and the limitations of these analyses. What these studies fail to address is the creativity and forms of resistance to constraints generated by working people. In the final sections, I focused on computer learning practice in the workplace and demonstrated how the structures of participation were rooted in the basic dynamics of the capitalist political economy. Far from being mere abstractions, issues of managerial control, organizational rationalization, routinization, alienation brought on by technological and work station design, and the experience of these things from a working-class standpoint had real material effects on people's learning. In the end, we see the relevance of an entire range of material structures for a full understanding of participation in computer learning practice.

At the same time, people were not passive victims of these material forces but often responded in creative ways. A brief discussion of Certeau's notion of *la perruque* helped to focus attention on examples of how people made do in the workplace, resisted managerial control by using tactical practices of subversion, and in so doing engaged in forms of computer learning. Each section demonstrated how material structures do not simply direct activity in some mechanistic way, but rather mediate it to provide gaps for learning. Throughout, it is clear that important class difference exist in access to and use of computers.

9   Contradiction and Commodification in Working-Class Computer Learning

> The taste of porridge does not tell us who grew the oats.
>
> *Karl Marx, Capital*, Volume 1

Reification is a term that Marx used in his later writing to describe a process through which people's living practices come to be understood as "things." Marx offered the first model of analysis that consistently problematized the reification of human activity under capitalism. The preceding pithy quote directs out attention to this process, and I use it to emphasize the key theme of this final analytical chapter: that broad sets of social, historical, and political-economic relations always lie just below the surface of the things we do. Learning practices are no exception to this rule, and in this chapter my goal is to show computer learning as a living human and specifically political-economic activity.

Sociocultural approaches to adult learning such as situated learning and activity theory inherently dereify learning. They move beneath the commonsense surface of learning, and they trace its social roots. At the foundation of these analyses is the concept of *contradiction*. Contradictions in communities of practice or activity systems are the driving force, the engine of learning. Learning, if it refers to nothing else, refers to a process of change, and according to Ilyenkov (1982), contradiction refers to the tensions within any system that bring about incremental quantitative change as well as occasional qualitative and transformational changes in that system. The concept is inherently historical and describes a key element of dialectic analysis of systems in motion as figured in the original work of Marx. The notion of contradiction focuses on the quantitative to qualitative change as "two temporally differentiated moments within the same process" (Ollman, 1993:15).

[T]he incompatible development of different elements within the same relation, which is to say between elements that are also dependent on one another ... bring such change and interaction as regards both present and future into a single focus. (Ollman, 1993:15–16)

Systemic tensions and conflicts that undermine an equilibrium and other qualities that sustain an equilibrium are manifestations of different movements within the process of contradiction. There is a constant push and pull that characterizes a system in motion as internal relations act upon each other and produce change.[1]

Engeström provides a basic example of how to understand the concept of contradiction in the context of activity theory by drawing on the example of doctor and patient activity within the medical system.

The primary contradiction of activities in capitalist socio-economic formations lives as the inner conflict between exchange value and use value within each element of the triangle of activity [see Figure 1.1 in this book]. A hypothetical work activity of general practitioners in primary medical care may serve as an illustration. The primary contradiction, the dual nature of use value and exchange value, can be found by focussing on any of the elements of the doctor's work activity. For example, instruments of this work include a tremendous variety of medicaments and drugs. But they are not just useful preparations for healing – they are above all commodities with prices, manufactured for a market, advertised and sold for profit. (Engeström, 1992:20)

Engeström goes on to discuss other levels of contradiction, but in general terms he provides a basic outline of how everyday practices can be examined for their political-economic character, their relationship to the commodity form, to capitalism, and, by extension, to class processes. In the situated learning approach, other theorists, such as Lave and Wenger (1991), supplement the core contradiction of the commodity form with the idea of *continuity and displacement*. For them, the core contradiction is rooted less in political economy than in skill differences between masters and apprentices, who struggle to dominate one another for the sake of the community (pp. 114–116). Despite the differences among these scholars, however, there is agreement that activity cannot be meaningfully understood without figuring some mechanism of contradiction, struggle, and transformation that drives systemic changes as well as changes in individual forms of participation, skill, and knowledgeability.

---

[1] Ollman outlines five distinct forms of movement that make up the process of contradiction: mutual undermining, mutual support, immanent unfolding, changing overall forms, and, finally, partial or permanent resolution (1993:50–53).

In computer learning, these changes are seen, for example, in individual interaction with the technology, in the forms of mature practice that develop, and in the general patterns of participation within groups and systems of activity as a whole. These refer to contradictions at the operational, goal, and motive levels of activity, respectively. However, forms of contradiction can also be traced in the interaction between different spheres of activity (computing in the home, the workplace, etc.). What is particularly important to an analysis of learning and the focus of this chapter, however, is the fact that these contradictions, even in their broadest forms, must not be relegated to mere background or historical context. For Marx through Ilyenkov (1982), Sweezy (1964), and Ollman (1993), as well as for original activity theorists such as Leont'ev (1978:11–14), it was believed that the failure to include these seemingly broad political questions leads to a failure to understand the dynamics and true meaning of the specific form of practice. In keeping with the activity theory tradition, I suggest that we must, in effect, broaden our perspective to better understand the detailed patterns and contingencies that define specific forms of concrete, everyday learning practice.

In the following sections, I explore the broader historical materialist dimensions of computer technology and learning in working-class life, with a focus on the process of commodification and its linkage to contradictions at what activity theorists call the *broader motive level* of activity. Though it builds on the earlier discussions, this focus offers one of the broadest forms of the argument that the adult learning process is never class neutral. Throughout, I draw on the work of Marx to show how the concept of contradiction helps us see the interrelations between commodity-form, use-value, exchange-value, fetishization, and alienation, on the one hand, and credentialization, education, and informal computer-based learning, on the other. I begin with a discussion of commodification that returns us to the basic principles of contradiction in the commodity-form in Marx's own work, connect this discussion to issues of learning, and then provide a detailed look at exchange-value and use-value-oriented working-class computer-based activity. As Marx established in the first chapters of *Capital*, the commodity form is the heart of capitalism and the type of class society it entails. Following this, I argue that by identifying the role of the commodity-form, as well as by identifying the processes of commodification within an activity, we are – necessarily – identifying living class processes within that activity.

The Commodity-Form and the Commodification Process

Although the idea of the commodity-form and the process of commodification may seem to be separate from computer learning, in this chapter I argue that under a sociocultural approach, they define fundamental dynamics of the learning process. As activity theory argues, the commodity-form is the source of the core contradiction in activity. It drives change in patterns of participation and provides the bases for an increasingly dominant motive of activity. Lave and Wenger's understanding of the role of the commodity-form in legitimate peripheral participation is different from the one described in activity theory but is nonetheless seen as central. Focusing on the use-value and exchange-value dimensions of learning in the context of schooling versus apprenticeship relationships, they point to the role of testing and credentialization in bringing about an important form of contradiction.

Testing in schools and trade schools (unnecessary in situations of apprenticeship learning) is perhaps the most pervasive and salient example of a way of establishing the exchange value of knowledge. Test taking then becomes a new parasitic practice, the goal of which is to increase the exchange value of learning independently of its use value. (Lave and Wenger, 1991:112)

It's a fairly straightforward claim that educational credentialization is an important example of the commodification of learning. However, at the same time, it's fair to say that this claim is rarely followed to its logical political-economic conclusions. In other words, learning translated into a credential is part of a value production process that is, in turn, involved in the exchange of labor power in the labor market. By extension, in claiming this, I am also arguing that learning is fundamentally a class process, namely, the buying and selling of labor power in a market that includes one's class standpoint in the exchange. More relevant to the focus of this book, however, is the question of whether or not the commodity-form plays a role in learning beyond credentialization and testing. Does it exist within everyday forms of learning, and if so, how might we begin to identify and understand it in these diverse and often fragmentary contexts? To my mind, fully understanding the nature of the commodity-form is best achieved by returning to first principles. A brief review of Marx's own analysis is useful in this regard and provides an important starting point for a political-economic analysis of the activities that make up working-class computer learning.

Volume 1 of *Capital* begins with Marx's most cogent analysis of the character of the commodity-form within capitalism. He describes it as the core building block of capitalism, linking it to the different circulation patterns of commodities and money. He outlines basic circuits of exchange, with commodities (C) and money (M) being exchanged for one another to form what he refers to as either a C-M-C or an M-C-M circulation pattern. I suggest that by beginning with these two basic patterns, we can understand the structuring effects of capitalism and social class on our everyday learning at the motive level of activity.

In circulation C-M-C, the money is in the end converted into a commodity which serves as a use-value; it has therefore been spent once and for all. In the inverted form M-C-M, on the contrary, the buyer lays out money in order that, as a seller, he may recover money.... The money is not spent[;] it is merely advanced.... We have here, therefore, a palpable difference between the circulation of money as capital, and its circulation as mere money.... The path C-M-C proceeds from the extreme constituted by one commodity, and ends with the extreme constituted by another, which falls out of circulation and into consumption. Consumption, the satisfaction of needs, in short use-value, is therefore its final goal. The path M-C-M, however, proceeds from the extreme of money and finally returns to that same extreme. Its driving and motivating force, its determining purpose, is therefore exchange-value. Marx, (1867–1868/1990:249–250, Vol. 1)

According to Marx, capital and the internal contradiction between use-value and exchange-value is at its core defined by the difference between the C-M-C and M-C-M circuits. The difference between these circuits is dependent on the projected plans for either direct use or further exchange. This distinction provides us with the bases for understanding the exchange-value and use-value orientations of many activities, including those involving computer learning. In turn, these different value orientations can be used to understand the hidden political-economic identity of learning practice. However, learning practice as either use-value- or exchange-value-oriented cannot be identified in absolute terms but rather is dependent on the analysis of the activity system (and system of systems) as a whole. Furthermore, commodities themselves always exhibit both use-value, broadly conceived, and exchange-value; likewise, human activity is always generated around a combination of these dominant value orientations as well. Nevertheless, we can still examine practices for their primary organizing value orientation. In plain terms, we can explore empirically whether activity is primarily organized around use-value generation and the direct satisfaction of individual/collective needs or whether it is primarily organized around the generation of exchange-values and eventual integration into some form of market relationship. At all times, it should be kept in mind that these alternative circuits of exchange and value orientations produce learning that may be identical in appearance, while distinctive in political-economic relevance, and class-based relevance. Drawing on this explanation, I suggest, provides the basis for identifying important distinctions between, for example, the everyday learning among the corporate elites seen in Chapter 6 and some of the everyday learning among working-class people seen elsewhere. Though the activities are similar in appearance, following Lukàcs, we see that the outcome of the learning "returns to" one group and is ultimately "appropriated from" the other group, giving the two processes very different class characters.

Returning to the ideas of testing, educational credentials, and exchange-value discussed earlier by Lave and Wenger (1991) for a moment, we can now see that the process they describe actually points to the production of exchange-value in the learning process, a process Marx associated with commodity fetishism and the process of reification. In explaining fetishism, Marx argued that labor power, the capacity to engage in useful activity that adds value, is unique because it is the only commodity whose use-value is defined by its ability to create exchange-value. No other commodities, without exception, have the power to do this. Marx was quick to point out that labor power – to which learning, knowledge, and skill can be thought to add value – despite being sold for a price (a wage) and being distributed in a market, is not the same as commodities like sugar, overcoats, or pork bellies because its value does not arise from the calculation of the quantity of labor expended in its production.[2] Rather, it is produced by human activities that are, strictly speaking, outside a capitalist labor process, that is, they produce value that has the potential to be appropriated for more than its market rate. This alternative form of value production takes place, for example, through forms of community- and household-based activity. Here participants do not seek to appropriate surplus value or maximize the

---

[2] This is one of the most basic contradictions that underlies the *human capital theory*. If we are to use the metaphor of capital (and imagine relations of capitalism that give it meaning) in terms of *human resources*, we must take all that goes with it. In other words, the development of human capital would be continuous with a process of appropriation of surplus value and, in a sense, *self-exploitation*. Human capital theory is therefore not adequate on two (related) counts: (1) it ignores the necessarily alienating ramification of self-exploitation and (2) it depends on the substitution of quantity (exchange-value) for quality (use-value). See Livingstone (1998, chapter 4) for further discussion.

profit of their collaboration on the basis of private ownership; rather, they more often are engaged in the satisfaction of direct human needs. Sharpening the basic observations of the role of the contradiction within the commodity-form that activity theory has identified, we can locate this contradiction in the process of commodification of labor power in human activity.

In terms of computer learning, it is clear that interviewees often describe practices that are organized as a commodity (i.e., computer literacy) production process. Despite drawing on informal, solidaristic learning networks in which collaboration is nonappropriative and noncapitalist, many interviewees described how their production of computer literacy was aimed at future exchange in a labor market. Indeed, understanding their practice in this way, in effect, legitimized it according to a dominant discourse of learning and, in particular, the discourse of human capital production. Activation of these forms of *human capital* discourses of learning, in fact, helped people create the mental distance necessary to identify their participation as (legitimate) learning practice. This objectification of one's activity parallels the processes Marx described as commodity fetishism and reification in that a whole social process is reduced to a commodity/thing. Learning, in other words, is legitimated upon conversion into an object for market exchange (i.e., M-C-M). It is clear that credentialized learning offers a means of capturing and bringing into relations of production the activities previously beyond the logic of commodification and capital. However, even without a formal system of credentialization, people can still be seen to orient their learning practice toward the moment of exchange in such a way that it sometimes forms a general organizing principle of activity, largely but not exclusively functioning at the motive level.

[It] cuts him off from his [*sic*] labour power, forcing him to sell it on the market as a commodity, belonging to him. And by selling this, his only commodity, he integrates it (and himself: for his commodity is inseparable from his physical existence) into a specialized process that has been rationalized and mechanised, a process that he discovers already existing, complete and able to function without him and in which he is no more than a cipher reduced to an abstract quantity, a mechanised and rationalised tool.... The transformation of all objects into commodities, their quantification into fetishized exchange-values is more than an intensive process affecting the form of every aspect of life in this way.... For the capitalist this site of the process means an increase in the quantity of objects for him to deal with in his calculations and speculations. In so far as this process does acquire the semblance of a qualitative character, this goes no further than an aspiration towards the increased

rationalization, mechanisation and quantification of the world confronting him. . . .
For the proletariat, however, the 'same' process means its own emergence as a class.
(Lukács, 1971:166, 171)

It is under these conditions that everyday activity can come to stand over working-class people as a fetishized commodity, alienated and separate from them, despite the irony that at present time very few of these people will actually get a chance to use these skills at work. Indeed, this suggests that the actual exchange-value of the skills is largely imaginary, irrespective of its power to organize practice.

At the same time, despite this form of integration and incorporation into relations in which capital dominates, there remain opportunities for and evidence of deviations. Learning organized on different principles continues to exist. However, use-value-oriented learning is not so easily identified. This offers, among other things, an important methodological challenge to analysts as well as to those groups, such as trade unions, that wish to make more organized use of these forms of learning as a transformational resource. This learning is not so readily converted into a thing and is not fetishized, but neither is it legitimized by a discourse of private economic gain, so it remains largely hidden from people's consciousness. Because direct use is the organizing motive of C-M-C circuits of exchange, there is no need to quantify what is essentially a fluid, ongoing social process. Engagement among people is not expected to be valorized as capital/time invested. It is a process that people do not instrumentalize and rationalize in this way. Thus, use-value orientation is more easily discussed as participatory, ongoing relations whose purposes are realized "in the doing." What's essential at this point, however, is simply to understand that by drawing on these two basic political-economic concepts, it becomes clear that activity for use and activity for exchange are fundamentally different dimensions of learning practice. In terms of the different structures they impose on the way people think and talk about their learning and in their role as an organizing principle of this learning, they speak to different meanings, purposes, and trajectories of development.

Before moving on to an analysis of the role of use-value and exchange-value dimensions of working-class computer learning, however, I want to briefly ground the ideas in interviewees' comments. Close inspection of the excerpts presented in the preceding chapters reveals a range of latent clues, each of which revolves around themes of instrumentalization and market rationalization of learning practice. These include the quantification of learning, the credentialization and standardization of learning, and, of course, cases in which people openly organize their learning around participation in the capitalist labor processes and labor markets. Clues to the identification of learning organized around the principles of use-value generation, although more diffuse, are equally available (if less frequent). Existing in a discursive vacuum, these practices were often identified negatively, by the things they were not. Most often, people's everyday practices were contrasted with the credentialism of formal schooling. Take this autoworker's description of the reasons that *weren't* involved in his taking a computer course.

> I didn't care if I passed the course or not. I was just going there saying, "*If I can pick up a few things, I'm happy.*" I didn't care. It wasn't about credits or nothing, so, you know, that's why I went. (W5)

Of course, the goal of the activity wasn't to *not* obtain a credential. This aversion to credentials plays a role in identifying the broader motive of the activity: primarily (though probably not exclusively) to satisfy his needs directly (to be "happy"). It is an activity whose meaning is found in the doing. Perhaps equally important is the fact that he feels, as many interviewees did, that he must defend his orientation.

One final point of introduction is made in the interviews with people who are members of a trade union. Discussions here included the relationship between learning, credentials, and collective bargaining. The comments of the following autoworker, for example, deal with the collective bargaining his union has done with his company over financial support for members who wish to take local college courses. He identifies the basic contradiction of the commodity-form when he contrasts learning for exchange and learning for the direct satisfaction of human needs. Underlying his description is an indication of how the tendency to commodify learning can be partially subverted by forceful representation of working-class interests. The excerpt begins with a description of the courses union members can take that would be paid for by the company. It is followed by a rationale for why the union bargained for such a broad definition of eligible courses.

> You could take dog grooming, any number of courses ... [t]he truth of the matter, I mean, going out and becoming a *computer whiz*, you might as well do it *for your own gratification* because it's not, unless you go into management, it's not really going to help you a whole lot in the workplace. *Not to be negative on education*, but that's just the reality. So

> that's why we wanted a wide range [for] people to be able to take *things that interested them*, whether it be wood carving, dog grooming, whatever, to do it for their own self-gratification. (W63)

Underlying the specifics of the case is a clear and concise explanation of the relations between use-value and exchange-value in relation to working-class computer learning. It demonstrates how the process of commodification can be identified within relations of learning and credentialization. The process of becoming a "computer whiz" can take on two quite different meanings as they become related to use-value and exchange-value orientations at the motive level of activity. It can "help you in the workplace" under conventional conditions of the commodification of one's learning/labor power, or it can be for your "own gratification." The description openly identifies a working-class standpoint in these relations and shows some of the ways that an organized working-class formation such as a trade union finds ways to respond to the commodification of learning to lessen the destructive competition, work intensification, and erosion of solidarity it can breed in an internal labor market. It is also important that we recognize the significance of the autoworker's comment about not wanting to be "negative on education," and indeed, he is doing nothing of the sort. Rather, he's identifying two different social processes for exactly what they are in class terms.

Exchange-Value Orientations in Computer Learning Activity

> If you're *computer literate* it *means you* should be able to basically *move a lot easier from one job to another job*. (W16)

> I engage in education and training to learn something else and *to make myself more marketable*. [We] really need more training in computers. (W37)

Examples of deviation aside, the preceding excerpts highlight the exchange-value orientation and goal direction of much of the computer activity that workers described in this research. In both formalized and informal learning processes, people's computer learning focused on skills upgrading and marketability, and was oriented not to the satisfaction of human needs directly but instead to a market exchange, earning a wage, and movement from one job to another. It also becomes clear, in looking at excerpts like these, how the broader structure of the activity, or motive level, is rooted in one's standpoint as a wage earner in a competitive market. Of course, the contradictions that coexist within activity are closely interwoven with the contradictions discussed in Chapter 3, where I described the basic components of working-class technological common sense. As a motive for computer-mediated activity, the exchange-value orientation makes visible the political-economic structure of even informal, everyday learning. The impulse toward the commodification of computer learning is also partially contradicted by people's experiences in the learning networks that we've seen among the most organized segments of the working class. Notions of computer literacy[3] seem particularly prone to be linked with the commodification and human capital discourses of learning. For example, in the practices of working-class parents in these interviews, discussions closely link commodification and computer literacy in terms of their children's educational needs. Indeed, the apparent importance of computers to the world of work and the labor market has elevated computer literacy, at least in the minds of many of the interviewees in this research, to the level of a *master literacy*. A brief excerpt from an interview with this autoworker provides an example.

R: Like when we were growing up we had to learn *math and English* in school, [computer literacy] should almost be the same now. *They should have to learn it.*

I: So it's very important for the future?

R: Oh, it should be a *mandatory* course.

I: And this is directly connected with the job market when they graduate and stuff?

R: Well, I mean, people are running around with little laptops in their cars. I mean it's just, you know, *you can't be without it.* (W16)

The "mandatory" character of computer literacy for working people and their children is rooted not in the usefulness or richness of the skills and knowledge forms themselves necessarily, but rather in its value for capital as exchanged on a labor market and brought to bear in the labor process. Who needs computer literacy? As we saw in Chapter 6, it isn't necessarily elites and corporate executives, but rather those who depend for their livelihood on selling their labor power for a wage.

---

[3] The definition and content of computer literacy have been the subject of debate that I've largely sought to keep separate from the analysis in this research, but see a wonderful, and to my mind still not dated, collection of essays on the different ways of thinking about computer literacy in *Social Science Computer Review* 7(1), where Robins and Webster (1989a) attempt to insert a critical voice into the technocratically oriented range of dominant perspectives on the subject.

Other forms of class processes and commodification within computer learning are more subtle and derivative. For example, we've seen frequent comments on the use of computer games among interviewees. How can we understand the processes of personal consumption and entertainment as part of the motive structure of activity? Do computer-mediated practices that are simply forms of commodity consumption necessarily express and produce class dimensions as well? For Marx, individual consumption of commodities does not appear to have been, strictly speaking, a distinctively class process.[4] In Volume 1 of *Capital* (1867–1868/1990:chapter 23), for example, he outlined two basic types of consumption in capitalist society. The first form was what he called *productive consumption*, in which people consume raw materials along with portions of fixed capital to produce exchange-value in surplus of the capital advanced. This is clearly a political-economic activity. The second form was what he called *unproductive* or *individual consumption*, in which people use their money to satisfy their subsistence needs. Marx didn't limit these to physical needs but included culturally conditioned needs, among which we might include specific forms of entertainment such as computer games. The play among these basic distinctions can be traced in many of the interviews in this research. Discussing how much time he spends learning about computers, for example, this chemical worker describes why the learning that other workers do in playing computer games is different. His offhand remark shows that, for him, game use can be partially defined by its relationship to legitimate (exchange) value production.

Yeah, well, I just can't, people will spend three times [the amount of time he spends learning about computers] playing bloody games. I just can't see that, there's just *no value added*. (W18a)

Why is it that the learning surrounding computer gaming (let alone the wide range of practical skills necessary for computer gaming on the job despite managerial surveillance) is not seen as valuable? More fundamentally, how is value used in the context of this reference to computer learning? Value is understood as what is useful to exchange in a market;

---

[4] Bourdieu's (1984) classic work in this area is an exception. In terms of Marx's discussion specifically, see, for example, *Capital*, Volume 2 (e.g., chapters 1 and 2) in the context of productive capital/consumption and in *Theories of Surplus Value*. Also, note that Marx did little to distinguish between needs that are essential for human survival (e.g., shelter, food) and those that are artificially induced as a cultural desire in a particular community.

it is what capital finds useful or, more precisely, profitable. In this context, computer gaming is a form of individual consumption rather than productive consumption, and thus it is disqualified, at least in this worker's mind, as legitimate learning activity.

However, more broadly, Marx recognized that the relationship between capitalist production, distribution, exchange, and consumption is not as simple as the basic distinctions between individual and productive consumption. He described how the two forms of consumption are in fact moments of the reproduction of capitalism and relations of social class as a whole. Bourdieu has been particularly astute in recognizing the way cultural consumption and economic reproduction are intertwined. For both, although the commodity, even in individual consumption, is put to a use that satisfies a human need directly, it is also part of a circuit of capitalist production, distribution, and consumption. Thus, even most individual consumption, no matter how innocently conceived, is implicated in a broader process in which class relations are ultimately reproduced.

In every aspect of daily life in which the individual worker imagines himself to be the subject of his own life he finds this to be a illusion that is destroyed by the immediacy of his existence. This forces upon him the knowledge that the most elementary gratification of his needs, his own individual consumption, whether it proceed within the workshop or outside it, whether it be part of the process of reproduction or not, forms therefore an aspect of the production and the reproduction of capital; just as cleaning machinery does, whether it be done while the machinery is working or while it is standing idle.... (Lukács, 1971:164)

At the same time, it is clear that individual consumption shouldn't always be thought of as a simple ratification and reiteration of the capitalist logic. Working-class computer gaming can represent something more than *class escapism* (Hakken, 1993). We need to recognize how, in use, a commodity always presents an opportunity for activation in unexpected ways. Computer gaming in the workplace, for example, provides goal-directed practice that requires creative collective social action and the development and sharing of new knowledge and skills in the workplace that have little to do with the direct interest of capital. As several interviewees outlined, these practices often lead to the breaking of security features of company computer systems and many other types of mundane subversion of workplace discipline. Such collective activities have the potential to build a feeling of membership and identities-in-practice that can lead to more conscious, formalized, and perhaps even class-conscious action. Certainly, among the interviewees in my research, issues of escapism, commodification, individual consumption, and productive consumption were tightly intertwined.

Use-Value-Oriented Computer Learning Activity: Communities and Social Change

Revolutionary practice or activity (not to be equated with the particular revolutionary activity of making a revolution) is ordinary day-to-day, hour-to-hour, human (historical) activity.... The distinctly human quality of our species is its capacity to practice revolutionary activity, a capacity, as we have said, that is, unfortunately, only sometimes self-consciously manifest. (Newman and Holzman, 1993:46)

Alternative practices, although not openly resisting forms of class domination, can nevertheless express the deep contradiction, embedded in the commodity-form, within computer-mediated activities. In some cases, as in the trade union activity mentioned earlier, alternative practices take the form of organized, conscious responses of collectivities representing class interests specifically. Other cases of practice that run counter to the basic commodifying tendencies of life under capitalism are less self-conscious but nevertheless are an active response to contradictions along the lines described in Certeau's (1984, 1997) notion of the tactical (see the previous chapter). These more subtle forms of practice take place in the interstitial spaces of dominant institutions. Whether brought on by the specific forms of technology in use, by elements of the social organization and division of labor within an activity, or by the interrelations between articulating activity systems, in all cases these practices are always responses from a particular class standpoint to the inner contradictions of activity. However, learning activity, whether it is wood carving or dog grooming or computer-based practice, is a process that needn't be and isn't always exploitive in nature.

Hakken's *Computing Myths, Class Realities: An Ethnography of Technology and Working People in Sheffield* (1993) examines how working people can engage with and understand computer technology in their everyday lives. He reports on a highly organized working-class community in northern England that produced a range of alternative computing practices including modes of computer-mediated learning that were not structured directly by the commodification process. These alternative practices revolved around what working-class Sheffielders understood as *socially useful* computing.

What was distinctive about the Sheffield region was the extent to which people there had pushed for local policies to influence computing. These policies aimed to channel computerization into 'socially useful production.' That is, they aimed to promote computer use that built on rather than replaced existing worker skills and local economic structures. In part as a consequence of strong worker education institutions, the policies encouraged 'community computing' in opposition to 'administrative computing.' (Hakken, 1993:28)

People in Hakken's work sought to develop specific computer practices in the community that were not oriented toward profit-making but instead sought to meet the needs of community members directly. Hakken comments that in some cases "working class people can bend computing to their own social purposes and thereby participate actively in the creation of computing culture" (1993:79). Examples of this form of countervailing social organization of computer-mediated activity documented by Hakken included workers' study circles; organized groups such as Computers for People; a women's Technology Training Workshop; and, a Community Operations Research Unit that offered technological support for other community groups. Each of these revolved around members' search for a way of using computing to extend democracy and expand the relations of collectivity and community (pp.179–180). What Hakken's research drives home is that there are distinct examples of alternative computer-based practice that exist in opposition to the processes of alienation and commodification.

Interviewees in my research also expressed alternative use-value orientations in computer practice, though there was little evidence of the formally organized computing cited in Hakken. Specifically, there was significant evidence of computer learning that went beyond both individual consumption and learning directed simply to gaining a formal credential. These were not revolutionary practices in the conventional sense, but were simply directed to building social connections among friends and family members in the home, neighborhood and workplace. In the following excerpt, we can see how some people carried out computer-mediated practices that contributed to communities in the local trade union and groups of workers on the shopfloor. The excerpt begins with my observation (as the interviewer) that the person had produced some (computer-generated) documents for his upcoming union meeting. He outlines how he learned his computer skills, reiterating many of the basic themes discussed in previous chapters. He goes on, however, to talk about the activities of another worker at the plant. This type of description paralleled practices reported by others in my research and indicates a hidden layer of computer-based activity oriented to the direct needs of participants.

I: I saw in preparation for the *union meeting* I saw your name on the bottom of a chart. Did you *prepare that chart?*

R: Oh, for the union meeting, yeah.

I: So you do some home computing?

R: I have a system at home. We moved a while ago and I haven't unpacked it yet. And I get paid to do it here [that is, paid to produce resins, during which he makes unsanctioned use of company computers to create documents], so.

I: There's access to a computer here?

R: Oh, for sure. I would say about half the membership has some sort of access to computers, like you have to be *authorized to be on the system,* but I mean half of them are almost *computer experts.* There's one guy here on the midnight shift, he's got kind of like a *catering service going for guys in his department.* He keeps it to his buddies, sometimes off-shift fellas. He's very proficient, he's probably more proficient in the computers than I am.

I: Caters to the off-shift? What do you mean?

R: Oh, brings in chocolate bars, coffee, stuff like that. He's got a coffee urn set up and covers his costs.

I: And how does he use the computer?

R: Yeah, he uses it. He's *not supposed to, but he has a menu set up on the company system.* We actually approached him, we wanted him to set up social committees for the union, because he is very good at that sort of thing, fifty/fifty draws, and, well, he organizes a party every year for the plant, like a Christmas dance, and he just raises money throughout the year with fifty/fifty draws and what not, he is just very good that way. . . .

I: Do you know if he has any *formal training in computers?*

R: *No, not to my knowledge,* but I think he started taking correspondence now. I don't know him that well. He works steady midnights. (W18a)

The activity described in the latter portion of the excerpt could be said to operate tactically within the interstitial spaces of the workplace. The interviewee's coworker does what he does out of enjoyment, contributing to the quality of life in his workplace despite rules that make his unauthorized use of the company's computer system a risk. His computer learning takes place at the operational level and outside of the interests of the company and their intended purposes for their computer systems. Catering to fellow workers takes the form of a cooperative system in which the costs of coffee and food are covered and people save money they'd otherwise spend on overpriced items from the company-run cafeteria. These practices work around the control of the workplace and even of the profit-making of the company cafeteria. They are an example of use-value-oriented, computer-based activity that was relatively widespread among the workers interviewed. These were cases of mundane, everyday activity that, although not opposed to the interests of capital in any direct or definitive way, was not aligned with these interests either. Other working-class computer-mediated activity outside of the factory that was also organized by the principle of use-value production included learning computers to help out in a child's local sports league, to support local trade union activity, to share cooking recipes with friends and neighbors, to share music, to keep up with friends and family, and so on. Through such activities valuable computer skills are generated. However, it is also this hidden system of knowledge production – hidden because it is denied and denigrated by participants themselves, as well as left unrecognized by educational institutions and workplaces – that has contributed to the imbalance between knowledge generation and knowledge use that David Livingstone describes as the *education–jobs gap* (1998).

One other basic form of use-value-oriented, computer-based activity that should be discussed before concluding this section can be identified by drawing on an excerpt from the partner of an autoworker I spoke with. Her description outlines one final way in which computer-mediated activity tends to resist incorporation into the processes of commodification. It has some similarities to the themes introduced in the discussion of the man who organizes coffee sales in the chemical plant. It involves a mundane but nevertheless direct deviation from legitimate market exchanges and highlights how computer learning contributes to alternative cooperative forms of economic activity. In discussions with her about computer learning, she said that she has spent a great deal of time learning about various types of database software. When I asked why, she explained the relationship between this learning and the goal of her activity, which was to share her passion for movies with friends and coworkers in her workplace as well as in her husband's.

R: I have my movie list on the computer. . . . It automatically puts it in
     alphabetical order and stuff like that. Then I can put in categories.
     Like I have cartoons, movies, miscellaneous, music, sports – like I have

them in categories, and then I print it up on the printer, so I have my list, and when I went to look for a particular ones, see, I have the numbers too – so I know where to find that movie.

I: Okay, so like a reference number, eh?

R: Yeah, and then for people, like I used to have one [list] I used to take to work with me because people from work would *borrow movies*, so they'd ask to see my list so they'd know what movies I'd had – stuff like that.

I: How big is your collection about?

R: Well the program numbers it, and it's up to nine hundred and – almost a thousand now.

I: So those are all movies that you have copied?

R: Yeah.

I: That's more than a video store.

R: Yeah, like I have movies, I have documentaries. Like I'm going to do this Beatles anthology thing [a six-hour documentary on television]. I'm taping one right now on the radio. . . . And, well I have three or four people who want me to make copies for them. Usually people call or just drop around, and they ask me to tape something for them or they borrow something. (W4b)

The quote from Newman and Holzman (1993) at the beginning of this section directed our attention to the notion of human historical activity, that is, activity that was not revolutionary in the conventional sense but nevertheless undermined core principles helping to organize social life in certain historical periods. What the woman in this excerpt went on to describe was the range of learning processes that helped her to construct her computer-based, informal, video library system for use by coworkers, neighbors, and family. It is an activity that stands in opposition to the two key principles of the capitalist logic: market system domination over other forms of exchange and private ownership of property. It is learning that is encapsulated in an activity system that not only counters, the commodification of skills but also subverts the for-profit exchange of goods and services. The significance of these and other informal systems of exchange that working people in this research talked about is that they were not organized around an impulse toward personal acquisitiveness and commodification. The idea of undermining the viability of employment for video shop workers wasn't lost on this woman, nor was the fact that movie producers invest a great deal to make movies, but what she did make clear was her belief in the unfairness of private ownership of what she felt was public communication.

Summary

This final analytical chapter has provided a discussion of commodification and learning from a working-class standpoint. It built on the analyses of computer learning already presented to bring into view an important means of identifying the way that apparently universal forms of practice are in fact differentiated and class-based. Based on an analysis of the contradiction inherent in the commodity form, I've argued that computer learning can be understood as a political-economic process through which people are incorporated into and sometimes resist incorporation into class processes. The recognition of these general dynamics of activity is not new to situated learning or activity theory. However, through a sustained conceptualization of use-value and exchange-value orientations in activity, important class dimensions were identified more clearly for investigation.

Use-values and exchange-values, including their apparently different patterns of transformation, are not separate from one another in the real world. Earlier discussions of overlapping spheres of activity anticipate this clarification in that, as I've claimed, it is misleading to see any hard and fast boundaries between economic and noneconomic activity. In this sense, learning at work is as much a communal activity as learning in the home or community is an economic one. However, as we begin to dig below the surface of reified things that people do, activity can be seen as having reproductive as well as nonreproductive and transformative dimensions. Returning to first principles in the form of a brief discussion of Marx's work was important for helping make the conceptual distinctions within activity theory and situated learning more clear. The examples of how people rejected dominant views of legitimate learning are extremely important in discussions of this kind, as they deepen our understanding of practice while at the same time refuting the deterministic tendencies of certain forms of class analysis. More important than balancing academic accounts of working-class life, however, these use-value orientations, revolving around the direct satisfaction of human needs and involving a tacit rejection of many of the organizing principles of capitalism, can serve as a starting point for making progressive use of the hidden learning capacities of subordinate groups.

10   Conclusions and Implications

Among the facts and claims that I used to start this book was the importance of recognizing social standpoints, especially my own, for understanding the argument I present. I can now outline this concern more accurately with the observation that every representation makes manifest a conviction. Honesty and method never make a representation of others innocent. The representation I've made of the people I've met, sometimes only briefly, supports the conviction that culture, as Certeau has so decisively put it, is plural and at the same time political in that it deals with possibilities – it makes the possible and impossible for us all. Yet, subordinate groups, in the face of material barriers, on their breaks, in their basements, kitchens, and neighborhoods, bear the burden of making this plurality. So I say, with a nod to a young Marx's original preoccupations, that we should take seriously the everyday life of people if we're to take one thing seriously. It may be the only real politics, the only real political economy there is.

In this book I've presented research on and discussions of literature in order to make visible the social as well as political-economic relations that shape adult learning and technology in working-class life, and by drawing on this research, the book could have taken a number of different directions. My purpose was to try to understand the full range of computer learning that working-class people engage in across a variety of social spheres – at work, in the neighborhood, and at home. Although access to schooling and training programs for working-class groups continues to be a problem, this research went beyond this issue. Social class affects more than access to formal education; it is embedded in the entire landscape of informal and everyday learning. The key challenge in presenting this argument was to make the processes of everyday learning visible or, more accurately, to make the social organization of everyday learning of working-class people visible. It was a challenge that, to my mind, proved to be too difficult for the majority of conceptual approaches to adult learning that I examined. In fact, I argued that these approaches displayed an interlocking set of class biases that systematically obscure, deny, and/or denigrate these learning processes, which working people tend to rely on most often. The solution to this initial problem was to turn to sociocultural approaches to learning, namely, situated learning and the Vygotsky-inspired activity theory; throughout, I've depended on these frameworks. Reflections on the work of Gramsci, Marxist-feminist theorists, and in particular Pierre Bourdieu, sharpen key areas of these frameworks, allowing an exploration of learning and technology in the lives of working-class people.

Among the findings of this exploration was that when working people talk about learning and computer technology, when we pay careful attention, we find that they are implicitly describing important class processes. The intersection of learning and technology provided a more or less direct link to discussions of the human experiences under advanced capitalism that defined a class condition. Paradoxically, in many ways, the last analytical chapter, Chapter 9, demonstrated that the learning process, that is, the process of social action and social change, among working-class people is key to both the reproduction and transcendence of class society. In this concluding chapter, I want to summarize and link the core arguments I've put forth in the book, offer several practical steps for the development of working-class practice in regard to issues of learning and computer technology, and finally, situate the main arguments in terms of the broader implications of key findings.

Computer Learning and Social Class: A Summary of Key Arguments

As a means of mapping the key arguments of the book, it makes sense to begin with a brief review of the way I approached the concepts of learning and computer technology (Chapters 2 and 3). Reevaluating the boundaries and meaning of the concept of adult learning was the first step in making visible the class relations inherent in people's computer learning. I suggested that the dominant tendencies of conventional adult learning theory play a role in the way that learning fits with contemporary social life. In other words, it is not coincidental that the individualization, universalization, and formalization of expert/novice relations, as well as the credentialization of learning, are effective means of integrating human activity with a process of exchange in a labor market. These are ideas that make sense under capitalism. Chapter 4 offered an analysis that helped to clarify several of the most difficult gaps in dominant understandings of learning. The detailed analysis of Larry and Roger learning together in the computer lab demonstrated the active everyday skills and abilities that are involved in even the most mundane computer-mediated activity. Here we got a sustained look at the tacit processes that underlie computer learning. At the center of this analysis was the claim that people can create knowledge collectively and are not necessarily bound by expert–novice relationships. This claim of the collective, social, and nonhierarchical dimensions of learning was, in fact, a counterargument to the dominant themes I outlined in the review of adult learning theory in Chapter 2. In the second part of this chapter, I analyzed human–computer–organization interaction in terms of organizational sequences of action. Gwen's activity presented further evidence of the class dimensions of computer learning focused on the workplace. We saw how the design features of the purchasing department's software mediated activity in the workplace. On the micro level, Oracle could be seen as the electronic embodiment of the core dynamics of capital accumulation and labor processes. Perhaps the most interesting aspect of the second case study, however, was how the creation of alternative sequences of action not only allowed workers to do their work efficiently but also shifted their forms of participation and hence caused them to learn.

Conceptualizing computer technology in a critical way was also important to the analysis. Looking at interviewees' perspectives on technology and their reasons for computer learning (Chapter 3) demonstrated the components and context of emergence for a working-class technological common sense. Connecting with the work of Gramsci, this common sense was a complex weave of dominant discourses and contradictory class experience. The core of this common sense was actively produced in the media as well as in people's workplaces, where narratives of technological progress were broadcast. Interviewees tended to mystify computer technology in their own lives and even conceived of computer literacy as a master literacy that everyone needed. At the same time, these notions conflicted with many experiences that people had in their own lives. What was good for capital, particularly at the point of production, diverged from what was good for the wage laborer when people took the time to reflect on concrete accounts of their own experiences. Also contradicting a core component of this common sense was the fact that people could develop fairly advanced knowledge and skill in using computers with little or no formal training, and that people typically found these skills to be far in advance of any requirements of the workplace. Although the working-class technological common sense was contradictory and fragmentary, it nonetheless played a key role in causing the majority of people, with varying degrees of enthusiasm, to begin computer learning.

Another set of arguments that I made in the book related to the further refinement of situated learning and activity theory approaches in light of my wish to trace the class dimensions of the entire range of people's computer-based practices. To begin with, I stated that understanding learning among subordinate groups who largely depend on the learning they do outside of formal courses requires a sociocultural approach to learning that can conceptualize the fragmentation of social life against which these groups struggle. The emerging recognition within the third generation of activity theory of the importance of understanding how different activity systems articulate with one another needs to be further elaborated. For my part, mostly in Chapters 5 and 9 but also in a variety of other places, I applied the notions of interstitial space (the generation of which itself requires a range of operational learning practices) and overlapping spheres of activity to understand how this fragmentation relates to class processes from a working-class standpoint. For the people I interviewed, computer learning was mingled with a range of goal-oriented practices and took place in a variety of locations, in many of which they experienced only limited discretionary control. Conceptualizations of learning limited to single spheres of activity, focused on narrow sets of goal-oriented practice and isolated from the full complement of practices through which working people produced the time and space necessary for interaction, will always miss what is essential to understanding this form of practice.

Building on this point, a second refinement contributed by the analysis involved a more thorough and more critical analysis of social standpoints in learning practice. The argument I presented in this book suggests that although, as Vygotsky pointed out, learning occurs whenever and wherever people have access to cultural tools, learning practices are both differentiated and differentiating in important ways. As I've noted repeatedly, recognition of the importance of social standpoints has already begun within situated learning and activity theory; however, the advancement of this program, particularly in the areas of major social divisions, can go much further. For these purposes, I've found the work of Marxist-feminist theorists indispensable. Specifically, it was the conceptualization of social class as an active process in which people engage from different standpoints that was key to highlighting the class dimensions of practice.

A third refinement relates to a reassertion of the importance of materialist analysis. In 1930 Vygotsky and Luria wrote as an epigraph, "... things are carried out with instruments and means" (quoted in Blanck, 1993:45), and to my mind it is the "means" that have not received enough analytical attention. In general terms, I emphasized the importance of integrating an explicit materialist component into the more general sociocultural approaches. Interviewees' relationship to various material structures and the distribution of time, space, and human energy in advanced capitalist society were the focus of Chapter 8 but informed discussion throughout the book as well. Related to this analysis in particular was the demonstration of the large degree to which working-class computer learning was gendered. The division of labor in working-class households – conditioned partly by class relations and partly by patriarchal relations – structured free and unfree time for discretionary activity. This distribution of material resources, in turn, was implicated in the patterns of computer learning. In this same chapter, I also explored how class differences relate to the distribution of home computer ownership. This analysis clarified the observations of recent educational surveys on how the capitalist class is reproducing itself through the use of computers. However, I also showed that despite this gap in private computer ownership, workers can still cobble together a learning environment. This analysis was extended to a discussion of how workers resist the material and organizational discipline in the workplace tactically to carry out computer-mediated learning. As a refinement on the sociocultural approaches to adult learning, we can conclude that the materiality of learning processes explains much about the directions and patterns of everyday learning among subordinate groups such as the working class. In terms of the situated learning approach specifically, I argued against the idea that skill differentials and the notion of mature practice can provide the sole bases for understanding the centripetal force of participation in communities of practice. Plainly, resources matter. They played a key role in shaping the learning patterns of working-class people.

A final refinement of the activity theory and situated learning theory approaches suggested by the analysis concerns the role that contradictions – specifically, the role of contradictions emerging from the commodity-form – play in understanding the character of working-class computer learning. In Chapter 9, I extended this idea to its logical conclusion by demonstrating how the conflict between use-value and exchange-value production, conceived as distinctive sets of orientations in activity, necessarily links learning to class processes. Basic Marxist concepts including fetishization and alienation, for example, can be applied, though I did not present a full discussion of their implications. Simply put, the contradiction of the commodity-form, to the degree to which it can be shown to operate, necessarily suggests important class dimensions of the learning process.

Having summarized the relationship between the major findings in the book and the approaches to learning theory I chose to take, in this portion of the chapter I want to review two other sets of findings and arguments that relate directly to the work of Bourdieu. The first one is the suggestion that there is a set of dispositional mechanisms that can be collectively referred to as a working-class learning habitus. Chapter 5 served as one of the main platforms for this argument, although the concept is implicated in several other places as well. This habitus was embodied in a set of dispositions, preferences, comportment, and sensibilities that defined the pattern of working-class learning. These dispositions were not stagnant but rather subject to re-formation in practice. This habitus emerged from people's position in broad sets of relations and, when fully expressed in materially stable conditions, gave rise to mutualistic and highly participatory forms of community. Further clues to the content of this learning habitus were found in the way participants collectivized and drew on each other's differences in interests, skills, and learning styles. Specific features of the working-class computer learning habitus were elaborated further in Chapter 6, where I traced an oppositional attitude toward formal education and training rooted in class experience. There I focused on the most conscious and formally organized expressions of class standpoints in computer-mediated learning. I began by establishing the important role played by class relations in the workplace. These affected people's computer learning both within and beyond the factory gates, again suggesting the existence of something more durable, that patterned forms of participation across multiple sites. In concluding Chapter 6, I also presented a brief analysis of class differences by examining a mini-sample of the dominant class groups. Here I looked at their practices and perspectives on learning, education, and technology, and radical differences in perspectives and practice emerged that helped clarify the distinctive features of working-class learning. Likewise, Chapter 7 demonstrated some of the ways in which the working-class learning habitus is developed through oral culture. Both talking about and talking within computer learning practice were used to store, transmit, and develop computer skills and knowledge in the everyday. Oral artifacts including specific narratives, sayings, and analogies not only presented information but also helped express and share interviewees' sense of their own standpoint in the social world. Now that I have reviewed the claims I've made regarding the learning habitus, it is safe to say that the concept is still in its early stages. Even in the analysis I provided, we saw that there were several variations. Although I'm convinced that there are clear tendencies that speak directly to class processes, it is clear that class processes alone do not adequately explain their origin. Gender and class produce forms of interaction that affect the learning strategies that are generated. Likewise, based on my brief indication of the role of ethnicity and language, race–class interactions in terms of the learning habitus should also be expected. The way these effects are mixed is, no doubt, another example of a local, moment-by-moment accomplishment with broad structural implications that requires careful investigation.

A second but more general thesis related to the work of Bourdieu concerns the parallel I draw between what he described as the processes of cultural distinction and the processes I describe as associated with the generation of learning capacity. It was the implicit, indirect ways that working people had of speaking about their learning, in contrast with the ease with which elite and executive class groups spoke about theirs, that first inspired this connection. I indicated that it was the degree of mental distance associated with, as Bourdieu puts it, distance from necessity that seemed to make it more difficult for working-class interviewees to articulate their everyday learning as learning per se. Access to proletarian public spheres, as discussed briefly in Chapter 7, undoubtedly plays a role in overcoming this, and certainly it was the case that trade union activists, those with ongoing access to just such an alternative public sphere, seemed to experience these constraints less than nonactivists. However, again, limited space makes this connection a suggestion rather than a full-blown argument, and therefore, this parallel between the process of distinction and its analogue in the area of learning should be considered preliminary.

Praxis and Working-Class Computer Learning

It's my belief that sociocultural analysis is well positioned to offer more than simply penetrating explorations of human activity. It can – indeed, in the tradition of intellectuals with an ethical commitment to a new society like Vygotsky I think it must – enter into the central debates of our times, and these debates shouldn't be limited to issues of formal education. Before looking at some of these broader debates, in this short section I want to outline various practical outcomes and policy suggestions that the analysis could encourage. To begin with, consider this statement from a working-class computer learner in Hakken (1993):

> I see technological development allowing a breakup of the working class demoralization. The scene is being set right now, for only socialism is capable of dealing with the silicon chip. (p. 22)

In considering policy perspectives on technological development, is it possible for us to take such an optimistic view of computer-based activity in advanced capitalist society? Is it enough to look for alternative uses for existing technological artifacts? The message suggested by the analysis in this book is that computer artifacts express deeply embedded hierarchical relations of design and development, but also that these relations narrow but do not dispose of the transformative potential of current technologies.

From a working-class perspective, perhaps the best hope of gaining socialized control over computer technologies lies in the democratization of the process of research and development (e.g., UTOPIA, 1985; Ehn, 1988; Shostak, 1999; Belanger, 2001; Sawchuk, 2001a, 2001b; Taylor and Briton, 2001; Suchman, 2002). In many ways, the analysis of the everyday computer-based activities of working-class people confirmed the relevance of this suggestion. The relationship between adult learning and technology in working-class life as presented in this book has been understood as full of contingencies and the potential for tactical responses on the part of working people, yet there is also a powerful reproductive character that runs through many of the practices I described. We saw, for example, that the practices of interviewees, shaped by forms of technological common sense, often lacked any resistance to processes of commodification. What's more, we can expect these tendencies to be particularly pronounced when people remain isolated as individuals and small groups outside of organized collective action, as the most vulnerable members of society often are. In this way, the labor movement as the primary means of generating an alternative proletarian public sphere continues to be one of the most important sources of hope. Specifically, the labor movement allows the collective impulses figured in the solidaristic networks examined in Chapter 5 to be harnessed to at least potentially affect the relations of design and development of computer technology (Sawchuk, in press). These same impulses were expressed in the type of organizing done by the working-class community in Sheffield, in the United Kingdom, as reported in Hakken (1993). On a broader level, beyond the democratization of the research and development process, the labor movement must continue to play a central role in democratizing the realm of paid work, which, as we've seen in the analysis, would reverberate in the other major spheres of activity (home and community) in a positive way. In other words, we've seen that experiences in the workplace do play an important role in people's perspective on computer learning and learning more broadly.

Another practical use of this research would center on new approaches to education among subordinate groups. Building on the discussion in the previous section, a curriculum for progressive educational processes could focus on consciousness raising around the class bias inherent in conventional educational thought and the demystification of technological forms, promoting the transformation of common sense into what Gramsci called *good sense*. At the same time, working-class groups clearly need to generate discretionary time, energy, and space so that they can respond collectively and creatively to the dynamics of advanced capitalism such as technological change. The labor movement and other organized expressions of subordinate standpoints such as the women's movement or global solidarity initiatives, community organizing among marginalized ethnic groups, and so on can all play a role in generating and coordinating these basic resources.

In terms of educational strategy, it also makes sense for organized labor and other social movements to build on existing modes of activity rather than trying to invent new ones. As labor educators know, working people can and do learn valuable lessons together outside of formalized courses. These less formalized means of organizing relations of learning, however, are not always the most efficient way to develop specific skills and knowledge. Provided that control lies in the hands of the learners themselves, formalized, pedagogically organized learning has a role to play in accentuating, shaping, and linking together the broader and more diffuse learning that people do in the everyday. This means that unions must bring the educational dimensions of the labor movement to the fore as an important organizing principle (Sawchuk, 2002). Whether this recommendation is taken seriously or not, however, what is clear is that working-class learning depends on informal networks. Learning within a critical and stable participatory community provides the best opportunity for working people to collectively establish, store, and transmit working-class perspectives on issues such as computer technology, education, and learning.

Toward a Knowledge-Intensive Capitalism or Working-Class Struggle? Implications of Working-Class Learning Networks

The most relevant findings of this book relate to the identification of informal working-class learning networks. Though this identification will have an intuitive quality for those of us who are in one way or another part of these communities, the book's contribution lies in a deeper understanding of the patterns of these networks, their operation, their determinants, and their implications for working people. There is an enormous surplus of knowledge production capacity among working-class people, though the purpose to which this knowledge production is directed is contradictory. Inevitably, the question that follows from this is, to what end could and should this enormous resource be directed? Beyond the basic assumption that people should have democratic control over the application of their collective capacities, what strategy would best serve those people and society generally? To my mind, this new knowledge of how working-class learning networks function suggests two major paths, each with its own implications for economic and social change. Roughly speaking, the choice appears to be between a knowledge-intensive capitalism or the further development of a broad-based working-class struggle. In this final section, I'll make some preliminary suggestions about the implication of these two pathways, though in the end it will become clear that each expresses a response to similar contradictions in advanced capitalism and that in this sense, they may be congruent.

The first path and its set of implications are aligned with an emerging identification of the untapped potential of employee learning networks as a key to the further development of capitalism. Without entering into a critique of management-led strategies, this path can be seen as an extension of human resource development, team learning, and ideas surrounding the notion of the *learning organization*. These ideas remain dominant on the North American business scene. However, in North America, beginning with the work of Berg (1970) and Carnoy and Levin (1985), and more recently extended in the work of Livingstone (1998, 2002), we see that there are major difficulties associated with applying human learning capacities effectively to the world of work. Livingstone (2002) has claimed that although we may already live in a knowledge society in which people are engaging in heretofore unheard-of amounts of learning, we may still be far away from something that might called a *knowledge economy* because much of this learning has not been utilized in the production process.

Teasing apart the implications of this first path also requires the recognition that cultural networks have been and will continue to be central to how work gets done. In North America, at least as early as the 1930s, with the emergence of the human resource movement and the studies at Western Electric's Hawthorne Works, there has been a basic recognition of this fact, and in Canada, national survey material on learning and work by Betcherman and colleagues (e.g., Betcherman et al., 1997) has demonstrated that the informal learning among workers continues to be a central, if poorly understood, phenomenon. The analysis that I've presented in this book adds depth to these observations but at the same time highlights an important contradiction. Specifically, we've seen that computer skill development of workers, although occurring informally, requires stable material conditions, opportunities to develop and engage in vibrant cultural communities, access to a public sphere that positively recognizes people's social standpoints, and so forth. However, when we compare these conditions for optimal informal learning with the reality of working-class life in North America, we see that socioeconomic trends run in the opposite direction. Poorer working conditions, limited career trajectories for the majority, little employment stability and downsizing, downward pressure on wages, and the growth of nonstandard work and longer work weeks (see Lowe, 2000; Vosko, 2000) are all the result of celebrated strategies of the business community. In short, the suggestion here is that business must orient itself away from these strategies if it is to have any hope of reinventing itself in the context of a true knowledge economy.

The second pathway for making full use of the potential of working-class informal learning networks comes with a different set of strategies and implications. This second direction suggests that these forms of knowledge production can be used to push an agenda that seriously challenges capitalism vis-à-vis a reinvigorated working-class struggle. Harnessing the capacities of working-class learning networks could be seen as an important step toward the reinvigoration of the labor movement and its program for progressive social change and economic democracy. In these terms, there is the prospect of enhancing the ability of unions to engage members effectively through expanded informal learning initiatives that hearkens to earlier, more effective periods of working-class mobilization. In one form or another, this sensibility has always informed the practice of organized labor, but perhaps one of the most explicit models for making gains in this way is to be found in syndicalist literature as a type of *cadre formation* (e.g., Guérin, 1970). The power that these networks provides for subordinate groups is immense. If integrated through a system of *organizational nodes* (e.g., events, courses, campaigns, festivals, etc.) of the formal structures of trade unions and other social movements, they can be further developed (Sawchuk, 2002).

From the perspective of the labor movement in looking back at the socioeconomic trends I have listed, the reversal of one in particular may be key. Here I'm speaking about mobilzation, following the limited but still largely successful example in France, around a shorter legal work week. This is a policy discussion that has roots at least 160 years old in North America alone and that has tended to cut across the entire range of social divisions (Hunnicutt, 1988). A shorter work week policy would reverberate through capitalist society by immediately tightening labor markets across the board. The spin-off from this in economic terms would be invaluable, providing more free time and a better distribution of resources to workers while having virtually no detrimental effect on the level of economic activity in general. Looking toward the long term, this policy could enhance the bargaining positions of workers, increase the mobilization of working-class groups of all kinds, support the learning networks we've seen in this book, and play a major role in positive, democratic socioeconomic change.

These two paths, as I've suggested, are a response to the internal contradictions of capitalism as a socioeconomic system and, despite appearances, are not mutually exclusive. Despite the notion that workers do not need the support of dominant institutions of work or schooling to create their own learning networks, the decimation of working-class communities within and beyond the workplace severely limits the potential for either business or labor to bring about something resembling positive social change. The most vulnerable segments of the working class, such as migrant laborers, nonwhite workers, working women, and the unemployed, experience even more limited opportunities to generate discretionary space for the development of learning networks, and as such are perhaps the most important starting point for intervention, no matter what perspective one takes. From the perspective of capital, however, reversing the socioeconomic trends listed here may be central to developing a knowledge economy, regardless of the fact that this may lead to the reestablishment of vibrant (and more or less oppositional) working-class cultural communities. Likewise, a broader labor movement invigorated through more effective use of its members' own capacities would itself be more effective in reversing many of these trends.

Appendix 1

Characteristics of Interviewees

ID	Age	Race/Ethnicity*	Sex	Schooling	Class	Household	Occupation
W1	35	Dutch Canadian	m	grade 12	mc	family1, di	machine operator
W2	–	–	m	grade 12	–	family1	machine operator
W3	49	Italian Canadian	f	grade 11	wc	single2	housekeeping (lo)
W4a	44	Scottish Canadian	m	grade 11	mc	family1, di	machine operator
W4b	44	German Canadian	f	grade 12	mc	family1, di	mail sorter (pt, ct)
W5	45	French Canadian	m	grade 12	mc	family2, di	machine operator
W6	50	Canadian	f	grade 11	mc	family3, di	machine operator
W7	51	French Canadian	m	grade 9	wc	family3, di	CNC machine operator
W8	34	Filipino Canadian	m	grade 13	mc	family3, di	machine operator
W9	42	Canadian	m	grade 12	mc	family2, di	shipper
W10	32	Polish Canadian	m	grade 11	mc	family1, di	technician repair
W11	48	Chinese	f	primary	wc	family2, di	machine operator
W12	53	Canadian	f	grade 12	mc	family2, di	machine operator
W13a	52	French Canadian	f	grade 12	mc	family2, mi	office clerk
W14b	22	Canadian	f	college	nc	single3, mi	office clerk
W15c	56	Canadian	m	grade 10	mc	family2, mi	warehouse supervisor
W16	36	Canadian	m	grade 12	mc	family1, s	quality technician
W17a	40	Canadian	m	grade 10	wc	family3, di	machine operator
W17b	48	Canadian	f	grade 13	nc	family3, di	driving instructor
W18a	35	Canadian	m	grade 10	mc	family3, di	machine operator
W18b	34	Canadian	f	grade 12	mc	family3, di	office clerk
W19	40	Irish Canadian	m	grade 13	mc	family1, di	machine operator
W20	44	Italian Canadian	f	grade 10	wc	single2	housekeeping (lo)
W22	48	Canadian	m	primary	wc	family2	machine operator
W23	27	Canadian	m	grade 12	mc	family1, di	machine operator
W24a	36	Ukranian Canadian	m	–	wc/mc	family1	union official

(continued)

Appendix 1 (continued)

ID	Age	Race/Ethnicity*	Sex	Schooling	Class	Household	Occupation
W24b	38	Ukranian Canadian	f	–	wc	family1	housemaker/retail sales
W25	27	Canadian	m	grade 12	wc	single1	machine operator
W26	39	Canadian	m	grade 12	wc	family1, di	machine operator
W27	63	German Canadian	m	trade	wc	family3	millwright
W28	27	Canadian	f	college	mc	family1, di	receptionist
W29	30	Canadian	m	college	mc	single1	machine operator
W30	37	Canadian/east coast	m	grade 10	wc	family1, di	machine operator
W31	42	Canadian	m	college	mc	family3, di	machine operator
W32	43	Canadian	f	college	mc/wc	single1	librarian
W33	34	Canadian	f	BA; BEd	mc	family3, di	office clerk
W35	34	Canadian	m	grade 10	mc	single1	shipper
W37	48	Canadian	f	grade 12	mc	single1	p/t office clerk
W38	58	Canadian	f	college	wc	single1	nurse
W41	63	Jewish Canadian	f	grade 11	wc/mc	family3, di	office clerk
W42	32	Greek Canadian	f	grade 12	mc	family1, di	janitor
W43	36	Chinese Canadian	f	college	wc	family1, di	office clerk
W44	57	Canadian	f	grade 12	wc	single1	office clerk
W45	50	Filipino Canadian	f	grade 12	lmc	family3, di	technician
W46	43	Canadian	m	grade 12	wc	family1	line worker
W47	47	Seke Canadian	m	trade	mc	family2, di	machine operator
W48a	32	Canadian	m	college	mc/wc	family1, di	machine operator
W48b	27	Canadian/martimer	f	college	mc	family1, di	office clerk
W49	49	Irish canadian	m	college	mc	family2, di	machine operator
W50	35	Canadian	m	grade 12	mc/lc	family1, di	machine operator
W51	32	Irish-Scot Canadian	m	grade 10	wc	family1, di	machine operator
W52	40	Italian Canadian	m	trade	mc	family1, di	millwright
W53	42	Canadian	f	grade 12	mc	family3, di	machine operator
W54	56	Canadian	m	grade 10	mc	single1	machine operator
W55	48	"Newfie" Canadian	m	university	mc	family4, di	machine operator
W56a	44	Creole	m	grade 12	wc	family1, di	machine operator
W56b	35	Eurasian Canadian	f	BA	mc	family1, di	human resources officer
W57	43	Canadian	m	university	mc	family3, di	machine operator
W58	–	Croatian	m	trade	mc	family2	machine operator
W59	33	Canadian	f	college	mc	family2, di	quality inspector
W60	32	Canadian	f	high school	mc	family2, di	office clerk
W61	39	Canadian	m	grade 10	mc	family2, di	machine operator
W62a	48	Italian Canadian	f	grade 8	mc	family3, di	material handler
W62b	–	Italian Canadian	m	grade 10	mc	family3, di	auto mechanic
W63	41	Canadian	m	high school	mc	family2, di	machine operator
W64	–	Canadian	m	high school	wc	family3, di	full-time union official

ID	Age	Race/Ethnicity*	Sex	Schooling	Class	Household	Occupation
W65	64	Italian Canadian	f	primary	mc	family3, di	machine operator
(Upper-Class Mini-Sample)							
C1	41	Canadian	f	BA, MA, LLB, BEd	uc	single1	languages teacher
C2	27	WASP	f	BA, MA	uc	single1	museum curator
C3	47	WASP	m	B.Comm., B. Acc	umc	family2	corporate executive
C4	60+	WASP	m	LLB	uc	family3	corporate executive
C5	49	refused	m	BA, LLB, BMan.	uc	single1	corporate lawyer

* = self-described; – = refused to answer; mc = middle class; nc = insists they are classless; wc = working class; uc = upper class; umc = upper middle class; di = dual income; mi = multiple household member incomes; s = one partner is a full-time student; family1 = living with partner and young children; family2 = living with partner and children 15+ years old; family3 = living with partner, no children/children gone; family4 = living with partner and adult relative(s); single1 = living alone; single2 = living with children only; single3 = living with adult relative(s) only; occupation = full-time paid employment; pt = part-time paid employment; ct = contract-paid employment (full-time hours periodically).

Appendix 2

Some Further Notes on Sequential Analysis of Human–Computer Interaction

The following is a partial line-by-line introductory examination of some of the features available in the transcript of interaction (Figure 4.1).

(Typical Opening Sequence)

Lines 1–2:   Roger performs an opening/summons-answer speech act (first pair part (FPP) of an adjacency pair [AP])

Line 3:   Larry responds (second pair part [SPP] of AP)

(Attempted Closing/Suspension by Larry)

Lines 33–34:   Larry provides an informative ("Oh, I'm not sure") in conjunction with a head and shoulder turn toward his own screen – which acts as a preclosing/suspension – that ends in an attempt at a closing/suspension in which Larry lowers his voice (saying "Shhh[it], wow") as if talking to himself (only) while appearing to be very engaged in the content of his screen.

(Some Troubles with Failed Closing/Suspension)

Line 35:   Either unaware of or unwilling to accept the closing attempt, Roger initiates another FPP, and with this we see that Roger's closing/suspension was unsuccessful. At the same time, however, although we can (as I've suggested) assume that Larry's actions in lines 33–34 were an attempt at closing/suspension, this is *not* a EM/CA-style claim but rather a traditional interpretive analysis. Rather, EM/CA in this situation awaits confirmation through an analysis of what sequentially follows.

Line 36:   This line provides a strong warrant for the suggestion of a (failed) attempt at a closing/suspension on lines 33–34 as Larry responds to Roger's FPP (line 36) in the same manner as in the first opening AP sequence (lines 1–3). Larry uses an SPP to an opening sequence because he (mistakenly) believed himself to have closed or suspended the interaction.

Lines 38–39:   Upon seeing that his closing/suspension has failed, Larry attempts to reiterate his closing in two recognizable ways here: (1) with an insertion sequence of his own (an FFP/question as opposed to a response, which would normally be expected in a question-answer AP) and (2) by turning physically to look for the facilitator, signaling his rejection of Roger's FFP/question on lines 35 and 37. In addition, Roger relinquishes his attempts to initiate a question-answer AP by providing the SPP of Larry's "insertion"-question (on line 38). Roger, in need of help, completes Larry's FPP (insertion-question) from line 38, provides a substantial pause signaling transition relevance, and shakily repeats "Third, third," finally eliciting a gestural response from Larry (with a turn of his head). Larry's calling over of the facilitator, Joe, is also an important part of Larry's attempt to suspend/close the interaction successfully. It is worthwhile noting that, at this point, we cannot be sure whether this is a true closing or merely a suspension of ongoing interaction. We cannot determine from the data whether Larry wants to end the conversation completely or merely suspend it until he and Roger are better equipped to handle the problem.

Lines 41–42:   In a final effort to succeed in closing/suspending, Larry looks for the facilitator once again, calling out, *"we're* kind of stuck here eh?" This is our first clue that Larry does not want to close the interaction but perhaps merely suspend it. Although it is still possible that Larry is merely being polite and truly intends to end the conversation, the use of "we're" strongly suggests that his engagement with Roger will remain relevant.

(Reopening)

Lines 48–49:   Larry, having completed his own typing, now initiates an AP/question, but *without* turning his head or shoulders. There is no opening/summons such as on lines 1–3. This fact is further confirmed by Roger's substantive answer (line 50) rather than mere acknowledgment of Larry's summons and answer.

Lines 53–54:   Larry, having experienced some serious problems in trying to merge his typewritten materials (lines 51–52), must now obtain serious verbal and visual information and decides to turns his head, shoulder, and chair toward Roger and his work space.

References

Apple, M. W. (1992). Education, culture, and class power: Basil Bernstein and the neo-Marxist sociology of education. *Educational Theory, 42*(2), 127–146.

Bansler, J. (1989). Trade unions and alternative technology in Scandinavia. *New Technology, Work and Employment, 4*(2), 92–97.

Barley, S. (1996). Introduction. In. J. Orr *Talking about machines* (pp. ix–xiv). Ithaca, NY: IRL Press.

Barthes, R. (1979). From work to text. In J. V. Harari (Ed.), *Textual strategies: Perspectives in post-structural criticism* (pp. 73–81). Ithaca, NY: Cornell University Press.

Belanger, M. (2001). *Course reader software.* Turin, Italy: International Labor Organization.

Bell, D. (1973). *The coming of the post-industrial society.* New York: Basic Books.

Bennett, K., and LeCompte, M. (1990). *How schools work: A sociological analysis of education.* New York: Longman.

Berg, I. (1970). *Education and jobs: The great training robbery.* London: Penguin.

Bernstein, B. (1971). *Class, codes and control* (Vol. 1). London: Routledge & Kegan Paul.

Bernstein, B. (1990). *The structuring of pedagogic discourse.* London: Routledge.

Bernstein, B. (2000). *Pedagogy, symbolic control and identity: Theory, research, critique* (rev. ed.). New York: Rowman & Littlefield.

Betcherman, G., Leckie, N., and McMullen, K. (1997). *Developing skills in the Canadian workplace: The results of the Ekos Workplace Training Survey.* Ottawa: Canadian Policy Research Networks.

Blanck, G. (1993). Vygotsky: The man and his cause. In L. C. Moll (Ed.), *Vygotsky and education: Instructional implications and applications of sociohistorical psychology* (pp. 31–58). Cambridge: Cambridge University Press.

Boden, D., and Zimmerman, D. H. (Eds.). (1993). *Talk and social structure: Studies in ethnomethodology and conversation analysis.* Oxford: Polity Press.

Bourdieu, P. (1977). *Outline of a theory of practice.* Cambridge: Cambridge University Press.

Bourdieu, P. (1984). *Distinction: A social critique of the judgement of taste.* Cambridge, MA: Harvard University Press.

Bourdieu, P. (1998). *Practical reason: On the theory of action.* Stanford, CA: Stanford University Press.

Bourdieu, P., and Eagleton, T. (1992). Doxa and common life. *New Left Review, 191*, 111–121.

Bourdieu, P., and Passeron, J.-C. (1977). *Reproduction in education, society and culture.* London: Sage.

Braverman, H. (1974) *Labor and monopoly capital: The degradation of work in the twentieth century.* New York: Monthly Review Press.

Briton, D., and Taylor, J. (2001). Online workers' education: How do we tame the technology? *The International Journal of Instructional Media, 28*(2), 1–13.

Burawoy, M. (1979). *Manufacturing consent: Changes in the labor process under monopoly capitalism.* Chicago: University of Chicago Press.

Butler, J. (1999). Performativity's social magic. In R. Shusterman (Ed.), *Bourdieu: A critical reader* (pp. 113–152). Oxford: Blackwell.

Calhoun, C. J. (1993). Introduction: Bourdieu and social theory. In C. J. Calhoun, E. LiPuma, and M. Postone (Eds.), *Bourdieu: Critical perspectives* (pp. 1–13). Cambridge: Polity Press.

Calhoun, C. J. (1995). *Critical social theory: Culture, history, and the challenge of difference.* Oxford: Blackwell.

Carnoy, M., and Levin, H. (1985). *Schooling and work in the democratic state.* Stanford, CA: Stanford University Press.

Certeau, M. de. (1984). *The practice of everyday life.* Berkeley: University of California Press.

Certeau, M. de. (1997). *Culture in the plural.* London: Minnesota University Press.

Charlesworth, S. J. (2000). *A phenomenology of working class experience.* Cambridge: Cambridge University Press.

Cockburn, C., and Ormrod, S. (1993). *Gender and technology in the making.* Newbury Park, CA: Sage.

Cockshott, W. P., and Cottrell, A. (1993). *Towards a new socialism.* Nottingham, UK: Spokesman.

Cole, M. (1988). Cross-cultural research in the socio-historical tradition. *Human Development, 31*, 137–157.

Cole, M. (1996). *Cultural psychology: A once and future discipline.* Cambridge, MA: Harvard University Press.

Cole, M., Engeström, Y., and Vasquez, O. (Eds.). (1997). *Mind, culture and activity.* Cambridge, MA: Cambridge University Press.

Cole, M., and Griffin, P. (1980). Cultural amplifiers reconsidered. In D. R. Olson (Ed.), *The social foundations of language and thought* (pp. 343–364). New York: Norton.

Collins, M. (1995). Critical commentaries on the role of the adult educator: From self-directed learning to postmodernist sensibilities. In M. R. Welton (Ed.), *In defense of the lifeworld: Critical perspectives on adult learning* (pp. 71–98). Albany: State University of New York Press.

Collins, P. H. (1997). Comment on Hekman's "Truth and Method: Feminist Standpoint Theory Revisited": Where's the power? *Signs, 22*(2), 375–381.

Collinson, D. (1994). Strategies of resistance: Power, knowledge and subjectivity in the workplace. In J. M. Jermier, D., Knights, and W. R. Nord (Eds.), *Resistance and power in organizations* (pp. 25–68). New York: Routledge.

Corrigan, P. (1979). *Schooling for the smash street kids.* London: Macmillan.

Curtis, B., Livingstone, D. W., and Smaller, H. (1992). *Stacking the deck: The stream-ing of working-class kids in ontario schools.* Toronto: Our Schools/Our Selves.

Dahrendorf, R. (1959). *Class and class conflict in an industrial society.* London: Routledge & Kegan Paul.

Dittmar, N. (1976). *A critical survey of sociolinguistics: Theory and application.* New York: St. Martin's Press.

Draper, J. A. (2001). The metamorphoses of andragogy. In D. H. Poonwassie and A. Poonwassie (Eds.), *Fundamentals of adult education: Issues and practice for lifelong learning* (pp. 14–30). Toronto: Thompson Educational.

Dreyfus, H. L. (1992). *What computers still can't do: A critique of artificial reason* (3rd ed.). Cambridge, MA: MIT Press.

Dreyfus, H., and Rabinow, P. (1999). Can there be a science of existential structure and social meaning? In R. Shusterman (Ed.), *Bourdieu: A critical reader* (pp. 84–93). Oxford: Blackwell.

Edwards, P. N. (1995). Cyberpunks in cyberspace: The politics of subjectivity in the computer age. In S. L. Star (Ed.), *The cultures of computing* (pp. 69–84). Oxford: Blackwell.

Ehn, P. (1988). *Work-oriented design of computer artifacts.* Stockholm: Arbetslivscen-trum.

Ellul, J. (1964). *The technological society.* New York: Vintage Books.

Engeström, Y. (1987). *Learning by expanding: An activity-theoretical approach to devel-opmental research.* Helsinki: Orienta-Konsultit.

Engeström, Y. (1992). Studies in expertise: Interactive distributed cognition at work. *Helsinki Research Bulletin,* n. 83.

Engeström, Y. (1996). Non scolae sed vitae discimus: Toward overcoming the en-capsulation of school learning. In H. Daniels (Ed.), *An introduction to Vygotsky* (pp. 151–170). London: Routledge.

Engeström, Y. (1999). *Expansive learning at work: Toward an activity-theoretical recon-ceptualization.* Unpublished monograph, University of California (San Diego).

Engeström, Y., Engeström, R., and Kärkkäinen, M. (1995). Polycontextuality and boundary crossing in expert cognition: Learning and problem solving in complex work activities. *Learning and Instruction,* 5, 319–336.

Engeström, Y., Engeström, R., and Vähääho, T. (1999). When the center does not hold: The importance of knotworking. In S. Chaiklin, M. Hedegaard, and U. J. Jensen (Eds.), *Activity theory and social practice* (pp. 345–374). Aarhus: Aarhus University Press.

Engeström, Y., Miettinen, R., and Punamäki, R.-L., (Eds.). (1999). *Perspectives on activity theory.* New York: Cambridge University Press.

Feenberg, A. (1999) *Questioning technology.* New York: Routledge.

Firestone, S. (1971). *The dialectic of sex.* New York: Bantam Books.

Fiske, J. (1993). *Power plays, power works.* London: Verso.

Foley, G. (1999). *Learning in social action: A contribution to understanding informal education.* London: Zed Books.

Freire, P. (1970). *Pedagogy of the oppressed.* New York: Continuum.

Freire, P. (1996). *Letters to Cristina: Reflections on my life and work.* New York: Routledge.

Freire, P., and Macedo, D. (1987). *Literacy.* New York: Bergin and Garvey.

Garcia-Orgales, J. (1992). *Technology adjustment research programme*. Toronto: Communications, Energy and Paperworkers' Union of Canada.

Garfinkel, H. (1967). *Studies in ethnomethodology*. Englewood Cliffs, NJ: Prentice-Hall.

Garrick, J. (1996). Informal learning: Some underlying philosophies. *Canadian Journal of Studies in Adult Education, 10*(1), 21–46.

Gentner, D., and Stevens, A. L. (1983). *Mental models*. Hillsdale, NJ: Erlbaum.

Giroux, H. A. (1979). Schooling and the culture of positivism: Notes on the death of history. *Educational Theory, 29*(4), 263–284.

Giroux, H. A. (1981). Hegemony, resistance, and the paradox of educational reform. *Interchange, 12*(2–3), 3–26.

Giroux, H. A. (1983). *Theory and resistance in education: A pedagogy for the opposition*. South Hadley, MA: Bergin and Garvey.

Giroux, H. (1987). Introduction. In P. Freire and D. Macedo (Eds.), *Literacy: Reading the work and the world* (pp. 1–27). South Hadley, MA: Bergin and Garvey.

Goffman, E. (1959). *The presentation of self in everyday life*. New York: Doubleday.

Goffman, E. (1961). *Asylums: Essays on the social situation of mental patients and other inmates*. New York: Doubleday.

Goffman, E. (1983). The interaction order. *American Sociological Review, 48*(1), 1–17.

Gouldner, A. (1954). *Patterns of industrial bureaucracy*. New York: Free Press.

Greenbaum, J. (1998). From Chaplin to Dilbert: The origins of computer concepts. In S. Aronowitz and J. Cutler (Eds.), *Post-Work* (pp. 167–184). New York: Routledge.

Gramsci, A. (1971). *Selections from the prison notebooks*. New York: International.

Guérin, D. (1970). *Anarchism: From theory to practice*. New York: Monthly Review Press.

Hacker, S. (1990). *Doing it the hard way: Investigations of gender and technology* (ed. D. Smith and S. M. Turner). Winchester, MA: Unwin Hyman.

Hakken, D. (with B. Andrews). (1993). *Computer myths, class realities: An ethnography of Technology and working people in Sheffield, England*. Boulder, CO: Westview Press.

Hamper, B. (1991). *Rivethead: Tales from the assembly line*. New York: Warner Books.

Harding, S. (1986). *The science question in feminism*. Milton Keynes, U.K.: Open University Press.

Harding, S. (Ed.). (1987). *Feminism and methodology: Social science issues*. Bloomington: University of Indiana Press.

Hart, M. (1990). Critical theory and beyond: Further perspectives on emancipatory education. *Adult Education Quarterly, 40*(3), 125–138.

Hartsock, N. (1987). The feminist standpoint: Developing the ground for a specifically feminist historical materialism. In S. Harding, and M. Hintikka (Eds.), *Discovering reality* (pp. 283–310). New York: D. Reidel.

Heap, J. L. (1991). Seeing snubs: An introduction to sequential analysis of classroom interaction. *Journal of Classroom Interaction, 27*(2), 23–38.

Heidegger, M. (1977). *The question concerning technology* (trans. W. Lovitt). New York: Harper & Row.

Heritage, J. (1984). *Garfinkel and ethnomethodology*. London: Polity Press.

Holland, D., Lachicotte, W., Jr., Skinner, D., and Cain, C. (1998). *Identity and agency in cultural worlds*. Cambridge, MA: Harvard University Press.

Holland, D., and Lave, J. (Eds.), (2001). *History in person: Enduring struggles, contentious practice, intimate identities.* Santa Fe, NM: School of American Research Press.

Holland, D., and Reeves, J. R. (1996). Activity theory and the view from somewhere: Team perspectives on the intellectual work of programmers. In B. A. Nardi (Ed.), *Context and consciousness: Activity theory and human-computer interaction* (pp. 257–281). Cambridge, MA: MIT Press.

Hunnicutt, B. K. (1988). *Work without end: Abandoning shorter hours for the right to work.* Philadelphia: Temple University Press.

Ihde, D. (1993). *Philosophy of technology : An introduction.* New York: Paragon House.

Illeris, K. (1999). *The three dimensions of learning: Contemporary learning theory in the tension field between Piaget, Freud and Marx.* Roskilde, Denmark: Roskilde University Press.

Ilyenkov, E. V. (1982). *The dialectics of the abstract and the concrete in Marx's Capital.* Moscow: Progress.

Industry Canada (Information Highway Advisory Council). (1997). *Preparing Canada for a digital world.* Ottawa: Federal Government.

Jermier, J. M., Knights, D., and Nord, W. R. (Eds.). (1994). *Resistance and power in organizations.* New York: Routledge.

Kerr, C., Dunlop, J. T., Harbison, F., and Myers, C. (1969). *Industrialism and industrial man.* London: Heinemann.

Knowles, M. (1970). *The modern practice of adult education: Andragogy versus pedagogy.* Chicago: Follett.

Knowles, M. (1975). *Self directed learning.* New York: Associated Press.

Knowles, M. S. (1977). *A history of the adult education movement in the United States.* New York: Krieger.

Knowles, M. (1980). *The modern practice of adult education: From pedagogy to andragogy.* Chicago: Follett.

Koch, M. (1996). Class and taste: Bourdieu's contribution to the analysis of social structure and social space. *International Journal of Contemporary Sociology 33*(2), 187–202.

Krahn, H., and Lowe, G. (1998) *Work, industry and canadian society.* Toronto: International Thompson.

Kusterer, K. (1978). *Know-how on the job: The important working knowledge of "unskilled" workers.* Boulder, CO: Westview Press.

Lash, S. and Urry, J. (1994). *Economies of signs and space.* London: Sage.

Latour, B. (1987). *Science in action.* Cambridge, MA: Harvard University Press.

Latour, B. (1994). On Technical Mediation-Philosophy, Sociology,

Lave, J. (1988). *Cognition in practice: Mind, mathematics and culture in everyday life.* New York: Cambridge University Press.

Lave, J. (1993). The Practice of Learning. In S. Chaiklin (Ed.), *Understanding practice: Perspectives on activity and context* (pp. 3–33). Cambridge: Cambridge University Press.

Lave, J., Murtaugh, M., and de la Rocha, O. (1984). The dialectic of arithmetic in grocery shopping. In B. Rogoff and J. Lave (Eds.), *Everyday cognition: Its development in social context* (pp. 9–40). Cambridge, MA: Harvard University Press.

Lave, J., and Wenger, E. (1991). *Situated learning: Legitimate peripheral participation.* Cambridge: Cambridge University Press.

Lee, E. (1997). *The labour movement and the Internet.* London: Pluto Press.

Leont'ev, A. N. (1974). The problem of activity in psychology. *Soviet Psychology, 13*(2), 4–33.

Leont'ev, A. N. (1978). *Activity, consciousness, and personality.* Englewood Cliffs, NJ: Prentice Hall.

Leont'ev, A. N. (1981). *Problems of the development of the mind.* Moscow: Progress.

Livingstone, D. W. (1987). *Critical pedagogy and cultural power.* Haddley, MA: Bergin and Garvey.

Livingstone, D. W. (1994). Search for missing links: Neo-Marxist theories of education. In L. Erwin and D. MacLennan (Eds.), *Canadian sociology of education* (pp. 55–82). Toronto: Copp Clark Longman.

Livingstone, D. W. (1997a). Computer Literacy, the 'Knowledge Economy' and Information Control: Micro myths and macro choices. In M. Moll (Ed.), *Tech High: Globalization and the Future of Canadian Education* (pp. 99–116). Ottawa: Canadian Centre for Policy Alternatives.

Livingstone, D. W. (1997b). The limits of human capital theory: Expanding knowledge, information learning and underemployment. *Policy Options, 18*(6), 9–13.

Livingstone, D. W. (1998). *The Education Jobs Gap.* Boulder, Colorado: Westview.

Livingstone, D. W. (2000). *Canadian national survey of informal learning.* Toronto: New Approaches to Lifelong Learning Network.

Livingstone, D. W. (2002). *Working and learning in the information age: A profile of Canadians.* Ottawa: Report prepared for the Canadian Policy Research Network.

Livingstone, D. W., Hart, D., and Davie, L. E. (1997). *Public attitudes towards education in Ontario (1996): The eleventh OISE/UT Survey.* Toronto: University of Toronto Press.

Livingstone, D. W., and Mangan, M. (Eds.) (1996). *Recast dreams: Class and gender consciousness in steeltown.* Toronto: Garamond Press.

Livingstone, D. W., and Sawchuk, P. H. (2000). Beyond cultural capital theory: Hidden dimensions of working class learning. *The Review of Education, Pedagogy and Cultural Studies, 22*(2), pp. 121–146.

Livingstone, D. W. and Sawchuk, P. H. (and contributors). (in press). *Hidden dimensions of the knowledge society.* Washington, DC: Rowman and Littlefield.

Lowe, G. (2000). *The quality of work: A people-centred agenda,* Don Mills, Ontario, Canada: Oxford University Press.

Lucio, M. M., and Stewart, P. (1997, Summer). The paradox of contemporary labour process theory: The rediscovery of labour and the disappearance of collectivism. *Capital and Class, 62,* 49–77.

Lukács, Georg (1971). *History and class consciousness.* Cambridge, MA: MIT Press.

Luria, A. R. (1976). *Cognitive development: Its cultural and social foundations* (M. Cole, Ed.). Cambridge, MA: Harvard University Press.

Martin, D. (1995). *Thinking union.* Toronto: Between the Lines.

Martin, D. (1998). The case of education in the labour movement: Pre-1970's. In G. Selman, M. Selman, M. Cooke, and P. Dampier (Eds.), *The foundations of adult education in Canada* (2nd ed.). Toronto: Thompson Educational.

Marx, K. (1845–1846/1996). *The German ideology* (R. C. Tucker, Ed.). New York: Norton.

Marx, K. (1861–1863/1987). Theories of surplus value. In J. Elster (Ed.), *Karl Marx: A reader* (pp.). Cambridge: Cambridge University Press.

Marx, K. (1867–1868/1990). *Capital* (Vols. 1–3). New York: International.

Mayo, E. (1945). *The social problems of an industrial civilization*. Cambridge, MA: Harvard University Press.

McChesney, R. W. (Ed.) (1998). *Capitalism and the information age: The political economy of the global communications revolution*. New York: Monthly Review Press.

McHoul, A. (1978). The organization of turns at formal talk in the classroom. *Language and Society, 7*, 183–213.

Mehan, H. (1993). The school's work of sorting students. In D. Boden and D. Zimmerman (Eds.), *Talk and social structure: Studies in ethnomethodology and conversation analysis* (pp. 71–90). Cambridge: Polity Press.

Mellinger, W. M. (1992). Accomplishing fact in police dispatch packages: The situated construction of an organizational record. *Perspectives on Social Problems, 4*, 47–72.

Menzies, H. (1996). *Whose brave new world?: The information highway and the new economy*. Toronto: Between the Lines.

Merriam, S. (1993). *An update on adult learning theory*. San Francisco: Jossey-Bass.

Mezirow, J. (1991a). Transformation theory and cultural context: A reply to Clark and Wilson. *Adult Education Quarterly, 41*, 188–192.

Mezirow, J. (1991b). *Transformative dimensions of adult learning*. San Francisco: Jossey-Bass.

Mezirow, J. (1994). Understanding transformative theory. *Adult Education Quarterly, 44*, 222–244.

Mezirow, J. (1996, Spring). Contemporary paradigms of learning. *Adult Education Quarterly, 46*, 158–173.

Middleton, D. (1996). Talking work: Argument, common knowledge, and improvisation in teamwork. In Y. Engeström and D. Middleton (Eds.), *Cognition and communication at work* (pp. 233–256). New York: Cambridge University Press.

Moerman, M. (1988). Society in a grain of rice. In M. Moerman and H. Sacks (Eds.), *Talking culture: Ethnography and conversation analysis* (pp. 68–100). Philadelphia: University of Pennsylvania Press.

Moerman, M. and Sacks, H. (1988). *Talking Culture: Ethnography and Conversation Analysis*. Philadelphia: University of Pennsylvania Press.

Moll, L. (Ed.). (1993). *Vygotsky and education: Instructional implications and applications of sociohistorical psychology*. New York: Cambridge University Press.

Moody, K. (1997). *Workers in a lean world*. New York: Monthly Review Press.

Mumford, L. (1991). Authoritarian and democratic technics. In J. Zerzan and A. Carnes (Eds.), *Questioning technology: Tool, toy or tyrant?* (pp. 13–21). Philadelphia: New Society Publishers.

Myles, J. (1991). Post-industrialism and the service economy. In D. Drache and M. Gertler (Eds.), *The new era of global competition: State policy and market power* (pp. 351–366). Montreal: McGill-Queen University Press.

Myles, J. (1991). Post-industrialism in the service economy. In D. Drache and M. S. Gertler (Eds.), Krahn *The new era of global competition: State policy and market power* (pp. 351–366). Montreal: McGill-Queen's University Press.

Naisbitt, J. (1982). *Megatrends: Ten new directions transforming our lives.* New York: Warner.

Nakhaie, M. R., and Pike, R. M. (1998). Social origins, social statuses and home computer access and use. *Canadian Journal of Sociology, 23*(4), 427–450.

Nardi, B. A. (1996). Activity theory and human–computer interaction. In B. A. Nardi (Ed.), *Context and consciousness: Activity theory and human–computer interaction* (pp. 7–16). Cambridge, MA: MIT Press.

Negroponte, N. (1995). *Being digital.* New York: Knopf.

Negt, O., and Kluge, A. (1993). *Public sphere and experience: Toward an analysis of the bourgeois and proletarian public sphere.* Minneapolis: University of Minnesota Press.

Newman, F., and Holzman, L. (1993). *Lev Vygotsky: Revolutionary scientist.* London: Routledge.

Newman, M. (1994). *Defining the enemy: Adult education in social action.* Sydney: Stewart Victor.

Noble, D. (1984). *The forces of production: A social history of industrial automation.* New York: Knopf.

Nofsinger, R. E. (1991). *Everyday conversation.* London: Sage.

Ollman, B. (1993). *Dialectical investigations.* New York: Routledge.

Ong, W. J. (1982). *Orality and literacy.* London: Methuen.

Orr, J. (1996). *Talking about machines: An ethnography of a modern job.* Ithaca, NY: ILR Press.

Ortony, A. (Ed.). (1979). *Metaphor and thought.* Cambridge: Cambridge University Press.

Percy, K., Burton, D., and Withnall, A. (1994). *Self-directed learning among adults: The challenges for continuing educators.* Lancaster, U.K.: University of Lancaster.

Poonwassie, D. H., and Poonwassie, A. (Eds.). (2001). *Fundamentals of adult education: Issues and practice for lifelong learning.* Toronto: Thompson Educational.

Porter, J. (1971). *The vertical mosiac.* Toronto: Toronto University Press.

Pratt, D. D. (1988). Andragogy as a relational construct. *Adult Education, 38*(3), 160–181.

Printing Industries of America. (1994). *Bridging to a digital future.* Alexandria, VA: Printing Industries of America.

Psathas, B., and Anderson, T. (1990). The practices of transcription in conversational analysis. *Semiotica, 78*, 75–99.

Reddick, A., with Bouche, C., and Groseillier, M. (2000). *The digital divide: The information highway in Canada.* Ottawa: Industry Canada.

Reich, R. (1991). *The work of nations: Preparing ourselves for 21st century capitalism.* New York: Vintage.

Resnick, S., and Wolf, R. (1987). *Knowledge and class: A Marxian critique of political economy.* Chicago: University of Chicago Press.

Robins, K., and Webster, F. (1989a). Computer literacy: The employment myths. *Social Science Computer Review, 7*(1), 7–26.

Rossing, B. E. (1991). Patterns of informal incidental learning: Insights from community action. *International Journal of Lifelong Education, 10*(1), 45–60.

Roszak, T. (1994). *The cult of information: A neo-Luddite treatise on high tech, artificial intelligence and the true art of thinking.* Berkeley: University of Calfornia Press.

Roy, D. (1952). Quota restriction and goldbricking in a machine shop. *American Journal of Sociology, 57,* 427–442.

Rubin, L. (1976). *Worlds of pain: Life in a working-class family.* New York: Basic Books.

Rubin, L. (1994). *Families on the fault line: America's working class speaks out about family, the economy, race and ethnicity.* New York: Harper-Collins.

Sacks, H., and Schegloff, E. (1974). "Opening up closings." In R. Turner, (Ed.), *Ethnomethodolgy* (pp. 233–264). London: Penguin.

Sacks, H., Schegloff, E., and Jefferson, G. (1974). A simplest systematics for the organization of turn-taking for conversation. *Language, 50,* 696–735.

Sadovnik, A. R. (Ed.). (1995). *Knowledge and pedagogy: The sociology of Basil Bernstein.* Norwood, NJ: Ablex.

Sargent, L (Ed.). (1981). *The unhappy marriage of Marxism and feminism: A debate on class and patriarchy.* London: Pluto Press.

Sawchuk, P. H. (1996). *Working class informal learning and computer literacy.* Unpublished M.A. thesis, Department of Sociology in Education, OISE/University of Toronto.

Sawchuk, P. H. (1997). Factory workers' informal computer learning: Some observations on the effects of progressive unionism. *Conference Proceedings of 27th Annual Standing Conference on University Teaching and Research in the Education of Adults.* London: University of London Press.

Sawchuk, P. H. (1998a). *Building informal learning networks into the curriculum: A discussion paper.* Toronto: United Food and Commercial Workers Union (Computer Education Working Group).

Sawchuk, P. H. (1998b). *Pedagogical/andragogical and informal-collective learning distinctions: Suggestions from a micro-analytic analysis of informal learning in an adult computer classroom.* Unpublished monograph.

Sawchuk, P. H. (1999a). The practices of structured participation: An emancipatory perspective on workplace learning. *Researching Work and Learning: A First International Conference* Leeds, U.K.: University of Leeds Press.

Sawchuk, P. H. (1999b). A cultural materialist approach to adult learning. *Proceedings of the 18th Annual Conference of Canadian Association for the Study of Adult Education.* Sherbrooke, Quebec: University of Sherbrooke Press.

Sawchuk, P. H. (2000). *Working-class computer learning: An historical materialist analysis of participation, practice and learning in the everyday.* Unpublished Ph.D. dissertation, Department of Sociology in Education, OISE/University of Toronto.

Sawchuk, P. H. (2001a). *Online learning for labour movement activists?* Toronto: NALL Working Papers Series.

Sawchuk, P. H. (2001b). The pitfalls and possibilities of union-based telelearning: A report of preliminary finding. *Proceedings of the Canadian Association for the Study of Adult Education Conference.* Quebec: University of Laval Press.

Sawchuk, P. H. (2002). Learning in the union local: The key to building strategic capacity in the labour movement. In S. Mojab and W. McQueen (Eds.), *Adult education and the contested terrain of public policy: Proceedings of the 21st Canadian Association for the Study of Adult Education Conference* (pp. 256–262). Toronto: Canadian Association for Studies in Adult Education.

Sawchuk, P. H. (in press). *Introductory report on the work, learning and technological design in the public sector project.* Toronto: Centre for the Study of Education and Work, University of Toronto.

Schön, D., Sanyal, B., and Mitchell, W. J. (Eds.). (1999). *High technology and low-income communities: Prospects for the postive use of advanced information technology.* Cambridge, MA: MIT Press.

Sejersted, F., and Moser, I. (1992). *Humanistic perspectives on technology, development and environment.* Oslo: Centre for Technology and Culture.

Selman, G., and Dampier, P. (1991). *The foundations of adult education in canada.* Toronto: Thompson Educational.

Sennett, R., and Cobb, J. (1972). *The hidden injuries of class.* New York: Vintage Books.

Shostak, A. (1999). *Cyberunion: Empowering labor through computer technology.* New York: M. E. Sharpe.

Simon, R. (1985). Critical pedagogy. In T. Husen and N. Postelthwaite (Eds.), *The international encyclopedia of education* (Vol. 2, pp. 1118–1120). Oxford: Pergamon Press.

Sinclair, J., and Coulthard, R. M. (1975). *Towards an analysis of discourse: The English used by teachers and pupils.* London: Oxford University Press.

Smith, D. E. (1987). *The everyday world as problematic: A feminist sociology.* Toronto: University of Toronto Press.

Smith, D. E. (1990). *Texts, facts and femininity: Exploring the relations of ruling.* New York: Routledge.

Smith, D. E. (1997a). Comment on Hekman's "Truth and method: Feminist standpoint theory revisited." *Signs: Journal of Women in Culture and Society, 22*(2), 392–398.

Smith, D. E. (1997b). From the margins: Women's standpoint as a method of inquiry in the social sciences. *Gender, Technology and Development, 1*(1), 113–135.

Smith, D. E. (1999). *Writing the social: critique, theory and investigations.* Toronto: University of Toronto Press.

Smith, D. E., and Whalen, J. (1994). *Texts in action.* Toronto: Unpublished paper, Ontario Institute for Studies in Education.

Sprouse, M. (1995). *Sabotage in the American workplace: Anecdotes of dissatisfaction, mischief and revenge.* New York: Routledge.

Statistics Canada (2000). *Internet use.* Ottawa: Government of Canada.

Sternberg, R. J. (1977). Component processes in analogical reasoning. *Psychological Review, 84,* 353–378.

Suchman, L. (1987). *Plans and situated action: The problem of human–machine communication.* Cambridge: Cambridge University Press.

Suchman, L. (2002). Practice-based design of information systems: Notes from the hyperdeveloped world. *The Information Society, 18*(2), 139–144.

Sweezy, P. (1964). *The theory of capitalist development.* New York: Monthly Review Press.

Thompson, E. P. (1963). *The making of the English working class.* London: Penguin Books.

Thompson, P. (1989). *The nature of work: An introduction to debates on the labour process.* London: Macmillan.

Toffler, A. (1980). *The third wave*. New York: Morrow.

Tough, A. (1967). *Learning without a teacher: A study of tasks and assistance during adult self-teaching projects*. Toronto: OISE Press.

Tough, A. (1979). *The adult's learning projects: A fresh approach to theory and practice in adult learning and education*. Toronto: OISE Press.

Usher, R. S., Bryant, I., and Johston, R. A. (1997). *Adult education and the postmodern challenge: Learning beyond the limits*. London: Routledge.

UTOPIA (1985). The UTOPIA project: An alternative in text and images. Stockholm: *Graffiti*, no. 7, Arbetslivscentrum (Swedish Center for Working Life).

Vosko, L. F. (2000). *Temporary work: The gendered rise of a precarious employment relationship*. Toronto: University of Toronto Press.

Vygotsky, L. S. (1978). *Mind in society: The development of higher psychological processes* (ed. M. Cole). Cambridge, MA: Harvard University Press.

Vygotsky, L. S. (1986). *Thought and language* (ed. A. Kozulin). Cambridge, MA: MIT Press.

Vygotsky, L. S. (1994). *The Vygotsky reader*. (ed. R. Van der Veer and J. Valsiner). London: Blackwell.

Wardekker, W. L. (1997). *Critical and Vygotskian theories of education: A comparison*. Amsterdam: Vrije Universiteit.

Weis, M. J. (2001). Online America. *American Demographics*. March (www.demographics.com).

Welton, M. (1995). *In defense of the lifeworld: Critical perspectives on adult learning*. Albany: SUNY Press.

Wenger, E. (1998). *Communities of practice: Learning, meaning and identity*. New York: Cambridge University Press.

Wertsch, J. V. (1991). *Voices of the mind: A sociocultural approach to mediated action*. Cambridge, MA: Harvard University Press.

Wexler, P., Martusewicz, R. and Kern, J. (1987). Popular educational politics. In D. W. Livingstone (Ed.), *Critical pedagogy and cultural power* (pp. 227–244). Toronto: Garamond Press.

Wilkinson, B. (1983). *The shopfloor politics of new technology*. London: Hinemann Educational.

Williams, R. (1963). *Culture and society 1780–1950*. Harmondsworth, U.K.: Penguin Books.

Williams, R. (1993). *Border country: Raymond Williams in adult education* (J. McIlroy and S. Westwood, Eds.). Leicester, U.K.: National Institute of Adult Continuing Education.

Williams, R. (1997). *Problems in materialism and culture: Selected essays*. London: Verso.

Willis, P. (1979). *Learning to labour: How working class kids get working class jobs*. Farnborough, U.K.: Saxon House.

Index

The Learning in Doing series was founded in 1987 by Roy Pea and John Seely Brown.